Black Women in the Ivory Tower, 1850–1954

UNIVERSITY PRESS OF FLORIDA

Florida A&M University, Tallahassee
Florida Atlantic University, Boca Raton
Florida Gulf Coast University, Ft. Myers
Florida International University, Miami
Florida State University, Tallahassee
University of Central Florida, Orlando
University of Florida, Gainesville
University of North Florida, Jacksonville
University of South Florida, Tampa
University of West Florida, Pensacola

Black Women in the Ivory Tower, 1850–1954

AN INTELLECTUAL HISTORY

STEPHANIE Y. EVANS

University Press of Florida
Gainesville · Tallahassee · Tampa · Boca Raton
Pensacola · Orlando · Miami · Jacksonville · Ft. Myers

12 11 10 09 08 07   6 5 4 3 2 1

Library of Congress Cataloging-in-Publication Data
Evans, Stephanie Y.
Black women in the ivory tower, 1850–1954 : an intellectual history /
Stephanie Y. Evans.
p. cm.
Includes bibliographical references and index.
ISBN 978-0-8130-3031-9 (alk. paper)
1. African American women—Education (Higher)—History. I. Title.
LC2741.E93 2007
378.1'982996073—dc22   2006022029

The University Press of Florida is the scholarly publishing agency for
the State University System of Florida, comprising Florida A&M University,
Florida Atlantic University, Florida Gulf Coast University, Florida International
University, Florida State University, University of Central Florida, University
of Florida, University of North Florida, University of South Florida, and
University of West Florida.

University Press of Florida
15 Northwest 15th Street
Gainesville, FL 32611-2079
http://www.upf.com

To Pamela Copley, my eighth-grade dance teacher at Utterback Junior High School in Tucson, Arizona, for teaching me that "dancers don't sweat, they glow." You saved my life. Rest in peace.

To Cherryl Arnold, my mentor and friend, for showing me that a black woman can live the good life. May God continue to bless you and keep you smiling. Ciao!

To John Bracey, my dissertation chair, for teaching me that "I am somebody." In addition to being a gentleman and a scholar, you are a master storyteller and a compassionate human being.

To members of the Association of Black Women Historians, for leading the way and supporting me as I follow.

Especially,
to Angela M. Crider, my sister, for inspiring me with her beauty and for always sharing her music.

Let's take a long walk around the park, after dark
Find a spot for us to spark conversation
Verbal elation, stimulation
Share our situations, temptations, education, relaxations
Elevations, maybe we could talk about Surah 31:18;
Elevations, maybe we could talk about Revelation 3:17;
Elevations, baby, maybe we can save the nation.

Jill Scott, "A Long Walk," *Who Is Jill Scott?* (2000)

Contents

Illustrations

Acknowledgments

Many people have offered me encouragement in the decade that it has taken to produce this work. Not all are named here, but none are forgotten.

I thank Meredith Morris-Babb and the staff at the University Press of Florida for supporting this project. The reviewers were especially helpful and made this manuscript infinitely more accurate and readable.

I offer gratitude to members of the Association for the Study of African American Life and History (ASALH), who have been generous with their time and professional guidance, especially Sheila Flemming-Hunter, Gloria Dickinson, Daryl Scott, and V. P. Franklin.

Thanks to scholars at Howard University's Moorland-Spingarn Research Center, especially Thomas Battle, Ida Jones, Donna Wells, and Joellen El Bashir, for allowing me access to the hallowed halls where the treasures are kept. I am grateful for assistance from archivists at Bethune-Cookman College, Middlebury College, Oberlin College, University of Pennsylvania, University of Chicago, Texas College, Shoreham and O.H.I.O. Historical Societies, the Sorbonne University, and the historian Marilyn Richardson. I am grateful for discussions with colleagues at Cornell, Berea, the Sorbonne, and the University of Cambridge.

Funding from the University of Florida College of Liberal Arts and Sciences, Paris Research Center, Center for Women's Studies and Gender Research, and African American Studies Program made this project possible. Thanks to Terry Mills, Angel Kwolek-Folland, Millagros Pena, Paula Ambroso, Debra Walker King, Colette Taylor, Melvina Johnson, and the Association of Black Faculty and Staff for encouragement. Go Gators!

I offer special thanks to Ms. Sharon Burney, who (along with her two beautiful daughters) staved off my periodic despair with creativity, humor, and good sense that is not so common. Thanks to Willie Baber, Stephanie J. Evans, Crystal Patterson, Imani Hope, Carrie Roberts, Taylor Ramsey, Louise Newman, Brian Ward, Jack Davis, Matt Gallman, Linda Behar-Horenstein, Keisha Duncan, and Pero Dagbovie for editorial suggestions. Without Susan Brady's professional editing service, this manuscript would be a hot mess; thanks for your keen eye.

The W.E.B. Du Bois Department of Afro-American Studies doctoral program at the University of Massachusetts, Amherst, provided rigorous and unwieldy workloads, for which I am eternally grateful. Thanks to my dissertation committee, John H. Bracey Jr., Robert Paul Wolff, Bill Strickland, and Alexandrina Deschamps, for your trust and patience during times when I had neither. Thank you to UMass professors, staff, my cohort, and my peers for demonstrating what "collegial" really means. UMass Women's Studies, Commonwealth Honors College, Five Colleges, and the Office of Community Service-Learning offered fruitful collaborations, which I appreciate tremendously.

Time I spent at the Swearer Center for Public Service (Brown University) and the Haas Center for Public Service (Stanford University) provided vital opportunities to test the validity of my research; special thanks to Kerri Heffernan and Nadinne Cruz. I am grateful to Rebecca Rockefeller, the environmentalist, for offering her insightful perspective. I am indebted to the National Black Graduate Student Association (NBGSA), Southern Regional Educational Board (SREB), and Sisters of the Academy for professional development opportunities and to Orlando Taylor of Howard University for sustained encouragement.

I extend special thanks to the students, staff, and administration of California State University, Long Beach. Go Beach! Without the Ronald E. McNair Scholars Program and TRIO funding, this book would not exist. Thank you Cherryl Arnold for investing in me personally and professionally (Ciao!). Thanks to Dr. Costa and my McNair peers, especially Mike and Amanda, and to President and Mrs. Maxson for their leadership. Women's Studies and Black Studies at CSULB, the Sally Cassanova Pre-Doctoral Program, the Academic Advising Center, and Patricia Rozee of the Office of Community Service-Learning offered immeasurable support. Also, my yearlong study of Greek and "dead White men" at St. John's College was expensive but invaluable; I'm glad to have been a "Johnny."

To all the students whom I have had the privilege to instruct, I hope this manuscript shows that you have taught me well. Blessings to my sisters in the Gainesville reading group, the Mu Upsilon Omega chapter of Alpha Kappa Alpha Sorority, Incorporated, and the Twelve Virtuous Women, for sisterhood that gives me faith, strength, courage, and wisdom.

I appreciate my parents, W. Annette Edmonds, Booker T. and Barbara McKim-Evans, and the Nalley family to whom this work is also lovingly dedicated. Last, I thank my family and loved ones across the globe who, with God's grace and mercy, have sustained me throughout this journey.

Amani Moto.

Abbreviations

AAUP   American Association of University Professors
ABWH   Association of Black Women Historians
AMA   American Missionary Association
ASNLH   Association for the Study of Negro Life and History
B-CC   Bethune-Cookman College
BGLOs   Black Greek-letter Organizations
FSUS   Florida State University System
HBCUs   Historically Black Colleges and Universities
ICY   Institute for Colored Youth
NAACP   National Association for the Advancement of Colored People
NACW   National Association of Colored Women
NCNW   National Council of Negro Women
NYA   National Youth Administration
PWIs   Predominantly White Institutions
SCLC   Southern Christian Leadership Conference
SNCC   Student Nonviolent Coordinating Committee
WC   Women's Convention, auxiliary group to the National Baptist Convention

Introduction

"This Right to Grow"

Higher Education as Both a Human and Civil Right

This RIGHT TO GROW is sacred and inviolable, based on the solidarity and undeniable value of humanity itself and linked with the universal value and inalienable rights of all individuals.

Anna Julia Cooper, Howard University, 1925

Anna Julia Cooper was born enslaved in approximately 1858. Despite racist and sexist barriers of the caste system in the United States, she earned a bachelor's and a master's degree from Oberlin College, attended graduate school at Columbia University, and then, in 1925, earned a doctoral degree from the Sorbonne University in Paris. Rather than simply bask in her own scholarly success, Cooper worked to improve higher education. She had experienced the inner workings of prestigious college and university systems— collectively known as academe or the "Ivory Tower"—and she attempted to increase access for women and African Americans into that exclusive network. With her critical approach to higher education, Cooper exposed the hypocrisy in American assertions of democracy, disproved claims of a social meritocracy, and discredited European notions of intellectual superiority. She knew that her academic attainment was achieved in spite of, not because of, existing academic institutions, and she effectively voiced her dissent against those who obstructed universal academic access. Cooper argued that all human beings have a right to grow. For Cooper, equal access to higher education was an essential part of human growth.[1]

Mary McLeod Bethune, the founder of Bethune-Cookman College, was an adept politico, renowned educator, and prolific writer. Having grown up in the late nineteenth-century South, Bethune, like Cooper, well understood the ramifications of denied access to education. Though an activist committed to many social issues, including suffrage, housing, fair labor, citizenship and peace, Bethune dedicated her life to supporting higher education access for African Americans in general and black women in particular. In contrast to Cooper, Bethune argued that education is a right of all citizens in a democracy. These two views of education—as a human right and as a civil right—form a complementary schema for understanding the academic participation of black women scholars of the past. These complementary definitions also present implications for increasing educational access in the future.

Bethune asserted that a university has three responsibilities: investigation, interpretation, and inspiration. The purpose of my research is to advance Dr. Cooper's vision of increased educational opportunity by addressing Dr. Bethune's three mandates. In this volume, I have three goals: to *investigate* the history of black women in higher education and to create a solid picture from formerly piecemeal images, to *interpret* the historic relationship between cultural identity and knowledge production, and to demonstrate how black women's experiences, ideas, and practices can *inspire* contemporary educators to transform the academy into an effective tool for increased social equity and opportunity.[2]

My two main arguments are that, first, black women's educational history complicates ideas of what an academic should do or be; and second, black women's intellectual history can outline a more democratic approach to higher education. Black women's perspectives can contribute to a physical democracy in academe, but these perspectives can also help to create an intellectual democracy—where all people have a voice. This history redefines the academy in interesting and relevant ways, at once challenging and then reifying elitist iterations of knowledge production. Black women scholars of the past did not simply challenge mainstream (that is, white and male) academic space. Their participation in the academy prior to 1954 revealed a unique standpoint at the crossroads of race and gender. Their performance as scholars speaks to the relationship between cultural identity and faculty roles in institutions. Further, this history deepens discussions of academic roles in society. By raising questions of how human and civil rights are intertwined with educational access, scholarly research, pedagogy, and community service, black women academics have significantly contributed to the annals of human thought. This contribution must be taken seriously if higher education is to realize goals of academic excellence and to interact responsibly with other social institutions.

Scope

Black Women in the Ivory Tower chronicles black women's struggle for access to increasingly advanced levels of formal education and presents philosophies of influential black women academics. The first part is an educational history; the second part an intellectual history. The scope of part 1, a narrative of degree attainment, lies between 1850, when Oberlin College conferred the first diploma upon Lucy Stanton, and the 1954 *Brown v. Board of Education* U.S. Supreme Court case. Although comprehensive studies of black women's academic participation are available, no work to date has adequately traced black women's attendance in higher education. A close reading of the historiography is imperative because scant attention has been paid to conflicting research methodologies and statistical inaccuracies often are repeated.

In part 1, I act as a cartographer, creating a qualitative and quantitative map of black women's collegiate history. In terms of geography, I reveal that early attainment opportunity was slightly greater in the North; that after Emancipation, the southern region generated the most college graduates; and that later, there was another shift to the North, this time for black women's graduate school attendance. By considering autobiographical accounts, social demographics, and national settings, I present unique perspectives of college life as well as patterns in the aggregate record.

Part 2 presents black women's philosophies of higher education from Anna Julia Cooper's 1892 *A Voice from the South: By a Black Woman of the South* to Mary McLeod Bethune's 1955 "Last Will and Testament." This part of the story, concerned with intellectual production, reveals how black women raised their voices as educators and contributed in significant ways to the development of higher education in the United States. The final chapter outlines how this history addresses contemporary academic issues.

Chapter Outline

Chapters 1, 2, and 3 constitute a quantitative overview of black women's educational attainment in the antebellum, Reconstruction, and Jim Crow eras. Chapter 1, "A Plea for the Oppressed," explores the antebellum period and highlights the social conditions in which black women pursued educational attainment. Chapter 2, "The Crown of Culture," tracks black women's push for higher levels of education between the Civil War and World War I, despite employment opportunities that were generally limited to agriculture, domestic service, or elementary education. Chapter 3, "Beating Onward, Ever Onward," outlines the growth in attainment between 1910 and 1954 and the development of a critical mass of black collegiate women. Throughout these first chapters, historic case studies are used as watermarks. Biographical sketches of Sarah Kinson, Lucy Stanton, Mary Jane Patterson, Mary Annette Anderson, and others are provided as signposts.

Chapter 4, "Reminiscences of School Life," considers African American women's reflections on their college experiences from the mid-1800s to the mid-1900s. After constructing the macrostory of institutions, geographic patterns, administrative dynamics, and national contexts, I offer a close look at six individual women, some well known, some obscure in the historical record: Fanny Jackson Coppin, Mary Church Terrell, Zora Neale Hurston, Lena Beatrice Morton, Rose Butler Browne, and Pauli Murray. I consider their lived experiences in the classroom, on campus, and in local communities. These women's reflections offer color and texture to the broader lines drawn in the earlier quantitative account.

Chapter 5, "I Make Myself Heard," places the six collegiate memoirs in an institutional context of black women's collective experiences. Particular attention is paid to differences at historically black colleges and universities (hereafter HBCUs) and predominantly white institutions (PWIs). Specifically, I highlight black women's appreciation of their educational access, their frustration with discriminatory policies, and the dedication to community uplift in their academic quests.

In chapter 6, "The Third Step," I investigate the conditions under which African American women pursued graduate studies and explore the disciplinary perspectives of early scholars. Here, I highlight the academic biographies of Eva Dykes, Sadie Alexander, Georgiana Simpson, and Anna Cooper, the first four recipients of the doctoral degree. These case studies tell of a passion for intellectual engagement and a dedication to pursue research that had practical implications for human and civil rights.

Part 2 offers an examination of Anna Julia Cooper's and Mary McLeod Bethune's insights on research (chapter 7, "The Yard Stick of Great Thinkers"), teaching (chapter 8, "That Which Relieves Their Hunger"), and service (chapter 9, "A Beneficent Force"). These two women were significant because both headed postsecondary institutions and were prolific educational theorists. I situate their ideas within a community of black women educators and make comparisons to educational philosophers of the Progressive era. In part 2, I explore black women's thought within the development of academic institutions in the United States, amid shifting educational ideologies, and during growth in educational attainment between the Civil War and the civil rights movement.

In chapter 10, I reflect on college access for African American women after the 1954 Supreme Court *Brown v. Board of Education* decision, articulate shortcomings in the philosophies of educators like Cooper and Bethune, and identify lessons that contemporary educators may learn from black women's experiences and ideas.

Interpretation of Educational History (Part 1)

By tracking black collegiate women's degree attainment, I have found four trends. First, they negotiated an intersection of racial and sexual contracts based on their unique standpoint. Second, black women articulated complex and useful educational philosophies. Third, as they earned college degrees and improved their social class, black women reflected the tension present in the larger national society between aristocratic and democratic ideals. Last, black women claimed public intellectual space and took time for scholarly endeavors despite social oppression, family responsibilities, and community pressures.

First, historic black collegiate women were caught in a unique social contract because of the intersection of their race and gender. Using a framework based on Rousseau's *Social Contract*, Carol Pateman's *Sexual Contract*, and Charles Mills's *Racial Contract*, in this research I posit the existence of a *standpoint social contract* for black women that is an intersection of the racial and sexual contracts. The framers of this nation's Constitution—without input from those designated as noncitizens—penned a foundational agreement that hinged upon black women's subjugated position. This contract mandated that black women be ignorant, silent, and subservient. Although black women are not a homogeneous group and differ in ethnicity, nationality, religion, occupation, and sexuality, their shared experiences created a recognizable standpoint, or social location, for black women. Common in their experience was their relation to this contract that excluded all Black women from political participation and social equity.[3]

Despite the failings of the original contract, I reclaim use of social contract theory by revisiting Rousseau's idea of a contract as an "act of association." In this history, I uncover evidence that African American women, especially those who entered the academy, attempted to fully participate in defining the national and international "common will." This record of black women's educational attainment refutes interpretations that portray them solely as objectified victims. Rather, I find that these historical narratives demonstrate that black women have crafted a social contract that exposes a contested relationship between individuals and public institutions, where black women have engaged in defining and determining their roles, even within oppressive structures. This research exposes dynamics of a social group's struggle for membership within institutions of knowledge production; using the idea of contract as a metaphor introduces a language that allows us to move beyond the "outsider within" victimization interpretations of black women's public history. In short, use of the term *contract* as a theoretical tool restores the agency of black women by recognizing their historic powers of negotiation despite ever-present structural barriers.

Second, this history reveals black women's articulation of insightful educational philosophies. Of the 114 women listed in the *Black Women in America: An Historical Encyclopedia* who are identified as educators by vocation, eleven wrote manuscripts before the 1960s. These works reflected the disparate experiences of black women, but each assumed that education should be fundamentally intertwined with moral responsibility and social justice. Of the educators in the *Encyclopedia*, eighteen earned doctoral degrees before 1955. Numerous others pursued legal, medical, and master's-level studies. Though not many obtained doctorates and few wrote full manuscripts, black women published journal articles, newspaper columns, and essays to inform and educate the public. For these intellectuals, there was no occupational pressure to produce a distinctive body of work, nor was there a market that welcomed or promoted their commentary. For those who did pursue the doctorate, their dissertation usually was not their last piece of published work. Family, work, and community-building responsibilities undoubtedly limited their publications in comparison to their male contemporaries, but they did publish relevant treatises on education.[4]

In *Reclaiming a Conversation: The Ideal of the Educated Woman* (1985), Jane Martin provided a counternarrative to traditional educational views. She conceded that scholars have recognized women as teachers and activists, but she asserted that not enough women have been granted the status of "philosophers." Martin argued that this refusal to acknowledge women as thinkers is tied to the narrow definition of "logical" thought and the claim that women are unequipped for orderly thinking.[5]

> Since the early 1970s, research has documented the ways in which such intellectual disciplines as history and psychology, literature and the fine arts, sociology and biology are biased according to sex. . . . on at least three counts the disciplines fall short of the ideal of epistemological equality for women: they exclude women from their subject matter, distort the female according to the male image of her, and deny value to characteristics the society considers feminine. . . . The implicit message is that women have never thought systematically about education, that indeed, they may be incapable of serious philosophical reflection on the topic.[6]

Though Martin's "conversation" advances gendered perspectives in this debate, it ignores race altogether. Given that in America, professions in primary and secondary education are female dominated, and that 80 percent of African American teachers are women, alternate experts need to be consulted and philosophies considered. In the canon of historic philosophical dialogues, black women are absent, but this history shows that the absence is not due to lack of black women's intellectual production.

The third theme I have identified in this history is the way in which black women's lives reflect the tensions present in the larger society between aristocratic and democratic ideals. Black women attended college based on a common understanding that the role of higher education was to prepare students for service toward social justice. As Stephanie Shaw wrote in *What a Woman Ought to Be and to Do: Black Professional Women Workers during the Jim Crow Era*, black women were educated to be "levers of service to society." Glenda Gilmore, Evelyn Higginbotham, and Cynthia Neverdon-Morton reiterated this theme in their research. My work builds on existing research by considering the dynamic role that advanced degree attainment played in black women's personal, professional, political, and social development.[7]

Black women's nineteenth-century activism in the abolition and temperance movements laid the foundation for the sororities and national associations of the twentieth-century club movement; college women were cornerstones in these service organizations. Yet, these ideas of service to community belied an ideological tug-of-war between aristocratic and democratic principles reflecting the larger identity struggle of academic institutions nationwide. Thus, the ideals of "service" and "social justice" were not always based on classless, egalitarian assumptions. Degree attainment was always balanced with a sense of attendant responsibilities, but access to privilege did not always result in a challenge of the hierarchical status quo. My investigation reveals detailed shortcomings in black women's ideals of racial uplift and woman-centered moral responsibility.

The final theme revealed in black women's educational history is that black women claimed public intellectual space in the face of many obstacles. Barriers to black women's college participation included violence, legal discrimination based on race and sex, and institutional variables like discriminatory classroom or campus policies. Black women college attendees fought to balance familial roles, church responsibilities, and organizational duties with their desire to access the individualistic privileges of academe. Black women wanted the right to whatever education might be available for any citizen of a democracy, yet the culture of community service required them to focus on learning what was necessary to secure a good job—usually teaching or nursing—to contribute to caretaking of their parents, and to raise a family of their own.

Black women scholars of the past found themselves in an ambiguous social position that continues to plague black women scholars today: college women were less likely to marry and have children because they did not fit neatly into either the black communities, which were undereducated and resource poor, or the white society to which their education acculturated them. Creating space within academic institutions and demanding quiet time to study was no small feat for early scholars.

Archival sources tell of the conflicting intellectual exchanges in which these early black women scholars engaged. On one hand, they were social activists, as demonstrated by Lucy Stanton's 1850 abolitionist graduation speech at Oberlin College entitled "A Plea for the Oppressed"; on the other hand, they sought entry into the elite halls of academia, as evidenced by Mary Annette Anderson's 1899 valedictory graduation speech at Middlebury College entitled "The Crown of Culture."[8]

The century between the eve of the Civil War and the heart of the modern civil rights movement was the most significant era in the development of educational institutions in the United States. The standardization of elementary and high schools and the proliferation of colleges and universities resulted in more widespread access to learning, formerly available only to the white, male, and upper class. In this century, a critical increase in African American women's educational attainment mirrored national growth. Black women's quest for educational, social, and political empowerment offers a germane site from which to measure the larger demographic shift, engage debates over vocational or liberal arts education, and expose inconsistencies between democratic equity and aristocratic elitism. While the social history tells part of this story, a consideration of the intellectual history is necessary to complete the picture of black women's academic life.

Interpretation of Intellectual History (Part 2)

Anna Cooper, Mary Bethune, and their contemporaries articulated educational philosophies that had four central themes: demand for applied learning; recognition of the importance of social standpoint and cultural identity in scholarship; a critical epistemology that both supported and resisted mainstream American ideals; and moral existentialism grounded in a sense of communal responsibility. Though Cooper and Bethune also taught at elementary and secondary levels, I explore these themes as they relate to postsecondary education.

Most black women educators insisted that learning be applied and that, in evaluating truth claims, experience should count heavily. Learning often provided a means of resisting oppression, and their knowledge claims were based on their own lived experience in an oppressive society. For them, demonstrated efficacy in social settings was the measurement of a theory's value. Too often, they witnessed political ideologues espousing ideals of democracy and equality while failing to put the ideals into practice for all people. Consequently, these women insisted that the meaning-making process be tied to real-world situations and that democratic ideals be matched with policy implementation.

Second, many black women educators kept their social standpoint and cultural identity at the fore of their treatises. They used dialogue rather than monologue as part of the teaching and learning process. To test truth claims, they conversed with their communities and brought their identities to bear on the discussion. Instead of placing a premium on "objectivity," they explicitly placed subjective knowledge at the center of understanding, although they did not assume that their standpoint represented that of other races. They rejected being objectified by scholars who attempted to speak for everyone.

In addition, black women in this research held themselves, and others, accountable for knowledge claims. They valued a critical approach to learning and effectively debated scholars who misrepresented black women's interests or perspectives. Gaining pedigree was not enough to earn respect as a scholar—scholarship was recognized by deeds. They produced qualitative and quantitative research to disprove falsehoods by those whom they considered educated fools and challenged claims of scholars or politicians when their egalitarian rhetoric did not match their practice.

Last, many black women academics voiced and demonstrated an ethic of care. Their ideas were based on an assumption of moral existentialism: social justice and civic responsibility were at the heart of all education—in thought and practice. Unlike traditional existentialism, the black women's brand did not find hope in individual existence but in the collective deeds of community service. Where some others questioned or ignored the social responsibility of the educated class, many black women scholars believed that those who were not serving the cause of justice for all simply were not adequately educated. Scholastic training was most important for activist purposes. Although black women's educational philosophies covered vast ground—including cultural identity's impact on educational access, administrative observations, teaching practices, and comments on curriculum preferences—moral guidelines were always present.

Cooper and Bethune contributed ideas on research, teaching, and service that support sociologist Patricia Hill Collins's argument for a "Black feminist epistemology." In *Black Feminist Thought: Knowledge, Consciousness, and the Politics of Empowerment,* Collins identified four dimensions of black feminist epistemology: (1) lived experience as criterion of meaning; (2) use of dialogue; (3) ethic of personal accountability; and (4) ethic of caring. Black women's educational philosophies provide a disciplinary portfolio that addresses these aspects of knowledge production.[9]

Cooper and Bethune embodied the oft-cited values of "scholarship, leadership, and service," or "head, heart, and hand," upon which American colleges were built. Nevertheless, these women's scholarly pursuits, educational practices, and numerous treatises were quite different from one another and reflected multilayered theoretical approaches. Both women were greatly influenced by the progressive and reform movements of their time, yet each experienced education in particular ways. Cooper wrote with an emphasis on Greek metaphors, linguistic analysis, and Romantic prose, reflecting her background in classical studies. In contrast, Bethune's work focused on political argumentation, plans for building her school, and strategies for organizational development, revealing a more pragmatic background. Their journeys as teachers and learners reflected their experiences as black women, but black women's identity and educational practice were neither static nor uniform.

Black women theorizing their social position is not a new phenomenon. As early as Phillis Wheatley (1770s), Maria Stewart (1830s), and Frances Harper (1850s), activists have publicly reflected on the meaning and experience of their social standpoints *as black women.* Cooper and Bethune are part of this historical, scholarly legacy and many others have contributed to the treasury of human ideas.

Theoretical and Methodological Frameworks

Collins described black feminist thought as a dialectical relationship in which black women resist the intersections of oppression, link their experience to ideas, acknowledge common challenges, investigate differences within black women as a group, reflect the dynamic nature of effective resistance, and support projects of other oppressed groups to advance universal freedom. Collins's work is the thematic core of this manuscript.[10]

John Hope Franklin's observations about historiographies offer a useful categorization of black women's educational research. In his essay "On the Evolution of Scholarship in Afro-American History" (1986), Franklin delineated four stages of scholarship: (1) the 1800s—when historians offered a basic demographic record of black presence in the United States; (2) the early 1900s—a list of black "firsts" in contributions to development; (3) from Jim Crow to the early civil rights movement—an era when historians documented violence, oppression, and discrimination; and (4) from the late 1940s to the early 1970s—when scholars traced African American revolt and resistance. Franklin did not assert that these stages were neat or static; rather, he outlined the general tendency of historians to approach black history from certain perspectives with specific assumptions based on the era in which they were writing.[11]

I converted this theory into a typology for my research: rather than simply record the presence, barriers, firsts, or resistance in black women's educational experiences, I used three categories—"presence," "oppression," and "contribution and creative resistance"—as methodological guidelines by which to record this history.[12]

With Collins's theoretical grounding and Franklin's categorization, I capture a complete picture of black women in colleges and universities by considering their role as both victims and victors—present and active in their own struggles for empowerment. Bettye Collier-Thomas has stated, "most of [the research on African Americans' educational experiences] is negative and tends to focus on Black people as victims, emphasizing their deficiencies and differences in comparison to whites."[13] Here, I view black women's experiences in a way that moves beyond a one-dimensional oppressed or savior narrative.

Purpose and Implications

A major purpose for this work is to challenge today's institutional leaders to increase educational opportunity. As some educational leaders have argued, diversity in higher education is imperative for academic excellence. Scholars who ignore the history of diversity in academia will remain poorly educated. This work shows that racial "minorities" have long contributed much to higher education and that their increased access to academia should be based on that contribution. Cultural diversity is central to an effective and productive intellectual democracy. Also, this work challenges marginalized populations to build on the gains made by those who excelled in the past. Further, contemporary social thought about race and education, like Tavis Smiley's *Covenant with Black America*, should depend on this history for much needed gender analysis.

Though historiography has consistently grown since the mid-1980s, shamefully little scholarly work about the history of black women exists, especially in the field of education. While a January 2005 guided keyword search for Library of Congress holdings yielded 434 references to Booker T. Washington and 752 to W.E.B. Du Bois, a search for two prominent African American women educators paled in comparison: Anna Julia Cooper (12 references) and Mary McLeod Bethune (95). The scholarly interest of researchers in educators such as John Dewey (495) and Jane Addams (241) far outweighs interest in black women educators. In addition, contemporary educators such as Paulo Freire (386) have garnered significantly more scholarly attention than black women who arguably offered just as much to the study of American education.

Authors in the edited volume *Philosophers on Education: New Historical Perspectives* (1998) raise important questions about the relationship between philosophy, history, education, and public policy. These questions include What are the aims of education? Who should formulate educational policy? Who should be educated? What interests should guide curricular choice? How should the intellectual, spiritual, civic, artistic, and technical dimensions of education be connected? Unfortunately, the philosophers chosen to answer these questions are all men in the European philosophical tradition, a choice that I contend does not provide a sufficient body of knowledge from which to assess educational meaning or policy.

Bethune and Cooper belong to a group of human beings who were enslaved during much of the time that popular "classic" philosophers—Hume, Locke, Jefferson, and others—were espousing their ideals. Moreover, some of these philosophers were aristocrats or slaveholders themselves. Black women's ideas can contribute to the dialogue that critically gauges the worth of "great men" who write "great books." Without this analysis, "classics" ring hollow.[14]

Recent scholarship by and about Black women in the academy shows almost unanimous discontent. In publications such as *A Broken Silence: Voices of African American Women in the Academy* (2002), *Sisters of the Academy: Emergent Black Women Scholars in Higher Education* (2001), and *Black Women in the Academy: Promises and Perils* (1997), black women college graduates and professionals narrate their experiences in terms of significant barriers caused by racism, sexism, and combinations of the two. Studies such as "Social Factors in the Positioning of Black Women in South African Universities" (1997) hint that this problem has international implications. This history illuminates the root causes of such widespread and enduring challenges that black women academics have faced and offers clues to potential solutions.

Black women have yet to reach demographic parity in the Ivory Tower. By fall 1999, a mere 1,706 black women were tenured as full professors of

161,309 total; this minuscule number is compared to 29,548 white women and 3,078 black men tenured as full professors. At the turn of the twenty-first century, the "community" of 176,485 faculty tenured as full professors at public and private research universities in the United States consisted of 91 percent whites, 75 percent men, 72 percent white men, 17 percent white women, 8 percent men of color (black, Hispanic, and Native American combined), and 2 percent women of color.[15]

Higher education is in need of massive reform to include the "heads, hands, and hearts" of the disenfranchised in order to make real the claims of a democracy heretofore unfulfilled. Black women's theoretical frameworks offer an effective litmus test for discussions of intelligence and academic freedom in educational institutions and the rights of education in humanity and society.

There once was a time when some scholars believed that the world was flat, the sun revolved around the earth, and that black women did not belong in the academy. The first two myths have been dispelled; let this book lay to rest the third.

Biographical Sketches—Cooper and Bethune

Cooper and Bethune expressed a vision of education heavily influenced by their complex social location as black women. The brief biographies below offer an entry point to the larger historical picture.

ANNA JULIA COOPER (1858?-1964)

Anna Julia Haywood was born enslaved in Raleigh, North Carolina, reportedly on August 10, 1858; she lived to be over 105 years old. She was the youngest of three, born to an enslaved black mother, Hannah Stanley Haywood, and an unnamed white father. In 1865, she began school at St. Augustine's in Raleigh and completed studies there in 1881.[16]

In 1877, Anna Haywood married George Cooper; the marriage license indicated that she was nineteen at the time. Mr. Cooper died only two years later; she never remarried. In July 1881, Cooper applied to Oberlin College in Ohio, and in 1884, she graduated with a B.S., specializing in mathematics. After graduation from Oberlin, she taught college courses at Wilberforce in Ohio for the 1884 school year, and in 1885, she returned to St. Augustine's, her alma mater, as a teacher. In 1888, Cooper was awarded an M.A. for mathematics from Oberlin based on her college teaching at Wilberforce. She then moved to Washington, D.C., to teach at M Street High School.

In 1901, she was appointed principal of M Street, where she led students to great academic achievements, including admission to prestigious colleges such as Yale and Harvard. Her dismissal from duties in 1906 cut short her Washington, D.C., career and reflected the politicized atmosphere of public education. From 1906 until 1910, she chaired the Department of Romance Languages at Lincoln University in Missouri. After Lincoln, Cooper returned to M Street (renamed Dunbar High School in 1916) as a teacher, not as principal. She worked there until her retirement in 1930. After leaving Dunbar, she assumed the presidency of Frelinghuysen University in Washington, D.C. (founded 1905), a school for working adults, where she stayed until her second retirement in 1941. She taught for over seventy years and continued to write and publish into her early nineties.

Cooper was a skilled lecturer: she addressed black clergymen in D.C. on the controversial topic of womanhood (1886); she spoke to the American Conference of Educators on the higher education of women (1890); she spoke at the Chicago World's Fair with Fanny Coppin and Fannie Williams (1893); she attended the first Pan African Congress in London (1900); and she addressed Quakers in New Jersey on ethics and race (1902). Her publications included a series of essays titled *A Voice from the South* (1892); a translation of *Le Pèlerinage de Charlemagne* (1925); a memoir, *The Third Step* (1945); and in 1951, at the age of ninety-three, she produced *Personal Reflections of the Grimké Family* about her social and intellectual life in D.C.

In December 1915, she became the guardian of five children, and during her lifetime she took care of many more in her home on T Street in D.C. She also volunteered at many social welfare agencies: she began a chapter of the Campfire Girls in Washington, D.C., served at a War Camp in Indianapolis, and supervised a playground in West Virginia. She cofounded the Colored Women's League in D.C., a predecessor to the National Association of Colored Women (NACW; founded 1896), and she was a supervisor and trustee of a black settlement house. She was also a dedicated member of the Alpha Kappa Alpha Sorority, Incorporated, and delivered the keynote address at the sorority's 1925 National Convention (Boulé), where she received the Sorbonne diploma.

Fortunately, Cooper's life and work have gained significant recognition since the 1980s. Her radical brand of feminist analysis has provided fertile ground for exploring the intersections of identity, epistemology, and ethics. Whereas historians have previously investigated her feminist or spiritual strivings, I now highlight her academic contributions.

MARY MCLEOD BETHUNE (1875–1955)

Mary Jane McLeod was born on July 10, 1875, in Mayesville, South Carolina; she died in May 1955 at her "Retreat" on the campus of Bethune-Cookman College in Daytona, Florida. She was the fifteenth of seventeen children and the first in the McLeod family to be born free from enslavement. Like most children during Reconstruction, she labored to help keep the family afloat, picking cotton or harvesting corn, but her family wanted a different life than agricultural work for her. In 1882, Emma Wilson, a black missionary, opened Mayesville Industrial Institute for black children at Trinity Presbyterian Church, and Mary began attending at seven years old. She graduated in 1886 at the age of twelve. That year she began study at Scotia Seminary (now Barber-Scotia College) in Concord, North Carolina. She graduated from Scotia in 1894 and, in July, moved to Chicago to study at Moody Bible Institute.[17]

After graduation in 1895 and unsuccessful applications to become a missionary in Africa, she briefly returned to Mayesville to assist Emma Wilson and then, in 1896, moved to Augusta, Georgia, to teach eighth grade at the Haines Institute. Haines was founded by Lucy Laney, who was part of the first graduating class of Atlanta University. Laney founded the school after teaching for twelve years in Georgia's public schools, and Bethune wrote of the powerful influence that Laney's work had on her own teaching and institution building.

After one year at Haines, Mary McLeod transferred to Sumter, South Carolina. In May 1898, she married Albertus Bethune and the next year had a son, Albertus Jr. At twenty-three, Bethune moved to Savannah, Georgia, and, six months after giving birth, accepted a position in Palatka, Florida. She then made history by founding what is now Bethune-Cookman College.

In *The Answered Prayer to a Dream: Bethune-Cookman College, 1904–1994*, historian Sheila Flemming wrote: "on October 4, 1904, she opened the doors of the Daytona Literary and Industrial School for Training Negro Girls in Daytona Beach; she started with $1.50, faith in God, and five little girls [ranging from eight to twelve years old]." The $1.50 was a down payment on a small building, and tuition was fifty cents per week for each girl. In two years, she had 250 students. Flemming chronicled the development of Bethune-Cookman College as an institution but also showed the central role Bethune played in building and maintaining her college.[18]

Because of her administrative savvy, Bethune garnered the philanthropic support of James Gamble (of Proctor and Gamble); Thomas White (of White Sewing Machine Co. in Ohio); and John Rockefeller, who had begun the

General Education Board grants for schools. In 1908, with the admission of male students, the name of the school was changed to Daytona Educational Industrial Training School. The curriculum was based on that of Booker T. Washington's Tuskegee Institute, and in 1908 Washington, whom Bethune greatly admired, visited her school. In 1911, Bethune founded the Patsy McLeod Hospital (named for her mother) with money donated by Andrew Carnegie; in 1927, the City of Daytona Beach took over the hospital's operations. In 1923, the school merged with Cookman Institute (founded in Jacksonville, Florida, in 1872). Bethune remained president until January 1943.

Bethune donated her life to community and public service. While at Moody Bible College, she visited and sang to prisoners, served the homeless at the Pacific Garden Mission, and counseled people on the south side of Chicago. In Florida, she established the Tomoka Mission at a varnish/turpentine migrant workers' camp, where she taught children and counseled adults. Over the years, she assisted the Red Cross, Planned Parenthood, National Sharecroppers Fund, Americans for Democratic Action, National Urban League, National Commission on Christian Education, Association of American Colleges, General Conference of the Methodist Church, and League of Women Voters. She served on the board of directors for the Southern Conference Educational Fund, American Council on African Education, Council of Church Women, Girl Scouts of America, Hyde Park Memorial for FDR, and the National Committee on Atomic Information.

Bethune was very deeply involved in the women's club movement of the early twentieth century: in 1917, she was president of the Florida Federation of Colored Women; in 1924, she was the president of the NACW; and in December 1935, she founded the National Council of Negro Women (NCNW), an umbrella organization for black women's clubs nationwide. Bethune was a member of Delta Sigma Theta Sorority, an organization intimately involved with the support of the early formation of NCNW. Bethune remained president of the NCNW until 1949 and served as a president of historian Carter G. Woodson's Association for the Study of Negro Life and History (ASNLH) from 1936 to 1951. In 1940, she became the vice president of the National Association for the Advancement of Colored People (NAACP).

Bethune was associated with the presidential administrations of Calvin Coolidge (1928 conference on child welfare), Herbert Hoover (1929 National Commission for Child Welfare and Commission on Home Building and Home Ownership), and Franklin Delano Roosevelt (1935 National Youth Administration, relief work, and job training). In 1936, she was appointed director of the National Youth Administration's Division of Negro Affairs, making her the first black woman to head a federal agency. In 1951, Harry

Truman appointed her to the Committee of Twelve for National Defense. Bethune was highly decorated: she was awarded the Order of Honor and Merit, Haiti's highest honor (February 1949); and granted eleven honorary degrees. She was honored by being portrayed on a U.S. postage stamp (1985), and Bethune-Cookman College still stands as a testament to her dedication to higher education and community service. The school enrolls approximately 2,600 full-time students each semester and still requires community service for graduation.

Mary McLeod Bethune: Building a Better World: Essays and Selected Documents, a valuable collection of Bethune's writing from 1902 to her death in 1955, showed that even though Bethune did not publish a single-authored manuscript, she contributed to texts such as *What the Negro Wants* (1944) and wrote hundreds of journal articles, letters, and opinion pieces. The editors of the Bethune collection, critiquing previous work on Bethune, wrote that "these early biographies all suffer from a lack of focus, omission of significant people and Bethune's work with them, and most seriously, the absence of primary sources."[19] Further, the authors asserted that "scholarly treatment of Black women in history demands expansive paradigms to accommodate their multi-layered identities and complexity." They attribute a "multiple-consciousness" to Bethune and other black women that extends beyond the "double-consciousness" of Du Bois.[20]

Beyond these limitations in existing scholarship, I argue that scholars have duly recognized Bethune as a premier educator in African American history, but they highlight her actions as an administrator or political figure rather than her contributions to social or educational philosophy. My research extends scholarship on Bethune, Cooper, and their contemporaries by considering their academic ideas in addition to their activist experience.

PART 1

Educational Attainment

"A Plea for the Oppressed"

Educational Strivings, Pre-1865

Before the Civil War, over 250 institutions offered college-level work; only a select few were open to black or women students. The most notable were Oberlin (founded in 1833), Antioch (1853), and Wilberforce (1856), all in Ohio; Hillsdale (1844) in Michigan; Cheyney (1837) and Lincoln (1854) in Pennsylvania; and Berea (1855) in Kentucky.[1]

Generally, efforts to educate black girls brought violent reprisals, even in liberal New England, as exemplified by mob violence that destroyed Prudence Crandall's school for black girls in 1833 Connecticut. If the climate in New England was hostile to the idea of educating African Americans, the rest of the country was downright murderous. Yet, in the cold, hard environment of colonial and antebellum America, seeds found fertile ground, and buds of hope began to bloom; black women earned their first college degrees in Ohio. Oberlin was the only college to graduate a significant number of black women before the Civil War.[2]

First Wave of Black Women's College Attainment

As has been widely recorded, Oberlin College was a beacon of light for antebellum black scholars, but in a geographically limited sense: the majority of students came from the North or Midwest. Migration patterns suggest that, before 1850, freedmen from the South mainly moved to Indiana or California and later to Kansas, Texas, or Wisconsin. Three major colleges made Ohio a key destination for black migrants, but the attraction was diminished by the economic or social prospects in the North and West. Still, there were at least 152 "identifiable black" college and preparatory students at Oberlin before the Civil War. There were 12 black women recipients of the Literary Degree (L.D.) and 44 black women candidates for that degree by the mid-1860s. Of this number, 23, almost half, were from Ohio, and only 13 were from southern states.[3]

The number of black women students at Oberlin continually grew, but they were confined to the Literary Course, regarded as the "ladies' course,"

Figure 1. Lucy Stanton Sessions. Courtesy of Oberlin College Archives.

Figure 2. Mary Jane Patterson. Courtesy of Oberlin College Archives.

Figure 3. Fanny Jackson
Coppin. Courtesy of Oberlin
College Archives.

which was designed to be less academically challenging than the course for males enrolled in bachelor's degree programs, or the "gentlemen's course." As in other schools, the curriculum at Oberlin was segregated by gender. In 1850, Lucy Stanton was the first black woman to complete the requirements for the L.D. at Oberlin.[4]

Stanton was born free in Cleveland, Ohio, in 1831. Her parents, Margaret Stanton and John Brown, were active in the abolitionist movement. As the president of the Ladies Literary Society and a graduation speaker at the 1850 commencement, Stanton delivered an address titled "A Plea for the Oppressed" that challenged the privileged class in the audience to actively participate in the struggle for African American freedom. As noted in *Homespun Heroines and Other Women of Distinction*, Stanton had a noteworthy but challenging career in education. She taught in Ohio, Mississippi, and Alabama before ultimately moving to Los Angeles in 1903 with her daughter, Florence. She was married and divorced twice, and because of her marriage status, her role as a single mother, and her race, some applications she filed to teach in the South were rejected. Nevertheless, she melded her learning and her social activism, becoming an influential member of her Los Angeles community. She died in February 1910.[5]

Twelve years after Stanton received her L.D., Mary Jane Patterson became the first black woman to earn the B.A. degree. A few students at Oberlin had substantial family support, and their families became central figures in the local communities surrounding the college. Patterson exemplified this case. She was part of an extended family of aunts, uncles, and cousins who owned a local grocery called "Patterson's Corner" in the Oberlin community.[6]

After graduation in 1862, Patterson moved to Philadelphia and eventually taught with Fanny Jackson Coppin, another Oberlin graduate, at the Institute for Colored Youth (ICY). She taught there until 1869, when she moved to D.C., where she worked until her passing in 1894. She became the first black principal of the Preparatory High School for Negroes in 1871 and retired from that position in 1884. Though Patterson earned an advanced degree for her time and held a high administrative position, that did not ensure financial stability. Responding to an invitation to visit Oberlin for alumni festivities, Patterson expressed regrets for not being able to participate because she was in charge of her family and had overwhelming financial responsibilities.[7]

Most black Oberlin attendees, like Patterson, were born free and came from families with the means to support their daughters' educations. Sarah Margru Kinson was representative of those exceptions who chose to pursue college studies despite their former status as slaves. One of the millions stolen from Africa, Sarah was aboard the *Amistad* schooner during the 1839 rebellion. After the famous 1841 U.S. Supreme Court case, Sarah returned to Freetown, Sierra Leone, West Africa. After five years in Africa, she ventured to the United States at age fourteen to attend Oberlin College. She studied at Oberlin between 1846 and November 1849, when she again returned to Africa as a missionary for the American Missionary Association. For a time, Lucy Stanton and Sarah Kinson roomed together. Sarah was a prolific letter writer to her benefactors, reporting about her learning process, aspirations, and perceptions of educational missionary work. Hers was but one of many remarkable stories about the twists and turns that took place in black women's lives during this time.[8]

Black women who attended PWIs during the antebellum era did not always suffer the mob violence that would plague black students in the 1950s desegregation efforts. Yet integrated school experiences revealed an undercurrent of race antagonism as well as cases of overt hostility, like that of Edmonia Lewis, who entered Oberlin in 1859. Lewis, of African American and Chippewa heritage, suffered a series of physical attacks by fellow students who accused her of poisoning two white female classmates and of stealing art supplies. Both charges were racially motivated and were proven false, but even after she was beaten up by white students (who were not punished), Lewis ultimately was denied the right to graduate. Though not all incidents at PWIs were so severe, black students were subject to racism by students, staff, and faculty, or by institutional policies that regulated curriculum, housing, meals, and social interaction.[9]

Frances (Fanny) Marion Jackson Coppin, arriving at Oberlin in 1860, graduated in August 1865. Coppin, born enslaved, followed Patterson's footsteps in the "gentlemen's course" and then taught and was principal at the ICY from 1869 to 1902. By 1865, only three black women had earned the B.A. (Patterson, Coppin, and Frances Josephine Norris from Georgia), and two were in candidacy (Elizabeth Evans from North Carolina and Georgiana Mitchem Adams from Peoria, Illinois).[10]

Most college students attended institutions in their home states; however, many families moved from the southern slavocracy to middle or northern states so their daughters could attend school. Oberlin, like Wilberforce, was a way station on the Underground Railroad and a hotbed of abolitionist activity, which greatly impacted the campus climate. However, life was not easy for black students, despite the relatively liberal attitudes in middle and northern states. For many, isolation was a significant part of their student experience. Despite attempts to include black students in campus life and the popularity some black students enjoyed, the lack of a critical mass had a chilling effect. Black women also were woefully behind in college access. The first black woman to attain the bachelor's degree did so two hundred years after a white male, forty years after a black man, and nearly twenty-five years after three white women received the B.A. from Oberlin in 1841.[11]

Education for Antebellum African Americans

In *The Education of the Negro Prior to 1861*, Carter G. Woodson outlined the ebb and flow of educational opportunities for African Americans during the colonization, enslavement, and nation building of the antebellum period. He identifies four eras of African American education between 1619 and the Civil War. From 1619 to 1750, the solidification of race-based enslavement narrowed opportunity, while from 1750 to 1800, the air of freedom exuded by American revolutionaries brought a relative loosening of educational restrictions. From 1800 to the mid-1830s, African Americans aspiring to be educated experienced a backlash due to the Haitian Revolution and the subsequent revolts by Gabriel Prosser, Denmark Vesey, and Nat Turner (and to reaction to David Walker's *Appeal*); and the period from the 1830s to 1860 was an era of intensified struggle for freedom. Though there were many formal and informal schools for Africans in America, the pre–Civil War era was largely barren of educational opportunity. Woodson's description of the antebellum period adeptly contextualized the arduous rise of the select few African American men and women who strove for education in the shadow of American slavery. While whites who attended college during the seventeenth century sought power over others, black collegians during the nineteenth century sought power over themselves. Heather Williams's *Self-Taught: African American Education in Slavery and Freedom* painstakingly details the extent to which black people endured hardship to educate themselves in the face of standardized violence and institutionalized terrorism. Although a college education was scarce for whites, it was essentially nonexistent for blacks.[12]

A few black men began attending college in the early 1800s. John Chavis is reported to be the first African American to graduate from college, having completed his studies in 1799 at Washington and Lee University in Virginia (formerly Washington Academy). However, due to lack of available documentation for Chavis, Alexander Lucius Twilight, who graduated from Middlebury College in Vermont in 1823, is commonly recognized as the first African American college graduate. In 1804, Lemuel Haynes, a pastor and American Revolutionary War veteran, was awarded an honorary M.A. degree from Middlebury College during its second commencement, but neither the degree nor the honor indicated blacks' regular access to college attendance. Among the first to be awarded degrees were Edward Jones, who earned a B.A. from Amherst College in Massachusetts in 1823, and John Brown Russwurm, an 1826 graduate of Bowdoin College in Maine who became editor of the influential New York abolitionist paper *Freedom's Journal*. In 1844, Howard University founding faculty member George B. Vashon became the first African American graduate of Oberlin College. Approximately one hundred African Americans, including only three women, earned the B.A. before the war's end.[13]

Though not many attended college, some African Americans attended schools before Emancipation. As in the evolution of the larger American school system, early formal education for black people represented a link between religious principles and rudimentary literacy. Most formal African American education began with Sabbath schools. Early Quaker and Catholic denominations advanced educational opportunity for black people in the South. Statewide education policies varied greatly. For example, Virginia banned education for those who did not adhere to the premise of white supremacy, whereas in North Carolina, Quakers were allowed to develop schools; the number of schools developed for blacks in those states reflected this difference. The disparate legacy of early educational opportunity in the South became clearer as states like North Carolina and Georgia easily out-paced restrictive states like Florida, South Carolina, Mississippi, and Alabama.[14]

The legal and social status of black women varied widely in different regions between 1619 and 1850; what can be said, generally, is that legal status combined with economic and social class played a very large part in determining who had access to formal education. Those families who could afford to send their daughters to schools for teacher training or liberal arts education, regardless of region, could do so only because of financial capital (earned in trades or agriculture), social capital (earned through elite kinship or white sponsorship), or a combination of the two. Though not all Africans were enslaved, the system of American apartheid forced Africans in America to seek intellectual development in a myriad of arenas outside of the developing formal school systems; black women were no exception.

Due to prohibitions in the South and unstable support for educational attainment in the North, free and enslaved black people in the antebellum era relied largely on their own initiative to learn to read, write, calculate, and study liberal or vocational subjects. The historians Woodson and Williams argue convincingly that black people willfully broke the law and conducted their own formal or informal learning despite the ever-looming threat of violent repercussions.[15]

By the mid-1800s, black women in the North and South had opened schools to educate black people. Catherine Ferguson (1793) in New York; Julian Froumountaine (1819) and Miss DeaVeaux (1838) in Georgia; Sarah Mapps Douglass (1821) in Philadelphia; and a group of French-educated Haitian nuns in Baltimore (1829) represented thousands of African American women who taught themselves, their families, and their communities to read and write during an era when it was either legally or socially prohibited. These women made significant contributions at a time when women's leadership was not readily acknowledged or accepted. Within schools that were not founded by women, especially those that met in black churches, women assumed most elementary and teacher training, but top administrative positions—which often required public speaking—were reserved for men.[16]

White northern missionaries developed many formal primary and secondary schools for free blacks. Many small schools in the North and Midwest offered instruction to black people prior to the Civil War. Though the curriculum in colleges differed for men and women, there was little gender segregation in African American's primary education. A few black women, like teacher Charlotte Forten Grimké, were freeborn, had educators in their families, and had obtained a normal or high school education. These early scholars expressed shock, dismay, and outrage at the lack of equality for blacks or women in the nation, and they advocated widespread change.[17]

Overall, black students suffered from poor curricula, small teaching staffs, and limited access to jobs that required advanced degree attainment. In the South, where the majority of black people lived, if education for blacks was tolerated, the school year was shorter for black children than for white children because of the privileging of field-labor schedules over school schedules, and less money was spent on physical facilities for black students. When there was support, much of the financial backing came from black communities themselves. Further, the common school (elementary) and normal school (secondary and teacher-training) curriculum reflected the prevalent racism of white America.[18]

Some black women became notable public figures and were certainly intellectuals, even though they did not attend college. A few activists, such as Maria Stewart and Frances E. W. Harper, had the advantage of grammar school or secondary education. Most, like Sojourner Truth and Jarena Lee, had little or no formal schooling but demonstrated advanced logic and critical thinking in the expression of their religious philosophies; they showed that intelligence was not dependent upon literacy. Truth could neither read nor write, yet she effectively articulated the complex relationship between race and gender and offered pointed critique of existing oppressive American hierarchies that barred freedom.[19]

Development of Higher Education in the United States

From the beginning of postsecondary education in the New World, there was question about the true goals of the academy. Though new colleges started out as crucibles for solidifying the morals of would-be colony leaders, a more pragmatic vision of the role of higher education soon emerged. As the political states and moneyed class grew stronger, the link between academic training and statesmanship became stronger. Increasingly, the development of the academy came to establish, serve, and protect the interests of a privileged few. Much of the funding for colonial academies—especially those that now make up the "Ivy League"—came from blood money of imperialist ventures against Asian, Native American, Latin American, and African nations or cultures. The return on the investment was the strengthening of an emerging American oligarchy. As early as 1693, the development of classical-vocational dichotomies became a moral and economic schism in institutional agendas. Debates about how students were to be trained and for whose benefit or about who was qualified for leadership became central to defining college study.[20]

Before 1850, the relationship of schools to religious groups such as Catholics, Congregationalists, Quakers, Baptists, Presbyterians, Anglicans, and Methodists also solidified. Sectarianism, reflected in churches' desire to have colleges adhere to their own religious paradigm, would be one reason for the rapid growth in college numbers. Schools often exemplified denominationalism or ethnic territorialism, which caused uneven development of antebellum and Reconstruction colleges.[21]

Due to the demands of rural life and the labor required of each family and community member, the notion of popular education was not pervasive in colonial America. Harvard (founded in 1636 in Massachusetts), the College of William and Mary (1692 in Virginia), and Yale (1701 in Connecticut) were founded for the very few who would be counted as citizens—"we the people"—in the colonial era.

During the Great Awakening of the eighteenth century, the common people embraced personal agency in their religious life; religion was no longer mediated solely by church leaders. College education experienced no such transformation. The academies moved further and further from their original moral strivings and became more oriented toward the material strivings of the elite men who attended. Though seminaries continued to enjoy academic growth, colleges moved toward secularism.

Much like the American political structure, higher education was not intended to be a popular endeavor. On October 28, 1636, the Massachusetts General Court passed legislation that provided for the founding of Harvard College; the Englishmen in the new country imagined themselves as "intending to lead lives no less than the purest, aspiring to serve God and their fellowmen in the fullest," and acknowledged a "responsibility to the future." To this group, "service" meant leadership, and leadership meant social dominance. The growth of higher education in the United States was sporadic; fits and spurts of growth attempted to match the growing demand. Yet a college diploma was still granted to only a select few. America entered the British-American War of the 1770s with only nine colleges. By 1776, there were only three thousand living graduates of American colleges. At the start of the Civil War, there were approximately 250 colleges, and perhaps as many as 700 institutions had tried and failed by that time.[22]

Once established, colleges quickly sought to distinguish themselves as elite. The 1819 Dartmouth College Supreme Court decision in *Dartmouth v.*

Woodward stipulated that, "once chartered, a college was beyond the control of the state," establishing the separation of public and private institutions. However, private colleges heavily depended on public funds. Once colleges gained prominence, they developed a selective amnesia and peddled a myth of self-reliance. As the historian Frederick Rudolph reported: "Speaking in 1873 against the creation of a tax-supported national university, President Eliot of Harvard advanced the argument that 'our ancestors well understood the principle that to make a people free and self-reliant, it is necessary to let them take care of themselves.'"[23] President Eliot was conveniently forgetting the "over one hundred occasions before 1789 [on which] the General Court of Massachusetts appropriated funds for Harvard College, which clearly was not capable of taking care of itself." Although they claimed private status, Harvard, Yale, Columbia and the like would not have survived without public funds.[24]

With public funding, the elite colleges did develop. Colleges experienced growing pains as faculties had great debates around subjects like physical education and administrations waffled over compulsory prayer and corporal punishment. Advanced study developed in a time of uncertainty about how closely students should resemble monks in their self-discipline and dedication. In 1831, two Harvard professors established an advanced teacher-preparation seminar in classics, and Thomas Jefferson's college in Virginia began to offer, in addition to the B.A. program, an M.A. program to those who completed advanced study in ancient languages, mathematics, natural philosophy, chemistry, moral philosophy, and two modern languages. The M.A. had been awarded at Middlebury early in the nineteenth century, but not until the 1830s did "graduate study" begin in earnest. Though the Harvard class did not last and the M.A. degree quality at Virginia had to be enhanced in order to qualify as "advanced," these events signaled a move from a college to a university system. Difficulties in funding, curriculum, administration, and growth foreshadowed problems that black colleges would grapple with as they developed later in the century.[25]

As the American college matured, students and professors alike institutionalized the glorification of ancient Greek culture. The architects of the Ivory Tower distorted history by erasing from scholarly memory contributions made in science, technology, religion, law, and the arts by peoples of Africa, the Middle East, Asia, indigenous populations, or any peoples other than an amalgamated European construct. The social significance of race was constructed, based loosely on unstable physical indicators. Ignoring significant biological and social variation, European—that is, white—studies dominated the New World academy. Fueled by an economic imperative to rationalize enslavement and world domination, whiteness was invented and, however questionably derived, rationalized by the academy in the name of science and logic. Though physical variation was a certainty, the significance assigned to it was an absurdity. Nonetheless, in the United States, the world began to be defined first through an English (white) aristocratic lens and then through an American (white) aristocratic lens. Black students who attended antebellum colleges like Oberlin were instructed in this "classical" canon that included Greece but excluded Africa.

A typical curriculum of the early nineteenth century consisted of Latin, Greek, logic, Hebrew, and rhetoric in the first year; logic, Greek, Hebrew, and an introduction to natural philosophy (later called physics) in the second year; mental philosophy (metaphysics), moral philosophy, and some form of economics, ethics, political science, and sociology in the third year; and review in Latin, Greek, logic, and natural philosophy, with an introduction of mathematics in the senior year. All subjects were considered to provide knowledge essential to the educated person, and all were taught from assumptions of white and male superiority. Debating, literary, and Greek-letter organizations developed as means for some to further differentiate themselves from the growing masses of students by claiming intellectual distinction beyond that bestowed by completion of the standard courses. Of these clubs, Greek organizations particularly captured the academic imagination, and Greek mythology became American mythology.[26]

After the French Revolution, French was added to the curriculum. The *Yale Report* of 1828, supported by Princeton, called for a solidification of the "classic" Aristotelian canon and reinstituted the call for "superior" education to reflect elite interests over those of the "laboring classes." Classic and practical agendas remained in tension. Then, in 1850, President Wayland of Brown University developed a study—equal in influence to the earlier *Yale Report*—that urged a shift toward practicality in college education. His complaint was that "the old course of study made no sense in an environment defined by the exploitative possibilities of an abundant continent." Profit motive, defined by the interests of a developing middle class, took the driver's seat in higher education. In the early nineteenth century, the wealthy had not made their money by going to college—they had made it from planting or trade. The extremely wealthy did fund the development of elite colleges, but in the mid-nineteenth century, it was the petit bourgeois who captured the curriculum to make the institutions generate social, political, and economic security for themselves.[27]

Such was the environment in which the Morrill Acts of 1862 and 1890 were passed and why they provoked so much debate. On one hand, heads of wealthy colleges opposed the establishment of public universities because it would popularize education and allot land to states, thus redistributing resources and wealth. On the other hand, the agricultural and mechanical focus of the state school curriculum would produce much-needed technology that enabled workers to generate wealth. When the acts passed, the first provided for the support of at least one college in every state, and the second renewed fund allotments and "stipulated that no appropriations would go to states that denied admissions to the colleges on the basis of race unless they also set up alternative facilities."[28]

These struggles between religious, industrial, agricultural, political, and aristocratic factions fed the curricular debates about what a college should prepare one to do or be. Race was central to the debate, but gender also was a site for constructing the identity of higher education in the United States.[29]

As in the early men's colleges, women's colleges originated as seminaries, training women for moral service, noble refinement, or both. The main reason some men could rationalize women's education was because it ensured morality and obedience—the proposition of developing women's intellect was seen as absurd: "The colonial view of woman was simply that she was intellectually inferior—incapable, merely by reason of being a woman, of great thoughts. Her faculties were not worth training. Her place was in the home, where man had assigned her a number of useful functions."[30] Thus, seminaries provided the first glimmer of hope; once the door was opened, there was no turning back.

In New England, Emma Willard (Troy, 1821), Catherine Beecher (Hartford, 1828), and Mary Lyon (South Hadley, 1836) took first steps to institutionalize white women's education. Georgia Female College in Macon, opened in 1839, offered one model of southern women's access, but the example was not widely followed in the region. Education for white women, as for African Americans, was initially established in the North, Midwest, or the western frontier.[31]

Oberlin was a forerunner of collegiate-level study. In 1837, Oberlin enrolled four female freshmen, three of whom graduated from the college department "gentlemen's course," earning a B.A. in 1841. Still, women's education was a rarity, and organizations like the American Women's Education Association (founded in 1852) worked to create uniformity and standards in the various women's institutions and to broaden opportunity.[32]

Building on the private school foundation, the state college movement began with the University of Iowa in 1855 and the University of Wisconsin in 1863, and then spread to Indiana, Missouri, Michigan, and California. State schools provided another arena of possibility, though they initially limited women's attendance to small numbers.[33]

That women of any race were intellectual beings was an uncommon position in the nineteenth century. Archaic views of women and scholarly study prevailed, and though enrollment increased, public sentiment about providing resources for women or African Americans to attend college was hostile at best, deadly at worst.

Social Conditions

Limited access to educational attainment was the least of the oppressions that black women suffered during this time. As the slave system solidified, strictures on mobility and intellectual development increasingly tightened. The formalization of slavery in the 1640s wove inequality into the very fabric of the emerging nation. In 1740, South Carolina became the first colony to draft a law against teaching black people to read or write, and most southern states quickly followed. However, even in the first wave of black women's educational attainment, a lawsuit was filed challenging racial segregation in education. In 1848, Benjamin Roberts, father to Sarah Roberts, sued the City of Boston for his daughter's right to attend a local school much closer to their home than the designated black school. Unlike the 1954 *Brown* decision, the Boston court upheld segregation, and a precedent for the "separate-but-equal" concept was embedded early in American educational history long before *Plessy v. Ferguson* (1896) established the doctrine on a national level. In the era that generated the disastrous Fugitive Slave Law of 1850, the dominant class attempted to smother black women's rights of self-definition and self-determination.[34]

As a pervasive system, slavery vanquished the chance for black people to grow academically and limited the choices for countless numbers of their descendants. For black people, the land of the free and home of the brave would have been more appropriately described as the land of the enslaved and home of race-based terrorism. In 1790, there were almost 60,000 free and 698,000 enslaved Africans in America. In 1820, there were 1,519,017 enslaved in the Lower South alone. Ninety percent of those enslaved lived in the South, and 95 percent lived in rural areas. In 1830, fewer than 3,000 enslaved Africans lived in the North. By 1860, the black enslaved population had skyrocketed: there were 3,953,760 enslaved in United States, approximately 3,953,696 of whom were in the South (mainly the Deep South states of Alabama, Arkansas, Florida, Georgia, Louisiana, Mississippi, South Carolina, and Texas). Ten percent of this number accounted for the "Mulatto," or mixed-race, who were enslaved. While a few had the privilege of having their head in a book, most had the peril of having their minds numbed by legally being owned by another human being and they were simply worked to death. Educational access and academic development were regulated by region; slavery in the United States foreshadowed generations of arrested development for many millions of African Americans, especially in the South.[35]

Between the hardship of fieldwork or domestic labor, separation from family, virtual immobility, low health status, high infant mortality, and poverty, African Americans suffered intellectually. Though Africans maintained agency as demonstrated by ingenious survival and communication skills, the dehumanizing effects of slavery created tremendous barriers to their reaching full scholarly potential. However, many blacks during the first wave of attainment achieved literacy without formal schooling. The narratives of Olaudo Equiano, Mary Prince, Frederick Douglass, and Harriet Jacobs demonstrate black literary production despite the limitations of enslavement.[36]

Where there was social space for formal schooling, black women formed clubs to link their personal development to the larger causes of abolition, racial justice, temperance, women's rights, and equal access to resources. Particularly in northern urban areas like Boston, Washington, D.C., and Philadelphia, where there was a relative critical mass of African Americans and some freedom to convene, the black women who had access to formal education before the Civil War formed scholarly and benevolent societies.[37]

A fundamental link between community service and education was grounded in the Quaker tradition, especially during late 1700s and early 1800s, yet for African American women, activism was more a matter of racial-group survival than of a distal sense of benevolence. Although nineteenth-century clubwomen were mainly free, literate, and living in the North, they were aware that many family and community members were still in the grip of slavery, and that amidst fugitive slave legislation, bondage was only a kidnapping away.[38]

Black women who were formally educated were indoctrinated into a specific type of knowledge: White missionaries provided instruction that was based on the assumption that black people were savages in need of civilizing, natural slaves in need of morality, brutes and sexual deviants in need of purity, or all of the above. There was a massive campaign of character assassination directed against black women that created a series of degrading and persistent stereotypes. The idea that black women could be learned *ladies* was rejected, even in the most liberal white communities. The quest by black women of this era for "true womanhood" often required that they assimilate a Victorian vision of white femininity in order to claim humanity.[39]

In the dominant society, black women were not seen as moral beings; black women's character was everywhere impugned. Conversely, access to college and marginal success in business trades developed a small cadre of black people who saw themselves as above the bar in terms of civility. The middle-class black community, comprised of activists involved in the temperance, social uplift, and abolitionist movements, often held that black women were more biologically capable than black men (or white people) of setting moral standards—which therefore made them more responsible for doing so. Both of these views held black women as exclusively moral or immoral, but neither view counted them as intellectual. Despite the limitations of colonial and antebellum education, black women left behind individual, social, and institutional legacies of learning that readied the ground for future enrichment. Lucy Stanton's "Plea for the Oppressed" foreshadowed a marriage of educational access and social activism that became connected to black women's scholarship within the changing identity of the American academy.[40]

"The Crown of Culture"

Educational Attainment, 1865–1910

Between the end of the Civil War and the beginning of World War I, many black women blossomed in fertile academic ground. Not only were three colleges developed especially for black women, but this era cultivated the first substantial crop of scholars to complete formal training that was on par with men's and to challenge the general assertion that they were incapable of higher learning.

This growth, though significant, was qualified; black women were admitted to schools but not always to the college department. For example, in 1866, ninety-six black students attended Berea College in Kentucky with ninety-one whites, but few blacks, and no black women, were enrolled in the college department. Most black women who graduated from college in the second wave of attainment did so in the South, but degrees were only sparingly granted and most in areas other than liberal studies.[1]

In 1892, Cooper wrote *A Voice from the South: By a Black Woman of the South*, a cornerstone in nineteenth-century critical feminist research and social commentary. In *Voice*, published a decade after she earned a master's degree, Cooper documented the limited opportunities that black women had at the end of the nineteenth century. She considered the "race problem" and the "woman question" related to economics, education, and political participation. The text did not focus solely on higher education but clearly linked educational attainment to economic and political advancement.[2]

Because Cooper's assessment of collegiate black women was insightful and groundbreaking, her study "The Higher Education of Women" is still widely cited. Subsequent research, however, demonstrated that her 1890 survey calculations were not accurate. Hers was an independent survey, and, as the twentieth century arrived, scholars like W.E.B. Du Bois and Charles Johnson conducted sociological research (with the advantage of a team of research assistants) that offered a more comprehensive account of the status of black women's educational attainment to date. Nonetheless, Cooper's study was an essential first attempt to measure black women's degree attainment.

Figure 4. Dr. Anna Julia Cooper.
Courtesy of Oberlin College
Archives.

Figure 5. Mary Church Terrell. Courtesy of
Library of Congress.

Figure 6. Mary Annette
Anderson. Courtesy of
Middlebury College Special
Collections.

Estimating the Second Wave of Attainment

In 1890, Cooper claimed that fewer than thirty women had earned a degree for college-level work, reporting: "I wrote a few days ago to the colleges which admit women and asked how many Colored women had completed the B.A. course in each during its entire history. These are the figures returned: Fisk leads with 12; Oberlin next with 5; Wilberforce 4, Ann Arbor and Wellesley with 3 each, Livingstone 2, Atlanta 1, Howard as yet, none." She then asked the principal of the Washington, D.C., M Street High School—the leading school for African American youth in the country—how many of their women graduates attended college; he reported only one, and she attended Cornell. Given these numbers, the state graduate count was dismal: Tennessee had 12 graduates, Ohio 9, Michigan 3, Massachusetts 3, North Carolina 2, and Georgia 1. According to this count, there were 15 black women graduates from northern colleges and 15 from southern colleges.[3]

By mid-twentieth century, more women than men earned college degrees annually; thus Cooper's demand for more female educational access would soon be met. Yet, the types of degrees available were still limited by sexist attitudes about women's capacity to learn; most women were enrolled in common schools for basic literacy skills or normal schools for teacher training.[4]

W.E.B. Du Bois's Atlanta studies of 1900 and 1910 were much more accurate in number. Du Bois calculated that by 1880, 54 black women had earned college degrees: Oberlin 31, Fisk 6, Wilberforce 6, Southland 4, Howard 2, and 1 each from Geneva, Shaw, Central Tennessee, New Orleans, and Straight. By Reconstruction's end, African Americans had earned an estimated 208 bachelor's and 10 master's degrees.[5]

By 1890, according to Du Bois's count, the number of black women graduates had risen to approximately 132, which was 100 more than in Cooper's calculation. In 1900, he cited a mere 252 black women out of the 2,541 black bachelor's degree awardees: Oberlin graduated 55, Fisk 31, Shaw 21, Wilberforce 19, Paul Quinn 13, Knoxville 10, Howard 8, Atlanta 8, Southland 8, Rust 7, Central Tennessee 7, Claflin 6, Livingstone 6, New Orleans 5, Philander Smith 5, Roger Williams 5, Iowa Wesleyan 5, Berea 5, University of Kansas 3, University of Michigan 3, Cornell 3, Geneva 2, Wittenburg 2, and Wellesley 2. One woman each graduated from Leland, Butler, University of Iowa, Adrian, Idaho, Mkendree, Bates, Virginia Normal and College, Clarke, Allen, Straight, Paine Institute, Branch, Arkansas, Vassar, and Mt. Holyoke. Only 23 percent of the students at liberal arts colleges like Howard, Atlanta, Fisk, and Shaw in the year 1898–99 were women; but the percentages for

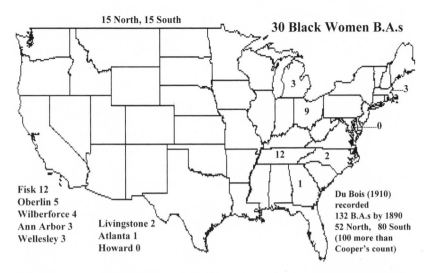

15 North, 15 South

30 Black Women B.A.s

Fisk 12
Oberlin 5
Wilberforce 4
Ann Arbor 3
Wellesley 3

Livingstone 2
Atlanta 1
Howard 0

Du Bois (1910)
recorded
132 B.A.s by 1890
52 North, 80 South
(100 more than
Cooper's count)

Map 1. Cooper, "The Higher Education of Women" (1890). Created by Stephanie Y. Evans.

women enrolled in teacher-training institutions were much higher. By 1910, black women's annual enrollment began to slightly outnumber black men's, but admission to professional schools was limited: that year, only two black women were recognized as lawyers. Except for the 1920s, after the return of veterans from World War I, the trend of black women having a higher college attendance rate than men continued throughout the century, but so did the trend of black women's denied access to graduate or professional schools.[6]

In 1890, black women's college graduation rate was evenly balanced between northern and southern states. Only two decades later, a significant demographic shift had taken place. The time had ended when the North was the paramount region for black women's educational opportunity; this was the age of southern institutional growth. I suggest two reasons for this shift: first, the solidification of the *Plessy v. Ferguson* Jim Crow segregation decreased attendance at formerly racially mixed institutions such as Berea College. Berea, founded in 1855 as a college for "Black and White together," succumbed in 1904 to the Day Law, which prohibited integrated schooling in Kentucky.[7]

Second, proliferation of HBCUs during the Reconstruction South opened up opportunity, even if growth was erratic. Though accreditation discrepancies would not allow a clear count of graduates, over fifty black-serving

Map 2. Du Bois, *College-Bred Negro* (1900). Created by Stephanie Y. Evans.

institutions came of age following the Civil War. HBCUs were significant because there was virtually no opportunity for black students to attend state PWIs in the South. Only three state schools in the South that admitted African Americans benefited from the Morrill Land Grant Act of 1862: Virginia, Mississippi, and South Carolina. Though the majority of black college women graduates were in the South, few were in state schools: by 1910, only 2 black women had graduated from state schools in Virginia, 2 in Mississippi, and 22 in South Carolina.[8]

Of 252 black women graduates by 1900, 118 had graduated from southern colleges (including Texas), and only 90 from northern and middle-state colleges (including D.C.). By 1910, 514 black women had graduated from black colleges in the South and only 144 from white colleges in the North or Midwest. In the second wave of educational attainment, the profile of the black woman collegian became overwhelmingly southern.[9]

In addition to northern and southern changes, westward movement increased. By 1900, 3 black women had graduated from the University of Kansas, and by 1910, 20 black women had graduated from colleges in the state. A few black families headed west during the California Gold Rush, decades before substantial higher education developed there. Eventually, black women entered western universities such as the Methodist Episcopal University of Southern California in Los Angeles.[10]

In addition to geographic changes, the variance in quality of education, curriculum, and institutional resources meant that college degrees were largely unequal.

College Classification and Regional Trends

The differences in research findings about numbers of college graduates reflect the disagreement over and changing assessment of exactly what qualified as a college. There were significant discrepancies between the 1900 and 1910 Du Bois Atlanta studies: the 1900 study estimated 2,332 black college graduates by 1899; the 1910 study estimated that a lower number, only 2,243, had graduated by 1899. The change in definition of a college between 1900 and 1910 explains the change in count of college graduates and demonstrates the difficulties researchers had providing accurate numbers.[11]

The 1900 Atlanta University study ranking system included four tiers: (1) Howard; (2) Fisk, Atlanta, Leland, Wilberforce, Paul Quinn; (3) Biddle, Shaw, Virginia Normal and College, Livingstone; (4) Lincoln. Seventy-two black women, a clear majority in the study, attended colleges of the first and second tier; only 28 attended third- and fourth-tier schools.

In 1910, researchers in the Atlanta Conference series updated the earlier report with a more comprehensive study. There were an estimated 34 HBCUs offering college-level work. The revised three-tier system reflected that of the 658 black women graduates, 421 graduated from ranked colleges. This number did not come close to the calculated 2,999 black men who had earned bachelor's degrees from top-ranked institutions.

The 1910 study used entrance requirements as a basis for ranking and counted eleven colleges in the first tier, including Howard, Fisk, Clark, Atlanta, Atlanta Baptist, and Spelman. The second tier included only three colleges, Lincoln, Talladega, and Wilberforce. The third tier included eighteen colleges, and the rank of "vocational schools" was added, listing nine schools, including North Carolina A&M, Tuskegee, and Hampton. The nine HBCUs that had professional schools were Howard, Wiley, Leland, Virginia Union, Knoxville, Spelman, Lincoln, Talladega, and Atlanta Bishop.[12]

Though there was a marked improvement in black institutions' ability to teach college-level work and a larger number of black students prepared to complete college-level requirements, debate about agricultural, technical, industrial, mechanical, normal, and liberal arts curricula expanded. There was little agreement about how to evaluate certificates, diplomas, and degrees, and these institutional changes took place amid drastic demographic

shifts of immigrant populations from Asia and Europe, providing more contention over what it meant to be an American or an educated American.
Rudolph explained that "none of this was like the old-time classical college. . . . Vocational and technical education had become a legitimate function of American higher education, and everywhere the idea of going to
college was being liberated from the class-bound, classical-bound traditions
which for so long had defined the American collegiate experience." Debate
over educational standards, remediation, and preparatory courses weighed
heavily during this period, and all but a few colleges had preparatory departments to bridge the gap between elementary and college course work.[13]

By 1910, 128 black men and women had graduated from Oberlin, and 54
black men and women had graduated from Harvard, Yale, Michigan, Cornell, Stanford, Catholic, Columbia, the University of Pennsylvania, and the
University of Chicago. Though in later periods more black women than men
annually earned bachelor's degrees, in early African American education,
access to advanced medical, legal, and liberal arts instruction (much like suffrage, political posts, and judiciary appointments) was first gained by black
men.[14]

Educator and researcher Lucy Slowe (1933) argued that HBCUs (notably Howard, Fisk, Atlanta, Shaw, Straight, and Tougaloo, all founded before
1870) "admitted women and men on the same basis." Anna Cooper (1890)
and Linda Perkins (1994) showed that this was not the case in the early days
of HBCUs' establishment. As Perkins pointed out, the highest-ranking institutions (Howard, Atlanta, and Lincoln) did not graduate large numbers of
women.[15]

The leading schools for black women college graduates were Shaw (82),
Bennett (71), Fisk (58), Clark (36), Atlanta (34), Wilberforce (24), and Howard (23). The smaller colleges also began amassing black women graduates:
Claflin (16), St. Augustine's and Walden (15), Shorter and New Orleans (14),
and Spelman (13).[16]

Colleges not ranked struggled to gain legitimacy in an era when the 1910
Carnegie Foundation Bulletin No. 4, by Abraham Flexner, institutionalized
regulations and accreditation for medical schools. By creating a standard
that did not take into consideration inequitable distribution of resources or
variation in educational goals, this report inspired mass closings of professional schools and colleges by those who had a vested interest in reducing
college access and limiting admittance into the medical profession. The 1928
Phelps-Stokes Report also advocated the closing of "inefficient" black institutions and the dissolution of ties with church bodies so white governmental
bodies would have increased power to regulate black schools. While both

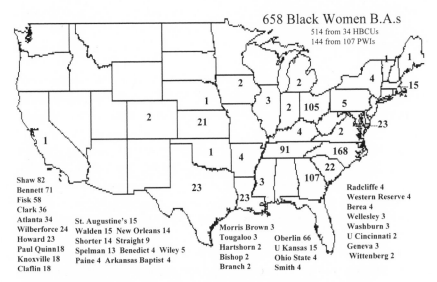

658 Black Women B.A.s
514 from 34 HBCUs
144 from 107 PWIs

Shaw 82
Bennett 71
Fisk 58
Clark 36
Atlanta 34
Wilberforce 24   St. Augustine's 15
Howard 23   Walden 15 New Orleans 14
Paul Quinn18   Shorter 14 Straight 9
Knoxville 18   Spelman 13 Benedict 4 Wiley 5
Claflin 18   Paine 4 Arkansas Baptist 4

Morris Brown 3
Tougaloo 3   Oberlin 66
Hartshorn 2   U Kansas 15
Bishop 2   Ohio State 4
Branch 2   Smith 4

Radcliffe 4
Western Reserve 4
Berea 4
Wellesley 3
Washburn 3
U Cincinnati 2
Geneva 3
Wittenberg 2

Map 3. Du Bois and Dill, *College-Bred Negro American* (1910). Created by Stephanie Y. Evans.

reports did offer much-needed standardization of criteria for institutions, they also provided gatekeepers effective tools with which to lock the doors to economic or professional advancement for African Americans by regulating HBCUs.[17]

Fledgling institutions where few black women graduated from the college department, like Arkansas Baptist (4), Paine (4), Tougaloo (3), Morris Brown (3), and Hartshorn (2), were not ranked or were ranked as third-tier schools; however, they were essential in providing preparatory, vocational, and normal school education for black women interested in improving their vocational skills and employment prospects.[18]

Generally, there was poor financial support for technical or vocational colleges, even though that was the most prominent college type. Hampton and Tuskegee were notable exceptions to this trend. The industrial framework perfected by Booker T. Washington suited the agenda of white philanthropists, and Washington was a skillful social engineer, so both schools garnered significant endowments from accrediting and funding bodies.

Southern states where black women graduates abounded were North Carolina (168), Tennessee (91), and Georgia (90). Of these, North Carolina produced a political network that became highly effective in advancing rights for black women. Repressive states like South Carolina (22 graduates),

Alabama (4), and Mississippi (3) solidified unyielding resistance to development in the areas that had the highest black populations.[19]

Comparatively, Ohio was the only northern state that maintained a critical mass of black graduates in the second wave of attainment: 105 total. Oberlin remained a leading institution for African American women: by 1910, 66 black women had earned B.A. and M.A. degrees. The next nearest PWI was University of Kansas with 15 black graduates. In the mid-nineteenth century, many black families moved to the Midwest, especially Ohio, because they were able to gain access to higher education, but the increased opportunities in the South and Midwest curtailed that flow.[20]

The 1910 *Atlanta* report provided two case studies of interest: University of Kansas and University of Iowa. University of Kansas admitted its first black student in 1870. By 1909, 16 black women and 15 black men had earned degrees. The gender proportion was not nearly as close in Iowa: 26 black men had graduated but only 8 black women. Some northern states fell behind midwestern and western growth. For example, although Pennsylvania had a strong history of women's literary societies and a large free black population, there was not an effective system of higher education for black women. By 1910, only 5 black women had graduated college in Pennsylvania, while 20 had graduated in Kansas and 23 in Texas. African Americans born in Pennsylvania were more likely than those born in any other state to get a college degree; however, they would get a degree in any other state than Pennsylvania.[21]

Historically Black Colleges and Universities (HBCUs)

Unlike Lincoln University in Missouri, which was founded by black Civil War soldiers, most black institutions contended with deep-seated administrative dilemmas: issues like having a predominantly white teaching staff, dependence on philanthropic or governmental support, and defining the financial trustees' role in determining curricular direction were recurring battles. Three types of administrative bodies—foundations, churches, and governmental bodies—presented substantial challenges within and between institutions.[22]

Foundations like the Peabody Education Fund (founded 1867), Carnegie Institute (1896), Rockefeller General Education Board (1903), Carnegie Corporation (1906), and Rockefeller Foundation (1913) financially relieved but also challenged administrators' ideologies. The foundations sought to control institutions and consolidate production as they had in business. They contended with religious bodies for power. The American Missionary Association (Congregationalist), Freedman's Aid Society (Methodist Episcopal Church), Home Mission Society (Baptist), and the Board of Missions for the Freedman (Presbyterian Church) also provided vital support but vied for control of black schools. These bodies administered funds such as the Phelps-Stokes, John F. Slater, Anna T. Jeanes, General Education Board, and the Rosenwald accounts to aid in the education of African Americans. But with financial support came curricular control. As in the first wave of attainment, church and commercial endeavors often clashed.[23]

Government regulation of public and private schools was a third dilemma for HBCUs. In *Black Colleges in America*, the authors detailed the tight web of money, curriculum, attendance, and governance in the development of HBCUs. In addition to reports produced by the philanthropic or church organizations, there were four national government surveys conducted between world wars that detailed the government's agenda for black schools. These reports included criteria for evaluating curriculum, which in turn impacted funding decisions. The reports (1916, 1917–18, 1928, and 1942) all encouraged the strengthening of teacher-training, agricultural, carpentry, and mechanical departments while suspiciously discouraging or recommending elimination of language and liberal arts classes.[24]

The struggle between foundations, religious denominations, and government bodies endured; none won total power to dictate institutional policy or curricular direction, but each fought for control of HBCUs. All three administrative bodies promoted principles of assimilation or white supremacy and narrowly defined academic capacity for black students, limiting the scope of what education meant for African Americans.

Amidst the growth of HBCUs, black women's colleges emerged. Three women's HBCUs of note blossomed: Bennett College in Greensboro, North Carolina (founded 1873, coeducational until 1926); Hartshorn Memorial College for Women in Richmond, Virginia (founded in 1883, established as a college in 1888, first college degrees awarded in 1892); and Atlanta Baptist Female Seminary (later named Spelman College) in Georgia (founded in 1881). Both Spelman and Hartshorn developed under the auspices of the American Baptist Home Missionary Society, while Bennett was associated with the Methodist Episcopal Church Freedman's Aid Society. By 1910, Bennett reported 71 black women college graduates, Spelman 13, and Hartshorn 2.[25]

Bennett graduated black women with college degrees before Spelman, but by 1910, Spelman outranked Bennett as a first-tier school; Hartshorn was not ranked in the top tiers. At the time, Bennett featured four major divisions: Biological and Physical Sciences, Social Sciences, Home Economics, and the Humanities. Though Bennett was founded almost a decade prior, Spelman bore the distinction of being the first college founded for black women in the United States. Since its founding by two New England missionaries in 1881, Spelman provided a continuous and unique collegiate opportunity for African American women. Spelman began with 11 students, and within a year, 200 black women between fifteen and fifty-two years old attended. Originally a normal, industrial, nursing, and missionary training school, the college department was established in 1897 and awarded the first college degrees in 1901 to two women. John D. Rockefeller donated repeatedly, and in 1924, the school was named Spelman Seminary after his wife, Laura Spelman Rockefeller. Both Bennett and Spelman institutionalized the "ideal" of a phenomenal black woman who was educated and dedicated to race uplift. The socialization process at black women's colleges provided a specific site for training in social standpoint negotiation.[26]

For black coeducational colleges admitting women, administrative efforts to match student populations with course offerings were tumultuous at best. North Carolina A&T, Scotia Seminary and Bennett College in North Carolina, Bethune-Cookman College in Florida, and Tillotson College in Texas switched back and forth from coeducational to single-sex status, reflecting gender uncertainties about what education was most appropriate for black women and how to meet the needs of a transforming demographic.

At coeducational schools like North Carolina A&T, when decisions between the sexes became an issue, women were unenrolled. An administrator justified the expendable status of women students by saying, "their presence in the college hampered the work, and there was an evident disinclination on the part of both sexes to engage in the harder kinds of manual labor in the presence of the other, both feeling called upon to wear their best clothes in order to impress the other." Despite the lack of solid rationale for this discrimination, women were not readmitted until 1926. The administrators wrote: "we gave co-education a patient trial for several years, but . . . we decided to abolish the girl department, and make the institution strictly a college of agriculture and mechanics. . . . In the first place, the girls are by nature not well fitted for agricultural and mechanical pursuits." These stereotypes were later discredited by studies showing women as the main agricultural producers worldwide, and during World War II (as the country needed extra factory labor for the war effort), women proved themselves able mechanics and engineers. But when schools were not stable enough to sustain both sexes in strict gender roles, women had to leave.[27]

Many historically black preparatory schools, colleges, and universities like Scotia Seminary and Palmer Memorial Institute in North Carolina; Institute for Colored Youth in Pennsylvania; Dunbar High School, Training School for Girls, and Howard in D.C.; Tuskegee in Alabama; and Bethune-Cookman in Florida became cornerstones of their local communities. The majority of black women college graduates obtained degrees from normal schools, which was the equivalent of a two- or four-year high school degree and two years of college study. This degree included a certification for elementary school teaching, but women also taught in the community through Sunday schools, youth leadership development, and mutual aid societies as much as they taught in the formal classroom.[28]

The educational boom that enabled millions of black Americans to gain school access was in line with advancements made in the larger society: "between 1890 and 1925 enrollment in institutions in higher education grew 4.7 times as fast as the population. The release from aristocratic ideals implicit in such a statistic was perhaps the most dramatic fact about the course of American higher education in the twentieth century." Though access to college increased nationally, social subjugation of African Americans minimized successes. For black collegiate women at white institutions, this meant occupying a precarious position.[29]

Black Students at Predominantly White Institutions (PWIs)

As with the first generation of college women, black women college students in the second wave ranged in economic status, ancestry, and goals. Though white women were described as "at the time the largest and most underprivileged of American minority groups," it is clear that black women were not only underprivileged but also intellectually underestimated, even when they did have relative privilege. In the North, particularly in New England, where there were only one or two black women college students in each state, most integrated fairly well. If born in that region, they attended integrated preparatory schools and the college entrance was fairly seamless, yet the path was far from smooth.[30]

In 1865, Cornell became the first prestigious college to become coeducational. Jessie Fauset, a 1905 graduate, was one of the first groups to break the color barrier there, when most white women's colleges remained closed. Where there were enough students to form a group, black women persevered by creating sisterhood and focusing on collective empowerment. This phenomenon of black women's clubs did not occur at the "Seven Sister" women's colleges, which effectively excluded black women from admittance.[31]

The Seven Sister colleges—Mount Holyoke, Vassar, Wellesley, Smith, Radcliffe, Bryn Mawr, and Barnard—were comparatively slow to grant access to black women. By 1910, Smith and Radcliffe had graduated 4 black women each and Wellesley 3. The first African American woman gained entry to Mount Holyoke in 1883, and the first to earn the collegiate degree did so in 1898. Barnard did not graduate a black woman until 1928 (Zora Neale Hurston), and Bryn Mawr did not grant a black woman a degree until 1931. Anita Florence Hemmings graduated from Vassar in 1897, and her daughter, Ellen Parker Love, graduated in 1927. Both passed as white. The first recognized black woman was not admitted to Vassar until 1940. Notably, those like Otelia Cromwell who did attend Seven Sister colleges often continued their education after graduation. Cromwell, who was from D.C., graduated from Smith in 1900 and went on to earn a Ph.D. in English from Yale in 1926.[32]

For those who did not desire to attend a state school or single-sex establishment, women's annexes to men's elite colleges developed in the 1870s. In 1874, Harvard first allowed women to sit for examinations and receive credit. In 1879, a group of Harvard professors began courses for women. Offered under the auspices of the Society for the Collegiate Instruction of Women, these courses constituted what was popularly known as the Harvard Annex. In 1893, the Annex became Radcliffe College. After Radcliffe came Barnard (sister campus to Columbia), Sophie Newcomb (Tulane), Pembroke (Brown), Jackson (Tufts), and Flora Stone Mather (Western Reserve).[33]

Options continued to increase for women. In 1872, there were approximately 97 major coeducational colleges and universities in the United States. Of these, 67 were in the West, 17 in the South, 8 in the Middle Atlantic states, and 5 in New England. By 1900, 71 percent of all colleges in the United States were coeducational, but, as reported in the Atlanta studies, few admitted black women.[34]

Most black women collegians who attended PWIs in the early twentieth century did not have a typical dorm experience because they were generally not allowed to live on campus. Administrators feared race mixing and argued for segregation based on sexual insecurities. But racism was pervasive regardless of the sexual tensions: dorms on single-sex campuses were also racially segregated or closed to black women.[35]

Contested physical space was matched by confrontation over academic space. Male scholars at leading institutions bristled at competition from female students, and, when pressure got intense, they resorted to claims that education defeminized women. Some argued that advanced studies made women unfit to marry because they lacked "necessary ladylike qualities that marriageable men were looking for"—namely, silent subservience. As women's enrollment increased, male scholars strove to designate science and engineering as male territory and segregate the curriculum by gender. Though some early women scholars did well and majored in mathematics, math too was claimed as something boys did better than girls.

Black women, therefore, had both racial and gender barriers to navigate. As with the earlier "ladies' course," institutions relegated liberal arts courses to a lower intellectual realm because women dominated the humanities. In this vein, honor societies, and by extension fraternities, segregated the student body and were bastions of white male ego, couched in euphemisms of "brotherhood."[36]

Honor Societies and Elite Notions of Education

Honor societies, particularly Phi Beta Kappa (ΦBK), were symbols of academic pedigree and illustrated the struggle between democratic ideals and aristocratic tendencies in higher education. Founded in 1776, the oldest and most prestigious secret society rose amidst the move from the religious Awakening toward reasoned Enlightenment. Reason, objective science, and secular values trumped the prior focus of education on spiritual growth and moral character. Though the honor society was based on academic excellence, Rudolph noted that "the Greek-letter fraternity and its counterpart, the social club, were intended to fill an emotional and social rather than a curricular vacuum." Honor societies, meant to reflect the "yearning of . . . fellowship of kindred souls," became an institution within an institution. Mary Annette Anderson, the first black woman graduate of Middlebury College and first black woman Phi Beta Kappa, was a member unlikely to be recognized as such a kindred soul.[37]

Born in Shoreham, Vermont, in 1874, Anderson began college after attending Northfield Seminary for Young Ladies, an integrated preparatory school in Massachusetts. She attended Middlebury College, coeducational since 1883, in the liberal state of Vermont, which was the first state to prohibit slavery in its constitution. While at Middlebury, she was a member of Alpha Chi, a small local sorority, and delivered the valedictory speech at her 1899 graduation ceremonies. Titled "A Crown of Culture," the speech surely presented a stark contrast to Lucy Stanton's 1850 "Plea for the Oppressed" graduation speech. The Civil War had ended, and even though post-Reconstruction setbacks warranted sustained activism, the abolition of slavery allowed black students like Anderson the luxury of speaking of higher education in terms of culture. Anderson experienced a world in

Vermont in the 1890s that was vastly different from the abolitionist campus in antebellum Ohio. Anderson graduated seven decades after Alexander Twilight in 1823, signifying that while black students were advancing in the ranks of elite status in education, women were still far behind men. After graduation, Anderson taught at Straight College in New Orleans for one academic year. She then moved to D.C. to teach at Howard between 1901 and 1907, after which she married and retired from teaching.[38]

Anderson's story demonstrates the discrimination against married women in employment. Although she remained in D.C. after her marriage, she no longer appeared in the Howard catalog, leading one to believe that she had resigned her position. This was the same limitation Lucy Stanton faced in the earlier wave of black women's collegiate history: at the time, it was tradition that once an educated woman was married, she ceased to participate in public work, particularly teaching. It is also interesting to note that Anderson's younger brother, John, was also a member of Phi Beta Kappa, underscoring the tendency of families to rise together.

Although conditions improved significantly between 1850 and 1899, the post-Reconstruction era saw the institutionalization of Jim Crow and a life of sharecropping and hard labor for most African Americans. Anderson's life as an educated black woman, recognized scholar, and dedicated teacher represents the ambiguous space that black women occupied between a life of leisure allowing participation in honor societies such as Phi Beta Kappa and the reality of the oppressed majority of black women. Discovering Anderson's history opens many doors for further research.

Until recently, novelist Jessie Fauset (1882–1961) was believed to be the first African American woman in Phi Beta Kappa. Fauset wrote of the discrimination she encountered while trying to reach the heights of academic life, but she nevertheless earned highest honors and became renowned for her writing. Fauset, an inductee in 1905 at Cornell, gained much recognition as literary editor of *Crisis*, the journal of the NAACP, from 1919 to 1927 and as a novelist during the Harlem Renaissance. Though graduating at the top of her class from the elite High School for Girls in Philadelphia, Fauset was denied the valedictory scholarship to Bryn Mawr because of her race. After graduation, she taught at the famed M Street High School from 1906 to 1919, earned an M.A. in French from the University of Pennsylvania in 1919, and studied at the Sorbonne in Paris during the 1925 academic year, for which she earned a certificate. She was also an honored member of Delta Sigma Theta Sorority. Fauset's case, like Anderson's, demonstrates the uneven access to higher education, even in the North. It also displays the perseverance that young black women scholars possessed despite that uneven access.[39]

African Americans at PWIs were caught between embracing religious principles and being recognized for their intellectual and reasoning abilities. Though the black church remained a central institution to black scholars, they continued to strive for inclusion in elite academic circles, with limited success. By 1900, there were approximately 12 black inductees in Phi Beta Kappa. But between 1901 and 1950, a mere 210 black members would be inducted, and chapters at HBCUs were suspiciously rare. Regardless of the increased strivings of black scholars, as Anderson's life work demonstrated, they would indeed advance in education but did not completely leave their moral strivings for community uplift.[40]

Social Responsibility and Education

As Shaw notes, black women were educated to be levers of service to society regardless of the type of institution they attended. The ideals of "service" and "social justice" were not always based on classless, egalitarian assumptions, but they were pervasive. Like many schools developed in European immigrant communities and in Catholic or Quaker schools, black schools depended on a significant positive relationship with the surrounding community. Racial segregation, however, made the African American school-community relationship even more essential for group survival. While definitions of community in black neighborhoods and HBCUs were largely defined by race, membership was not racially exclusive.

Shaw offers a definition of community that illuminated the missions of HBCUs during their inception:

Community in this instance was more than a neighborhood. Interests, rather than buildings and borders, determined membership. Community therefore defied boundaries and tended toward dispersion rather than concentration. Community was also more than a romantic metaphor for racial solidarity. Composed dynamically of a diverse group of people, it was a social institution or an arrangement of people who possessed a common understanding of history, mutual interests in the present, and shared visions of the future for the group and all its members. But community was based on more than philosophical impulses; it was also rooted in activism—theory balanced with practice.... Thus community was both a product and a process—a sociopolitical entity

that was the product of collective consciousness and a process for producing that consciousness as well.[41]

Despite, or perhaps because of, the barriers presented to African Americans'
educational attainment, college attendance was inseparable from community engagement and social responsibility. Though there was much disagreement on the appropriate curriculum, proper employment, or correct methods by which to uplift the race, black women generally internalized uplift
ideals and lifted as they climbed the walls of the Ivory Tower.[42]

As college enrollment grew, black women developed their own social,
scholarly, and service clubs. The first black Greek-letter organization, Sigma
Pi Phi, or the Boulé, was founded in 1904 by black male college alumni in
Philadelphia. This organization built on the century-long tradition of literary
and abolition societies, Black National Conventions, Free African Societies
(founded by Richard Allen and Absalom Jones), and the first black male
secret society—the African Lodge of Free and Accepted Masons (known
as the Prince Hall Freemasons), founded in 1775 in Massachusetts. In 1906,
Alpha Phi Alpha Fraternity, founded at Cornell, became the first black Greek-
letter organization (BGLO) on a college campus. In 1908, nine black women
on Howard University's campus, led by Ethel Hedgeman Lyle, formed Alpha
Kappa Alpha Sorority, the first college-based black women's Greek-letter organization. They incorporated in 1913 to ensure perpetuity of ideals. Black
sororities began during the second wave of attainment but grew strong
roots in the third wave. Sororities were founded on college-educated black
women's networks that developed in the mid-1800s. Mary Church Terrell,
Anna Julia Cooper, and Mary Jane Patterson founded the Colored Women's
League, an organization that contributed to the development of the 1896
National Association of Colored Women (NACW), which had such a large
impact on black women's national presence. These organizations were an
intersection of popular womanhood ideals, academic ambition, and desire
for public voice. They at once confirmed and subverted women's stereotypical social roles.[43]

A thin line existed between portraying black women as social servants
and black women as servile. As a typical example of the latter, the historian
William Alexander prescribed black women's duty as agents of community
uplift in a way that revealed persistent repressive attitudes toward women
in higher education. To Alexander and others, women were to be educated
only about the domestic sphere:

and these interests are chiefly confided to women, particularly as the attention of men is otherwise directed. . . . Principles elevated, firm, and founded on reflection, joined to her natural gifts can alone render her capable of fulfilling that mission of instruction for which she is designed. . . . That for this end she was sent into the world, to live for others rather than for herself; to live, yes, and often to die for them. Let her never be persuaded to forget that she is sent into the world to teach man that there is something more necessary than the claiming of rights, and that is the performing of duties . . . that there is something more than intellect, and that is purity and virtue. Surely this is woman's calling . . . [fulfilled by] helpful hands [and] wise self-distrust.[44]

So, in 1887 Alexander advised, women had to choose between public rights and intellect or private virtue and duty; the latter, of course, more suited their station. Black men often put black women on a pedestal, but in doing so, they subscribed to the same limiting definitions of womanhood espoused by the dominant culture. This resulted in disagreement on the "proper" education for black women, which mirrored inconsistencies and dualities in the larger American educational system.

Higher Education and Social Change—Manufacturing the Oligarchy

Aristocratic "gentlemen" and labor-focused entrepreneurs overcame their differences: land, assets, policy, and colleges became intertwined, transferring power within a closed circuit of elites. Even as more Americans attended college and vocational education took hold, private education, high admission fees, and legacy enrollments represented efforts to keep the moneyed elite relatively separated from the riffraff. There were huge rifts between European immigrants from Ireland, Russia, Germany, Poland and elsewhere; Jews and Catholics experienced similar struggles. But with promulgation of white supremacy, these groups could, at some point, assimilate and benefit from unearned race privilege in a way that communities of color could not.[45]

Nationally, colleges were grappling with controversial topics at the turn of the twentieth century: appropriate learning for men and women; faculty roles and responsibilities; the utility of "classical" subjects like Greek in an agricultural and mechanical era; the practicality of requiring mathematics for admission or graduation; funding low-income students; articulating mission statements; and "the elective principle," or what role students should have in choosing their own course of study.[46] Once students were admitted, how to measure learning and how to instill accountability—especially for elite students—became paramount. Should students test out of grade levels? Should students be subject to random tests to ensure competency and dedication to study? As the country grew wealthier, college became a social endeavor, a leisure activity, and a badge of upper-middle-class status. University attendance became a statement of monetary worth and a rationale for sustaining the accumulated riches of those few who could afford to attend.[47]

By the early twentieth century, college was compulsory for the rich. Often, when a student's social status was secured, apathy became apparent: "a member of the faculty at the University of Michigan in 1906 confessed, 'The relative number of students who do not know just why they are at the University is increasing.'" For upper-middle-class white students, college was clearly not as much matter of survival as it was for black and poor students, and this was reflected in student attitudes toward academic work. Higher education's social role was as dynamic and unstable as American identity itself.[48]

In 1895, Booker T. Washington's "Atlanta Compromise" speech and his 1901 *Up from Slavery* made him a nationally recognized spokesperson on race relations. W.E.B. Du Bois, an 1895 Harvard Ph.D., published *The Souls of Black Folk* (1903), challenging Washington's interpretation of educational imperatives for black Americans. Their dialogue took place amid larger tensions in a rapidly developing country where anti-immigrant legislation directed against the Chinese and Mexicans deepened animosities between ethnic groups, and Native American removal or termination policies belied national growing pains. These national crises were exacerbated by worldwide discord. As the first Pan-African Congress met in 1900 in London, signaling a burgeoning international coalition of the African Diaspora, European antagonisms escalated, resulting in world war.[49]

Through these cataclysmic changes, black women kept climbing toward full citizenship and a voice in decision-making processes. Because of the large number of teachers needed and the feminization of teaching, social work, and nursing occupations, black women attended high school and college at greater rates than African American men. Further, the systematic incarceration of black men and limits on available occupations for college graduates negatively impacted men's attendance rates. Nevertheless, childbearing, familial, and communal responsibilities undoubtedly impacted most women's ability to make necessary gains in obtaining formal education.

The masses of African Americans suffered from continued economic repression of sharecropping and debt peonage coupled with political oppression. In most cases, conditions such as mass migration that was a result of white violence (as a push factor) and industrialization with subsequent urbanization (as a pull factor) made stable and steady education for black children nearly nonexistent. Despite the oft-noted overwhelming demand for access to education after Emancipation, and although illiteracy rates dropped dramatically, substantial access to equitable education eluded masses of African Americans.

Of all barriers to education, violence was especially prevalent. After Emancipation, white violence grew steadily and was unmitigated by law or custom. Legal repression was not enough to keep black people in their subjugated "place," so physical violence was employed to punish those who did acquire education, an elevated economic position, or both. White citizens attempted to beat any desire to succeed out of those who would dream of any other role than complete economic, social, political—and intellectual—submission.[50]

Where enslavement and antiliteracy laws reigned supreme in antebellum eras, African Americans were subjected to endless violence, economic intimidation, and political disenfranchisement once they were declared "free." White domestic terrorism—signaled by the 1867 founding of the Ku Klux Klan in Tennessee—increased lynching between the 1880s and 1930s. Violence challenged black development at every turn. In historian Leon Litwack's account:

> In the 1890s, lynchings claimed an average of 139 lives each year, 75 percent of them black. The numbers declined in the following decades, but the percentage of black victims rose to 90 percent. Between 1882 and 1968, an estimated 4,742 blacks met their deaths at the hands of lynch mobs. As many if not more blacks were victims of legal lynchings (speedy trials and executions), private white violence, and "nigger hunts," murdered by a variety of means in isolated rural sections and dumped into rivers and creeks.[51]

Between 1882 and 1898, there were at least fifty black women lynched; of these, at least three were visibly pregnant. Thus, statistically, for every five black women who had graduated with a college degree by the turn of the twentieth century, one black woman had been lynched.

In an atmosphere such as this, access to literacy did not guarantee freedom or justice, but overall, it did improve the quality of life. African American activism and organizational self-help galvanized, and by the eve of World War I, thousands of black educators were uplifting the race through education. The second wave of black women's education was a royal affair for the fortunate few. Though Anderson's "crown of culture" was adorned with the thorns of uneven democracy, black women wore it with pride and wielded their college degrees for the betterment of others. In the next era, the third wave of attainment, they continued to pursue excellence, with heads bloodied, but unbowed.

3

"Beating Onward, Ever Onward"

A Critical Mass, 1910–1954

Droves of migrants to northern and urban areas; the modernization produced by two world wars; cultural renaissance in popular cities like Harlem, St. Louis, and Chicago; the Great Depression; and the intensification of mass mobilization for citizenship rights all had great impacts on black women's college experiences in the third wave of educational attainment. While the growing majority of black women attended undergraduate colleges in the South, the access to graduate studies, though slow, again drew them to northern urban institutions like the University of Pennsylvania, University of Chicago, and Columbia University in New York. Like her predecessors, the third-wave graduate often left her school state after graduation to find a teaching job, and her final location often depended on what type of degree she attained.[1]

Measuring Attainment between World Wars

As the Progressive era advanced, so too did the educational status of African Americans. The 1910 Atlanta University study estimated that 5,000 black students had earned diplomas, certificates, and degrees in normal, vocational, college, and professional areas, with 2,964 completing college-level work. However, these numbers, like Cooper's, did not stand up to research conducted in later years. In Charles Johnson's *The Negro College Graduate* (1938), the estimated 1910 numbers were 9,828 African American graduates, including 3,856 completing college-level work. The 1910 Atlanta study counted only 658 black women who had earned a bachelor's degree compared to 2,999 black men. Though Johnson's study did not calculate pre-1910 numbers by gender, surely his numbers were drastically higher than Du Bois's given the difference of 4,000 in the number of estimated total students.[2]

At the end of World War I, the numbers of African American degree earners had swelled to 7,304 bachelor's, 145 master's, and 25 doctorates. Though black women's annual college attendance rate was higher than men's, their attainment of B.A.s from top-ranked schools was woefully behind that of African American men and white women. As universities expanded and the campus became less of a community and more of a conglomerate, honors programs, like honors societies, became a haven of intimate interaction. As a "revolt against the impersonalization," honors programs, starting in 1922 at Swarthmore College, attempted to return some sense of an aristocratic ideal in the face of the popularization of higher education.[3]

Black women generally did not have entree to such programs or the preparatory classes that determined eligibility. They were also kept out of the more prestigious schools that would offer preparation for graduate school. Civil rights activist Dorothy Height recalled how she was kept from entering the Barnard class of 1933 because they had a quota of two black girls per year. Though her qualifications made her a clear choice for admittance, when she appeared at the interview and they found she was black, her application was denied. She ended up attending New York University, graduating with a B.A. in religion and earning an M.A. in educational psychology from Columbia University. Overall, black women were on average thirty years behind black men and white women in earning the bachelor's, thirteen years behind in the master's, twenty-four years behind in high honors like Phi Beta Kappa, and fifty years behind in earning the Ph.D.[4]

Charles Johnson, a renowned sociologist, painted a detailed picture of the development of blacks in higher education between world wars. He surveyed 116 PWIs and 56 HBCUs that identified 25,923 living black graduates who had earned bachelor's, master's, doctoral, law, medicine, dentistry, pharmacy, law, or theology degrees. Like the earlier Atlanta studies, Johnson's 1938 research supplemented institutional statistics with a survey sample of 3,518 men and 1,994 women graduates.

Of the 43,821 (cumulative) college degrees earned by black students listed in Johnson's study, 71 percent of the degrees were academic and 29 percent were professional. Graduation from HBCUs totaled 37,397 (85 percent), which far outnumbered the 6,424 (15 percent) graduating from PWIs. This era also represented a vast increase in what became community-college education. Though many attended colleges that were not high-ranked or even accredited, postsecondary education became an ever-more attainable goal. Johnson found that most African Americans in the study earned their degree between 1926 and 1936, with a 115 percent increase occurring between 1920 and 1928.[5]

In her 1942 dissertation at Columbia University, "Education and Marginality: A Study of the Negro Woman College Graduate," Marion Cuthbert revisited Johnson's survey data set of 1,994 women and conducted a new sur-

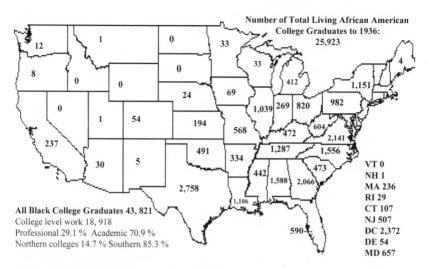

Map 4. Johnson, *The Negro College Graduate* (1938). Created by Stephanie Y. Evans.

vey of her own with a sample of 172 college and 58 noncollege women. A decade after Cuthbert, Jeanne Noble published "The Negro Woman's College Education" (1956) and calculated that 106,470 black women had attended four or more years of college by 1950. This reflected an attendance rate of 2.1 percent of the population by black women compared to a 1.6 percent attendance rate by black men, a 4.4 percent attendance rate by white women, and a 6 percent attendance rate by white men. Noble also conducted a questionnaire survey of her own to determine contemporary outlooks.[6]

As with earlier studies, Johnson's, Cuthbert's, and Noble's statistical analyses were problematic. The estimations were subject to the changing definitions of what constituted a college, the varied number of reporting institutions responding to surveys, and unevenly recorded U.S. Census data based on slippery categories of race. Though the Census was the most comprehensive population study, until 1960 it distinguished only between white and "other" races, without a complex breakdown of ethnicity. Yet, regardless of the actual number of degrees black women earned, these three researchers located a majority of degree holders and surveyed a significant number of black women college graduates. With their surveys, they also provided insight into those graduates' experiences and attitudes.[7]

Between 1870 and 1936, Cuthbert estimated that black women respondents had earned 1,495 degrees, 847 diplomas, 29 vocational diplomas, and 87 certificates. It is impossible to accurately calculate the number of black women college attendees who left before finishing a degree program. Numbers were not conclusive, even for a narrow time period of one year. For instance, historian Barbara Solomon estimated that in the 1939–40 academic year, 21,418 women enrolled at HBCUs compared to 16,311 men, but she also expressed frustration at the inability to accurately determine numbers of graduates at either HBCUs or PWIs because of inconsistent recording. Black women were attending college in record numbers, outpacing black men at increasingly higher rates, though at lower degree levels, but, as with prior studies, exact calculations were elusive.[8]

Regional Trends

Of the estimated 25,923 living black graduates, 19,883 earned their diploma, certificate, or degree in the South, compared to 3,017 in New England, 2,675 in the Midwest, and 348 in the West. Like Du Bois, Johnson separated degrees by college rating and accreditation; only 18,918 earned degrees for college-level work. Despite mass migration to the North, New England schools that historically had been at the forefront of black education all but shut off educational opportunities to African Americans. Though black students were still admitted to some schools, they did not stay after graduation. In Maine, where John Russworm graduated in 1826, only 7 black graduates lived in the state by 1938. Vermont, home to Middlebury College, which counted Alexander Twilight and Mary Anderson among its alumni, had no black living graduates as residents. This phenomenon reflected the powerful pull of large urban centers and the staying power of the South: unless scholars were from New England, there was no incentive to go to school there; if they did, there was little incentive to stay after they completed studies.[9]

By devaluing anything black, particularly a HBCU degree, and limiting black enrollment at PWIs, older white northern colleges maintained their claim as elite, "superior" institutions. So, while a trickle of black students were always admitted to New England schools, the numbers never amounted to the flood experienced in New England in the first wave of attainment or in other regions during the second and third waves. Massachusetts, with a long history of attainment, had only 173 living African American graduates compared to California's 165. Johnson's study also revealed a continued lack of educational opportunity for black students in South Carolina, Mississippi, Alabama, and Florida. The complexity of the southern region is of great interest. Deep South states like Florida and Mississippi had abysmal records of college access, while North Carolina and Georgia were havens for black collegians. Early access significantly influenced later attendance patterns in these states.[10]

Johnson's work highlighted the major centers of black intellectual life. Black college graduates were born and lived in Pennsylvania but were still largely educated out of state; and the high residence of black graduates in New York (16 percent) and Illinois (11 percent) showed that blacks who settled in those areas remained long after the migration and renaissance of earlier decades. Of the total living graduates, 2,372 claimed Washington, D.C., as home; of that number, 1,777 held college-level or professional degrees. This was by far the leading location for black intelligentsia. The whole state of Texas had only 2,758 graduates, with 2,477 of those completing college-level work. Those gravitating toward D.C. also settled in surrounding areas. Though Virginia had gotten off to a slow start, graduating only 2 black women from state schools by 1910, there were 2,141 graduates and 1,022 degree holders, men and women, by 1938.[11]

After World War I, there was a significant decline in African American professional degree attainment due to the entrenchment of Jim Crow laws. Of those few who earned professional degrees by 1936, most were in the medical field: 37 percent were in medicine; 25 percent in dentistry; 14 percent in pharmacy; 13 percent in law; and 11 percent in theology.[12] Black scholars and professionals continued to construct their own paradigms and, although attempts continued to gain the status, recognition, and legitimacy enjoyed by white institutions, black collegians made substantial gains on their own terms at HBCUs and in surrounding communities.

Race Uplift, Politics of Respectability, and the Bourgeoisie's Defense of Themselves

The financial struggles of Bethune-Cookman College (B-CC) exemplified the lack of support awarded to HBCUs and the limited funding for women's advanced liberal arts preparation. In a 1938 report, Ward Madison of the Rockefeller Foundation argued, "it is clear that with its enrollment of 202 students (17 of whom were high school students) and inadequate library and vocational facilities, that B-CC was suffering from budgetary woes." Though the Rockefeller Foundation did provide funding, and Mr. Rockefeller himself donated personal items (such as an electric organ from his home in Ormond Beach), the college did not have nearly the support it needed or warranted. The third wave of attainment witnessed unprecedented growth in the educated class, but war and deep recession disproportionately affected communities of color. Poor funding of HBCUs was an outgrowth of poor funding for black schooling at primary and secondary levels.[13]

Often there was one primary school and one secondary school in a town or county expected to accommodate all skill levels and overcrowded conditions. One student recalled: "there were two schools for Negroes. One had classes from first through tenth grades, the other, almost seven miles from home, had grades eleven and twelve." Although the schooling available for black students was limited in funds and physical resources, the dedication of the teachers and surrounding communities was legendary. At the end of World War I, there were 22,528 black women teachers of the 30,074 African Americans in the profession.[14]

Funding for black schools came from government and philanthropic bodies but also from various constituencies within black communities. As in the larger U.S. society, there existed an underground economy in black communities: crafts or skill-based income (cooking or hair care), lotteries or gambling ("running numbers"), bootleg or smuggled products, and illegal (though some would argue not immoral) activities provided alternative means of making money. Even those workers and entrepreneurs who did not attend college, labeled as "lower-class," significantly contributed to institutions and supported students who did attend. Most important, HBCU funds and material resources came from alumni who formed the fluctuating black middle class.[15]

Many graduates invested in mutual aid societies, life insurance firms, or funeral homes, and when they made small fortunes, they gave back to HBCUs. One such exemplar was Maggie Walker. Maggie Lena Mitchell Walker graduated from Richmond Normal School and was recognized as the first black woman bank president. She was on the boards of Hartshorn College and Virginia Union University and was an early member of the National Training School for Girls in D.C. Through her work with the Eastern Star, the woman's auxiliary to the Prince Hall Free Masons, her capital fund drives garnered thousands of much-needed dollars for those schools.[16]

As in the second wave of attainment, black women formed networks of communication and coalition. This is not to say that all black women educator-activists worked directly together. While there was no sustained correspondence or organizational connection between Cooper and Bethune, the relationships between sororities, national women's organizations, board of directors, and advocacy groups formed a one- or two-degree separation in their parallel activities. Among the groups dedicated to social uplift, the black Greek-letter organizations (BGLOs) involved a cadre of students dedicated to community activism on and off campus who were largely representative of the emerging black middle class. As the "Divine Nine" (four sororities and five fraternities) emerged, they embodied the same duality of social service and "cultured" elitism present in the larger academic system and social structure. After the founding of Alpha Kappa Alpha Sorority in 1908, Delta Sigma Theta (1913) and Zeta Phi Beta (1920) were both founded at Howard. Then Sigma Gamma Rho (1922) was founded at Butler University in Indianapolis, Indiana, as the fourth sorority and the first established on a historically white campus. Cooper being an AKA and Bethune a Delta represented a pattern of formalized sisterhood within the nation's black women leaders.[17]

Although the black fraternity and sorority movement gained currency in the mid-twentieth century, not all campuses had chapters. The secular overtones met with the same resistance on some black campuses in the 1920s as they did on some white campuses in the 1700s and 1800s. Also, the elitism that often accompanied such groups was considered detrimental to the communal uplift central to HBCU missions. Accordingly, Tuskegee did not host chapters until the 1940s, though other social and service clubs existed.[18]

Though divisions formed in the sorority movement, black women effectively organized and coalesced for community empowerment—and individual achievement. All four of the first African American women to earn a Ph.D. were in a sorority: two in Alpha Kappa Alpha, and two in Delta Sigma Theta.[19]

After advancing NACW, Terrell was a founding member of the College Alumnae Club (CAC) in D.C., begun in 1910 at her T Street home. The club, like the Boulé, included only members who held bachelor's degrees from a list of approved colleges. The CAC had three objectives focusing on social, intellectual, and civic collaboration. Their service work included mentoring local high school girls and providing scholarships for students of Armstrong and Dunbar High Schools. By 1923, the CAC maintained over one hundred members and sponsored special events to foster a community of scholars. One event honored Eva Dykes and Georgiana Simpson as recipients of the doctorate. Simpson became CAC president as the organization evolved into the National Association of College Women.[20]

The black women's club movement consisted of "sororities, secret societies, religious and professional organizations." These groups were effective community organizers but were plagued by internal divisions between leadership, rank-and-file members, and allies. There were bitter disagreements over what educated black women should learn and whether the primary function should be social or activist. Externally, prominent men like W.E.B.

Du Bois and educator John Hope criticized the organizations' thrust of women into traditionally male arenas and charged that members exhibited a "clubwoman's swagger" that was more show than substance. Internally, there were constant critiques of what Ida Jackson called "better than thou" approaches to social service and community uplift. Further, members' attitudes and actions routinely revealed divisive agendas. Black clubwomen carried out administrative coups, filibusters, and stonewalls reminiscent of the most powerful boardrooms or staterooms. Family status, region, economic class, ethnicity, educational type or level, and church affiliation all mediated closeness or hostility in black women's interpersonal relationships. In 1935, Bethune created an umbrella federation to facilitate collaboration between existing groups; it was an "organization of organizations." The National Council of Negro Women (NCNW) transformed black women's clubs into issue-focused advocacy groups and capitalized on the social networks developed and sustained by the 1896 founding of the NACW. But still, there was plenty of dissension in the ranks.[21]

Sororities also served as a means of creating coalitions with white women activists: both Jane Addams and Eleanor Roosevelt were honorary members of Alpha Kappa Alpha. It seems that the organizations, though dedicated to service, also were addicted to prestige. Mary Terrell excluded activists like Ida B. Wells, Josephine St. Pierre Ruffin, and even Bethune from leadership roles; these power plays had to do with geographic struggles for power but were also grounded in economic and educational class antagonisms by those like Terrell who claimed the national spotlight based on elitist ideas. Through church, club, and school, black women served; however, even as they challenged hegemony, they advocated middle-class values and perpetuated exclusion. Evelyn Higginbotham termed this phenomenon the "politics of respectability," and Ula Taylor named this Progressive era service-based middle-class dogma "the iron cage of uplift." Taylor denounced the ideology of uplift because it blamed the victims of American capitalist culture and held the socially disadvantaged responsible for improving disintegrating conditions caused by elitism that clubwomen simultaneously undermined and upheld.[22]

There were many assumptions implicit in popular "uplift" ideology: (1) because of women's moral superiority, black women were the only ones capable of affecting social change in the black community; (2) black women of low moral standing were responsible for the degradation in the black community; and (3) the dominant society was neither capable of nor responsible for changing the social status of African Americans. Thus, those who reified a psychology of self-help and racial uplift often failed sufficiently to challenge the oppressive systems responsible for the subjugation of black people.

In 1937, Florence Read, a white woman who served as president of Spelman College from 1927 to 1953, wrote "Defense of the Women's College" in *Opportunity*. She highlighted advantages of attending a women's college, including opportunities for a personal relationship with faculty and a chance to study nursing, domestic science, mission education, or teacher training—all women-dominated service fields. She also wrote, "when Negro women realize that it is 'up to them' to bring about better housing, to insure higher standards of health, to raise the taste of social and cultural life, and generally improve the ways of living, then there will come a steady revolution towards those goals." The popularity of mission schools, like the Moody Bible Institute in Chicago where Bethune attended, attested to the universal notion of black women's primary accountability for community development through service. The uplift creed potentially created a martyr or savior complex for activists and ignored the agency of lower-class blacks who were not simply waiting to be "saved" by those who claimed themselves or who were appointed race leaders.[23]

An image of exceptionalism was central to the middle-class black movement: in order to be acknowledged as a member of civil society, one had to remain distant from the baseness of the majority black group. The middle class was ultimately caught between the rock of primitivism and the hard place of bourgeois aspirations. Not being "like the others" became a compliment for which many strived, and the quest for exceptional status fueled the talented-tenth and uplift mentality long after Du Bois had distanced himself from the concept because of its misinterpretation by both blacks and whites.[24]

Despite internal conflicts of the black bourgeoisie, their efforts to achieve autonomy from white social and institutional control remained steady. In the 1920s, students at HBCUs, particularly Fisk in 1924 and Hampton in 1927, rebelled against white administrative, teaching, and curricular dominance. The student and community protest was so effective that Fisk's President McKenzie resigned in 1925. For various reasons—including political expedience and economic survival—black administrators often accommodated racist mandates, but many black students rebelled against the white administrative agenda and reflected the multiple layers of black collegians' social thought.[25]

In his groundbreaking *Education of Blacks in the South*, historian James Anderson looked closely at the Fisk and Hampton rebellions; in *The New Negro on Campus: Black College Rebellions of the 1920s*, Raymond Wolters also detailed campus unrest at Fisk, Howard, Tuskegee, Hampton, Wilberforce, Florida A&M, and Lincoln (Mo.) that foreshadowed the student protest of the 1960s. Both texts presented the underlying conflict between black students, administrators, community members, and white administrators or trustees in the struggle to define educational opportunities for black students at HBCUs and interactions with local communities surrounding the schools.[26]

African American students were invested in corrective measures to dispel stereotypes and construct what they felt was a more appropriate image. A large part of campus, club, and social work involved vindication and black people's "defense of themselves." The African character for centuries had been maligned—from colonial aristocrats to common white citizens—and the tradition of vindicating the black race in the white popular imagination was paramount in all of African American cultural and intellectual production.

In the 1970s, sociologist St. Claire Drake identified vindication as a central thread in past African American history scholarship. In addition to "race uplift" and "vindication," I have identified "reclamation" as a third central thematic focus in African American women's social thought. Whether through pan-Africanism (1900s), black nationalism (1920s), the black history movement (1940s), Afrocentricity (1980s), or womanism (1980s), black women communicated with their African ancestors as much as they attempted to provide a corrective image in the European mind. Both Cooper and Bethune revered their mothers, and Bethune claimed that her African ancestry gave her considerable powers of extrasensory perception and dream interpretation. As black women wrote to inspire collective growth and wrote against white character assassination, they also wrote in communication with their foremothers toward a reclaimed, if romanticized, African womanhood.[27]

Race uplift, vindication, and reclamation were often salient within the black women's community work. However, because not all challenges to women's intellectual rigor came from whites, women had to diligently fight against views within black communities that diminished their intellectual capabilities, especially those that, at first glance, seemed benign or flattering. Such a case, "Our Girls," an entry in the fall 1927 edition of *Bulletin of Tennessee A&I State College*, features a fictitious dialogue between two male students who sing the praises of Tennessee State college women. The male discussants praise women's modesty, physical attractiveness, and fashion sense "that rivaled a Paris shop review." Historian Elizabeth Ihle countered, "Though flattering the image of young black women was seen as necessary to combat the constant charges of promiscuity, mannishness, and ignorance constantly made against them, these qualities are not the most relevant to a college student's pursuit of a degree." Black women fought on many fronts to maintain what I call their academic self-esteem.[28]

The 1928–29 Fisk handbook provides another example of such back-handed flattery: "the college girl of today starts for a high standard of womanliness which includes scholarship, good health, justice and fair play, self-control, a love of beauty, courtesy toward all and an essential goodness of heart. These standards are foremost in the ideals long held by Fisk women." The wording is consistent with the honor codes of their contemporaries, but the moral restrictions placed on black women, under the guise of protection, were strict and the limitations unbearable to some. The *Howard University Student Manual,* like those of most HBCUs, detailed specific living, visiting, travel, and behavior codes—it even prohibited women from driving without permission. Though praises of black women collegians were sung, independence and self-determination was blocked at every turn.[29]

Pressure for women to be scholarly (but not too smart), fashionable (but not gaudy), and any number of other contradictions, was ever-present. As a critical mass of women grew on campus—"upward of 100,000 members"—the dean of women's position emerged to handle social issues, assist with campus policy, and provide academic guidance. Lucy Slowe, the first to hold this position at Howard, was among the forerunners of women deans. Slowe was "a founding member of Alpha Kappa Alpha Sorority, a charter member of the District of Columbia College Alumnae Club, a founding member of the National Association of Deans of Women and Advisors to Girls in Negro Schools, and the dean of women at Howard University from 1923 until her death in 1937"; she was, as Ihle affirmed, "enormously influential." Slowe gave speeches from Columbia, South Carolina, to Columbia University in New York—and even a national radio address. She carried the message that "students grow into well-rounded women through doing things that challenge their whole being." She detailed many co-curricular opportunities that Howard's students should have access to beyond traditional studies and exams and used her education to challenge narrow definitions of college women's academic opportunities.[30]

Slowe gave many speeches and wrote journal articles criticizing institutional and familial restrictions put on black women. Her advocacy for expanded women's roles on and off campus went against the grain and set a precedent for the expansion of female student freedom. According to Slowe, part of the job of the dean of women was to instill morality in students but also to inspire them beyond traditional limits of what amounted to a curricular corset.

Margaret Murray Washington, Booker T. Washington's third wife, took the "Woman's Department" to another level. Lucy Slowe had broken ground at Howard, but Margaret Washington was entrusted with major operations at Tuskegee that led to the growth of the entire campus. Margaret Murray graduated from Fisk University, was immediately hired as a teacher at Tuskegee in 1889, and—long before her marriage to Booker T. in 1892—was promoted to "Lady Principal." Married to Booker T. Washington for twenty-two years (and outliving him by a decade), she dedicated her life to the success of Tuskegee and touched the lives of black women of all stations. Even Bethune called her "Big Sister." Washington was also a member of Delta Sigma Theta Sorority, held the presidency of NACW from 1912 to 1916, and in 1921 founded the International Council of Women of Darker Races: she was an exemplar of the local, national, and international networks of African American college women.

Administrators like Slowe and Washington, regardless of station or type of college, expected young black women to commit to community service; deans of women across the country led by example. On all fronts, black women were expected selflessly to give of themselves. Their struggle to define themselves did not necessarily refute the responsibility of service, but they argued for freedom of choice in how they would contribute to social betterment. They held contentious relationships with gendered perceptions of race uplift and racialized views of gender progress. Marjorie Baltimore, an undergraduate in the 1930s, wrote, "the Fisk woman has by intellectual and social work proved her willingness to fall in line with the great race movement." She then outlined the role that Fisk women played in civic organizations and the importance of resisting both racism and sexism, insisting that "Radicalism is sometimes necessary for emancipation." After World War I and during the Depression, gender roles began to reconstrict, and Baltimore wrote against the return to conservatism and in favor of women's sustained participation in civic and academic activities.[31]

Beyond curricular and social self-determination, black women's research reflected their desire to investigate and interpret the world their own way. As researchers, they chose topics relevant to black women. In four case studies below, Slowe (1933), Cuthbert (1942), Player (1948), and Noble (1956) demonstrate methodologies that reflected their organizational realities and discussed findings in terms of their own needs and desires. Black women scholars of the third wave of attainment demonstrated an effort to defend their names and speak their own truths, especially through scholarly research. Their negotiation of a standpoint social contract is evident in their academic production.

Four Black Women's Approach to Educational Research

Emergence of the sorority and club movement was but one significant change in black women's college experience: as Lucy Slowe cited in her 1933 "Higher Education of the Negro Woman," the industrial revolution, international connectedness, and woman's suffrage altered what it meant to be an educated black woman in the new century. Slowe critically evaluated institutional curricula and policies in order to adequately prepare her students for the changes that modernization and economic depression so swiftly brought. She sent surveys to seventy-six colleges asking them to assess the preparation of black women for social science analysis and leadership skills. The results revealed that of the 14,813 black women enrolled at the forty-four responding colleges, only 8 percent (615 women in political science and 560 in economics) were pursuing degrees relevant to the changing social status of women. Slowe argued that women's political independence garnered by suffrage in 1920 warranted an increased focus on political and economic studies. She lamented the fact that, because of lingering stereotypes, there were few opportunities for black women to gain leadership experience in student government organizations or councils.[32]

Slowe suggested curricular alternatives commensurate with the shifts in industrial, domestic, political, technological, and social realms. She commented on the changes in industry away from domestic service and the reduction of black women engaging in home work (like taking in laundry). She saw an increased role for restaurants, cafeterias, hotels, and cleaning shops in the service industry for which black women needed to be prepared.

For those who did have access to postsecondary education, Slowe protested that the "curriculum all pointed toward training teachers." Where there was a mass movement of black women to the teaching profession during Reconstruction, the solidification of the Jim Crow system and enforced segregation after World War I frustrated collegiate women with ambitions to excel in the professional labor force beyond the field of teaching.[33]

In her publications, Slowe challenged the strict regulation of black women college students in comparison to their male colleagues, observing, "The belief exists that college women must be shielded and protected to such an extent that the most intimate phases of their lives are invaded by rules and regulations." When the unconditional rules, particularly at HBCUs, were slow to change, some women ran into trouble and chafed under stubborn

restrictions; vivid examples of the conditions that Slowe identified are recorded in the memoirs discussed in the following chapters.[34]

After Slowe, Marion Cuthbert, who worked closely with Charles Johnson,
analyzed 1,994 black women survey respondents. She revealed noticeable
shifts in black college student demographics and stark contrasts between the
women and men students. Not surprisingly, women (59 percent) were twice
as likely as men (29 percent) to be single, and women (51 percent) were more
likely than men (38 percent) to be married but have no children. Evidently,
the more time a woman devoted to her studies, the less time she made for
courtship, marriage, childbearing, and child rearing. Because black women
were more likely to work outside the home (whether or not they were in
school), having a family meant working during day and night hours. Men,
on the other hand, could study, work, and be married because they were not
held responsible for the private domestic duties that consumed women after
the public workday. Cuthbert noted and discussed the black male-female
relationship tensions in both the public and private realm.[35]

Of the 1,994 women respondents, 1,178 were unmarried, and those who
were wed generally married in their social class. Yet only about 300 reported
spouses in professions requiring a college degree. The most-represented
spousal occupations included business owners (120), elementary school
teachers (108), medical doctors (72), ministers (40), lawyers (22), and college
professors (13). In his 1933 *Mis-education of the Negro*, Woodson correctly
pointed out that the most economically successful African Americans often
were not those who had earned degrees. Because more women attended college than men, the marriage patterns of the 1930s reveal that black women
married within their economic social class, even if not within their educational class. Regardless of whether they married someone in their educational class, women sought partners with comparable social status. In sum,
educational class did not always determine economic class, but generally,
those designated middle class by money or degree stuck together.[36]

Cuthbert's respondents articulated a feeling of belonging neither in the
black community nor in white society; they were marginalized in both college and community setting. Cuthbert named the study in reference to this
sentiment and deemed black academic women a "marginal majority." Cuthbert's thesis was that black college women did not fit comfortably in the
dominant culture whose middle-class Eurocentric values they had accepted,
nor did they fit in most black communities, the majority of whose members
had not gone beyond high school and some of whom reveled in being "low
class." This displacement after being "educated" foreshadowed cognitive dis-

sonance that still occurred for black women scholars in the later twentieth century.

Given their racial and gendered standpoint, the question loomed large, What type of education was fitting for black women? In the spirit of Anna Cooper and Lucy Slowe, Willa Player researched the curricular and organizational structure of Bennett College in order to determine what form of education was suitable for students at a post–World War II black woman's college. "Improving College Education for Women at Bennett College," Player's 1948 Columbia dissertation, coupled Johnson's and Cuthbert's employment and economic analysis of black college women with 317 alumni responses to a survey constructed by Bennett faculty. The results were used to implement curricular and administrative changes suitable for modern education.[37]

Player grouped 144 topics into nine categories, including "earning a living, community leadership and citizenship, home and family life, religion and philosophy of life, mental and physical health, recreation, and general problems" that African Americans faced. Based on student responses, she proposed ten institutional changes, including efforts to continually survey students for cues on revamping the curriculum; critical evaluation of campus policies; tracking technology and changing work opportunities so student training fit employment opportunities; increased alumni contact to survey efficacy of Bennett's education; and greater attention to students' individual needs. Fittingly, after extensive research and campus work experience, Player became the first black woman president of Bennett College in 1955.[38]

Player's institutional survey was only one methodological tool effective in measuring black women's collegiate participation. Before World War II, an overwhelming number of college attendees were club and sorority women. In Cuthbert's 1942 sample of women, 75 percent reported being involved in a sorority. It makes methodological sense, then, that Jeanne Noble used black sororities as the source for conducting her survey in 1954. Noble sent out 1,000 questionnaires, identifying women through the four black sororities, Alpha Kappa Alpha, Delta Sigma Theta, Zeta Phi Beta, and Sigma Gamma Rho. Signaling another important overlap between researcher and subject, Jeanne Noble served as national president of Delta Sigma Theta Sorority from 1958 to 1963.

Noble cited that of the over 106,000 black women college students, 42,000 were members of the four major sororities. Her study was representative of a particular type of college woman, but it was representative nonetheless. After 1955, due to the drastic increase in college attendance and the allure of exclusivity, the number of sorority members would never again reach 40 percent. Yet, for the pre-*Brown* years, Noble's methodology was especially useful given the sparse attendance of black women at PWIs. Sigma Gamma Rho was a key connection for this study: it was the only sorority founded at a PWI. All seven Sigma Gamma Rho founders were career schoolteachers, two of whom earned M.S. degrees, so this demographic was important to study but, without the aid of a sorority network, would have been difficult to locate.[39]

Noble's study provided fascinating insight about how black women college graduates conceptualized their education in the tumultuous time between world wars. Though Noble's 1955 dissertation was based on a January 1954 survey, the 1956 publication date allowed her to situate the significance of her study in light of the U.S. Supreme Court's *Brown* ruling, giving it particular historical relevance.[40]

In her work, Noble asserted that studying black women was important because they comprised a unique college demographic: (1) there were more black women in college than black men; (2) more black women than white women worked outside the home; and (3) black college women placed more emphasis on the vocational aspects of education as compared to white women's focus on liberal arts. When asked about the least important aspects of education, Noble's participants responded that learning for learning's sake was not a luxury black women could afford.[41]

Noble concluded that black women deserved the right to study as individuals without the burden of race responsibility or gender limitations guiding their every academic move. Like Slowe before her, Noble called for an equalization of educational and occupational opportunity. She claimed that the goals of education should be self-discovery, self-acceptance, and self-fulfillment—luxuries of the individual self that black women were not historically afforded. Noble did not argue against social service; she simply asserted that social work was not the sole responsibility or vocational capability of black women. This desire for individual fulfillment and personal advancement exposed a fatigue and frustration that many black women experienced from a century of race uplift they had shouldered. It reflected the tension between the ability to study to enrich one's soul and the responsibility to serve the community, support one's family, and act as a role model.[42]

Of the 1,000 questionnaires Noble distributed, 412 were returned: 264 respondents had graduated from coeducational HBCUs, 104 from white coeducational colleges, 29 from black women's colleges, and 16 from white women's colleges. This demographic was representative of the overall population in that the majority had graduated from HBCUs, but it was disproportionate in the number of white women's colleges, which were still largely segregated. Noble readily admitted the limitations of her sample, but the information did allow a consideration of the evolution of both the respondents and the researchers.[43]

In Noble's study, black women cited in letters, journals, and memoirs how racism and sexism in the curriculum, classrooms, campus, and social realms weighted their every step of academic growth. Black women researchers documented the individual and institutional barriers to academic advancement, but the national challenges were equally significant.[44]

National Scene

The Harlem Renaissance—heralded by Johnson's *Opportunity*, defined with Alaine Locke's 1925 *The New Negro*, and furthered by Works Progress Administration programs—popularized black cultural expression in complicated ways. The high/low culture dichotomy trapped black women in saint/jezebel stereotypes. On the West Coast, before and after Harlem's vogue, Hollywood mangled the image of African Americans. In 1915, D. W. Griffith's *Birth of a Nation* was released. The stereotypes of black man as brute, white man as hero, white woman as damsel, and black woman as whore were solidified (with advanced celluloid technology) into the national psyche. The 1939 production of *Gone with the Wind* legitimized the racism initially presented in *Birth of a Nation* and did additional damage to black women's image. The film, lauded for its use of new technology and its production on an epic scale, was acclaimed as an instant classic. It continues to be heralded as "one of the best films ever made," but the NAACP's Walter White clashed with the filmmakers and the black actors over damage done to black people's character by the derogatory portrayals.[45]

The image of African Americans as lazy, giddy, inept, and intellectually listless mesmerized the public, and, despite Hattie McDaniel's triumph as a recipient of an Academy Award, black women were damned to portray shiftless maids and mindless servants. In *Contempt and Pity: Social Policy and the Image of the Damaged Black Psyche, 1880–1996*, historian Daryl Scott has demonstrated how social scientists both reflected and projected negative stereotypes of black psychological states that also appeared in popular culture. Though black self-image and group definitions were complex and changed over time, the black persona was essentialized and black women bore the brunt of portrayals of ignorance. No matter how many black women attended college, they were still seen as possessing no more wit, mental stability, or moral fortitude than the air-headed, habitual liar represented by

Butterfly McQueen's character "Prissy." Both McDaniel and McQueen tried to balance their work in Hollywood with attempts to change, even in small ways, the vapid culture of the motion picture industry. Despite their best efforts, black women were molded into images that they found difficult to shatter, regardless of education or vocation.[46]

Popular image was but one significant barrier to education; violence that began in the first and second waves of attainment grew between world wars to epidemic proportions. The statistics on the number of African Americans who were lynched can never reflect the reported and unreported rapes, mass murders in race riots (such as those that took place in the "Red Summer" of 1919), or the decimation of entire black communities like Ocoee (1920) or Rosewood (1923)—both in Florida. The economic roller coaster of prosperity and poverty between wars disproportionately impacted black communities. Economic depression was directly linked to increases in race-based violence. White brutality was rationalized at every institutional level, and even the bid for a congressional bill against lynching failed.[47]

Fighting for equal access to education was challenging in the face of such obstacles, but the struggle through community organizing continued. One major accomplishment in the 1920s was black parent-teacher organizing. In 1926, the year that Woodson began Negro History Week, Selena Butler founded the National Congress of Colored Parents and Teachers and advanced black educational support networks that (with churches) became the core information centers for the civil rights movement.[48]

After World War I broadened African Americans' political awareness and global involvement, the black nationalism of Garvey's "Back to Africa" movement exploded in the 1920s and 1930s. The Pan-African activist motion fanned old embers of African emigration. Garvey's Universal Negro Improvement Association (UNIA) provided thousands of black women an opportunity to educate themselves and their communities about social, cultural, spiritual, and political issues relevant to black people. Amy Euphemia Jacques Garvey, who was formally educated in Jamaica before immigrating to New York, was a large part of the organization's effectiveness. Initially less popular but ultimately more enduring than the UNIA, the NAACP also built on national networks developed during the postbellum Negro Conventions. With foundational support from Ida B. Wells, Mary Church Terrell, Daisy Bates, and others, the NAACP became central in the civil rights movement.[49]

Before *Brown*, small but important gains were made in professional, political, government, and business realms. Overall, black women still were relegated to low-skilled labor, mainly in the domestic field, which neither required nor supported advanced scholarly development. Working in the service industry was as honorable work as any; being confined in such occupations due to lack of opportunity was discrimination that black people had faced since coming to the Americas.[50]

In *A Different Mirror: A History of Multicultural America*, Ronald Takaki tells of barriers to education for Latinos, Native Americans, and Asian Americans in addition to African Americans and European immigrants. The nuances of each group's relation with social systems are significant, but the overall theme of exclusion by emerging white society is clear. Like Africans, any non-whites were pressed into labor and mind-numbing service. Takaki reports a Mexican American's comments in the 1920s: "I have heard many teachers, farmers and members of the School Board say, 'What do Mexicans want to study for when they won't be needed as lawyers? They should be taught to be good; they are needed for cotton picking and work on the railroads.'" It was apparent to those kept outside the gates of the Ivory Tower that higher education was desirable; it was equally clear to the gatekeepers that denying access to education was the key to controlling workers. Takaki reveals that a farmer in Texas explained:

> If I wanted a man [to work] I would want one of the more ignorant ones. . . . Educated Mexicans are the hardest to handle. . . . It is all right to educate them no higher than we educate them here in these little towns. I want to be frank. They would make more desirable citizens if they would stop about the seventh grade.

Though physical labor was as admirable work as any, lack of choice to attend college was evidently central to maintaining a labor force that would not be able to negotiate for property ownership, voter rights, living wages, or any number of other rights that "good citizens" in a democracy would deserve.[51]

There were other developments between world wars that made the terrain to educational opportunity rough. Most notable was the 1925 Scopes trial. The eighteenth-century dispute between Awakening and Enlightenment worldviews matured into the nineteenth-century debate between religion and evolution—God and Darwin furthered an argument that, by World War II, impacted all levels of education. Religion, science, art, government, labor, race, gender, and family all influenced institutions; accordingly, black women's collegiate experiences were inseparable from historic time and place.[52]

In 1925, Anna Cooper wrote, "the impulse of humanity towards social progress is like the movement in the currents of a great water system . . .

beating onward, ever onward towards its eternity, the Ocean." The first century of black women's degree attainment was a forceful "beating onward, ever onward." This dynamic history between the 1850s and 1950s demonstrates the shifting barriers to black women's intellectual citizenship, the determination with which these barriers were faced, and the fruit of decades of sustained striving. This history also shows social contracts through which black women had to creatively negotiate and provides a geographic canvas for the personal stories presented next.[53]

"Reminiscences of School Life"

Six College Memoirs

Autobiography provides a rich source from which to consider the development of African American collegiate women. Though historically unreliable as a stand-alone document, a first-person account (as seen in John Hope Franklin's *Mirror to America*), adds much detail to the scene drawn by the collective, quantitative story. The six autobiographical case studies presented in this chapter reveal themes in the conditions, emotions, motivations, and opposition that black women experienced in college classrooms, campuses, and communities.[1]

This range of college experiences, from Fanny Coppin's in the mid-nineteenth century to Pauli Murray's in the mid-twentieth century, represents admirable dedication to individual cultivation. Though additional narratives are added in the next chapter's contextual essay, the central figures considered here are Fanny Jackson Coppin, Mary Church Terrell, Zora Neale Hurston, Lena Beatrice Morton, Rose Butler Browne, and Pauli Murray. Each offers a fascinating magnification of her understanding of the "right to grow." Many black women who began college did not complete graduation requirements because of lack of funds, desire to work for civil rights, or frustration with racism and sexism in the hierarchy of the university, so these accounts are especially poignant because five of the six women progressed to graduate-level study.

In an article titled "Collegiate Womanhood" in the *Fisk Herald* (1930), Marjorie Baltimore explained that the multiple barriers attendant in the "double bind of race and sex," for black women, amounted to more than the sum of its parts. The case studies below demonstrate the exponential nature of the barriers that arose from this double bind. Yet the stories move beyond victimization by defining college as struggle, adventure, and success. The accounts are compelling for their detail and humanize the national demographic numbers. First, basic biographical details are presented, followed by each woman's reflections on college life.[2]

Frances (Fanny) Jackson Coppin (1837–1913)

Fanny Coppin was born enslaved in the nation's capital to Lucy, also enslaved. It was rumored that Fanny's father was a white "senator from Carolina." Fanny's aunt Sarah purchased her freedom at the age of thirteen or fourteen for $125. Fanny attended school in New Bedford, Massachusetts, and then in Newport, Rhode Island. In 1860, Jackson began the "ladies' course" at Oberlin, and the following year she began the more rigorous "gentlemen's course." She graduated from Oberlin in August 1865 and immediately began teaching at the Institute for Colored Youth (ICY) in Philadelphia. As a result of her excellence in teaching, Coppin was appointed by the Quaker Board of Managers to the position of principal, which she held from 1869 to 1902. In 1881, she married Levi Coppin, fifteen years her junior, and they were both involved in the African Methodist Episcopal (AME) Church. In 1902, the Coppins conducted missionary work in Cape Town, South Africa.[3]

Coppin was intimately involved with the community surrounding the ICY, especially in settlement homes for black women. She also wrote children's texts and served on the board of the Home for the Aged and Infirmed Colored People from 1881 to 1913. She gained recognition through her weekly column, the "Women's Department," in the *Christian Recorder*, and articles in the *Philadelphia Press* and *Boston Commonwealth*. Her public addresses included a speech titled "The Intellectual Progress of the Colored Women of the United States since the Emancipation Proclamation," given at the Congress of Representative Women at the Columbian Exposition (1893 Chicago World's Fair).[4]

Coppin's *Reminiscences of a School Life and Hints on Teaching* (1913) documented her administration and pedagogy at ICY and also included travel diaries and biographical narratives of students. In this collection, she revealed challenging aspects of her college years, but she also recalled fruitful relationships in Oberlin and Philadelphia.[5] *Reminiscences* melded genres: it was at once autobiography, memoir, textbook, and organizational history. In 1903, a year after her retirement as principal, the school was moved to Cheyney, Pennsylvania, and renamed Cheyney State Teacher's School. Through efforts of her former students, Coppin has been recognized as a champion of black teacher education and Coppin State College in Maryland was named in her honor.[6]

In 1859, only 32 of Oberlin's 1,200 students were black, and by 1861, blacks comprised only 245 of 8,800 Oberlin's cumulative population. In 1860, the year Coppin entered Oberlin, 199 of 1,311 students were enrolled in the "gentlemen's course"—only one, Mary Patterson, was a black woman. Coppin recalled: "The faculty did not forbid a woman to take the gentleman's course, but they did not advise it. There was plenty of Latin and Greek in it, and as much mathematics as one could shoulder." Though French was not offered, Coppin took private lessons in addition to her regular schedule of classes.[7]

Although Coppin was an excellent student in the advanced courses, she felt pressure to prove her scholastic competence and justify her desire for harder work:

> I never chose to recite in my classes at Oberlin but I felt that I had the honor of the whole African race upon my shoulders. I felt that, should I fail, it would be ascribed to the fact that I was colored. At one time, when I had quite a signal triumph in Greek, the Professor of Greek concluded to visit the class in mathematics and see how we were getting along. I was particularly anxious to show him that I was as safe in mathematics as in Greek. I indeed, was more anxious, for I had always heard that my race was good in the languages, but stumbled when they came to mathematics.[8]

Black students reported feeling fear, insecurity, and pressure in an atmosphere that not only was competitive, but where white students and instructors doubted their intellectual capability.

Coppin critiqued professors' resistance to her enrollment in Greek and discussed the intersection of race and gender in her educational experience. She did not explicitly charge Oberlin with racism or sexism; however, she stated that the demand to prove one's mental abilities was ever-present for black and women students. Beyond faculty, the public pressure to establish a right to attend school was staggering. Coppin understood that for her, unlike her white colleagues, success or failure in any academic endeavor would reflect on all black people.

She commented that, despite the pressure, the environment was not overtly hostile. Many, like Oberlin's President Finney, deplored the indignities that black people suffered in antebellum America. Some students demonstrated sensitivity to racial conditions and displayed soothing compassion toward those most affected. Coppin confided: "At one time, at Mrs. Peck's, when we girls were sitting on the floor getting out our Greek, Miss Sutherland, from Maine, suddenly stopped, and looking at me, said: 'Fanny Jackson, were you ever a slave?' I said yes: and she burst into tears. Not another word was spoken by us. But those tears seemed to wipe out a little of what was wrong."[9]

Coppin had received teacher training in Rhode Island, and the faculty at Oberlin assigned her a course to teach, with the understanding that if students rejected a black instructor, the assignment would be revoked. All went well. Of her teaching assignment, she admitted:

> fortunately for my training at the normal school, and my own dear love of teaching, tho there was a little surprise on the faces of some when they came into the class, and saw the teacher, there were no signs of rebellion. The class went on increasing in numbers until it had to be divided, and I was given both divisions. One of the divisions ran up again, but the Faculty decided that I had as much as I could do, and it would not allow me to take on any more work. . . . [I was] teaching my classes, besides 16 private music scholars, and keeping up my work in the senior class.[10]

Though she was tapped as a student teacher and proved popular at the task, she had insecurities because she had internalized the dominant culture's perception of her scholarly credibility.

In the midst of the Civil War, at one of the few coeducational institutions that admitted black and white students in the United States, Coppin experienced a wide range of freedoms. Oberlin's liberal atmosphere was not typical: "I had been so long in Oberlin that I had forgotten about my color, but I was sharply reminded of it when, in a storm of rain, a Philadelphia streetcar conductor forbid my entering a car that did not have on it 'for colored people,' so I had to wait in the storm until one came in which colored people could ride."[11]

She was aware of the privilege Oberlin provided and used it to assist in the education of others. She began a literacy night class for freedmen and recalled:

> It was deeply touching to me to see old men painfully following the simple words of spelling; so intensely eager to learn. I felt that for such people to have been kept in the darkness of ignorance was an unpardonable sin, and I rejoiced that even then I could enter measurably upon the course in life which I had long ago chosen.[12]

Coppin wrote of students' right, after mastering basic skills, to choose their direction in education. Because of obstacles she had faced, she asserted that race, gender, or economic class should not determine a specific track of study. She claimed the right to think, adored academic study, and denied the public demand that she remain ignorant or play dumb because she was a black woman born enslaved.

Mary Eliza Church Terrell (1863–1954)

Mary Church was born in Memphis, Tennessee, in 1863. Though neither of her parents was educated beyond the secondary level, Terrell's father became wealthy buying Memphis real estate after the yellow fever epidemic of 1878. Because of his social standing, he knew statesmen like Blanche K. Bruce, a Reconstruction senator from Mississippi. While at Oberlin, Terrell received an invitation from Senator Bruce's wife to attend a function in D.C., indicating her high social status. Terrell graduated from Oberlin in 1884 with a B.A. After graduation, she taught for one academic year at Wilberforce, then took a two-year tour of Europe, during which she visited and studied in France, Germany, Italy, Switzerland, and England. Upon her return, she earned an M.A. from Oberlin in 1888.[13]

Mary Church taught at Dunbar High School in D.C., where she met and married Robert Terrell, an 1891 graduate of Harvard Law School. The D.C. school board appointed her superintendent in 1895, the first woman to hold the post. In 1892, she cofounded (with Anna Cooper and Mary Patterson) the Colored Women's League and in 1896 became the first president of the National Association of Colored Women (NACW). In 1909, she was a founding member of the NAACP and later became an active member of Delta Sigma Theta Sorority.

Terrell enjoyed a busy public-speaking schedule, delivering addresses at places like Spelman College, the Brooklyn Institute of Arts and Sciences, and Radcliffe College. Being multilingual, she delivered a speech in Berlin, in German, at the 1904 International Congress of Women. She received an invitation to serve as a U.S. delegate to the Women's International Congress for Peace and Freedom (WICPF). In 1919, she traveled to the WICPF meeting with Jane Addams, the U.S. organization's president, and Moorfield Storey, president of the NAACP. Terrell delivered an address, also in German, at St. Peter's Cathedral in Zurich. Years later, in 1921, Terrell and Addams again collaborated to discredit false charges that African American troops mistreated German women during World War I. Terrell was outspoken against racism in public areas, employment, housing, and education.[14]

In 1940, she penned an autobiography, *A Colored Woman in a White World*, and painted a colossal portrait that detailed her experiences in school, work, and social life. Her story revealed a fascinating perspective on figures like Frederick Douglass and Susan B. Anthony, both of whom she knew personally, and offered insightful commentary on a range of public figures from Marian Anderson to Adolf Hitler. The autobiography was written in grandiose language: besides lauding her own activist efforts and detailing her whirlwind travel, she built extensive verbal monuments to her husband, who had become a powerful African American judge in D.C. Besides being a premier scholar and traveler, she picketed in the nation's capital—dressed to the nines—fighting to desegregate cafeterias, theaters, and public transportation.[15]

Terrell attended Oberlin two decades after Coppin and, for many reasons, had a less stressful experience. She was born free, attended school after the Civil War, came from a wealthy family, and was educated from the age of six at a "Model School" attached to Antioch College, where renowned educator Horace Mann was president. Terrell's life was certainly easier than Coppin's, but she too felt obligated to vindicate the African race. Of her primary school years, Terrell wrote:

> I was covered with confusion and shame at the thought [of having enslaved ancestors], and my humiliation was painful indeed. . . . I resolved that so far as this descendent of slaves was concerned, she would show those white girls and boys whose forefathers had always been free that she was their equal in every respect. At that time I was the only colored girl in the class, and I felt I must hold high the banner of my race.[16]

Terrell provided insight into historic elementary education practices by referring to critical incidents: a teacher "boxed her ears"; she was asked to play a Negro servant in a play (she refused); and she confronted fellow classmates, white and black, who made racist remarks against Chinese students. Terrell's tenure at Oberlin was relatively easy, but her recollections exposed racism at all levels in the supposedly more egalitarian North.[17]

Terrell did well at Oberlin. In addition to her Greek and Latin studies, she attended Bible study regularly and enjoyed it but wrote: "when I tackled geometry in the preparatory department of the college I met my Waterloo sure enough! I struggled hard to do the work, but I did not understand how to go at it properly and I barely pulled through the course. How I loathed plane geometry! It wounded my pride and 'hurt my feelings' because it was so hard for me to understand. I did a little better in solid geometry, but I did not set the world afire even in that." She also expressed frustration with learning to draw but proved proficient at literature. When as a freshman she was elected class poet, she wrote "The Fallen Star," in which she imitated Longfellow's hexameter in *Hiawatha*.[18]

Although many black women embraced challenge, some were careful not to advance too far. Terrell wrote: "some of my friends and schoolmates urged me not to select the 'gentlemen's course,' because it would take much longer to complete than the 'ladies' course.' They pointed out that Greek was hard; that it was unnecessary, if not positively unwomanly, for girls to study that 'old, dead language' anyhow; that during the two extra years required to complete it I would miss a lot of fun." Many women students internalized this message that they should mute their striving. Terrell's friends warned her that, "worst of all, [taking the gentleman's course] might ruin my chances of getting a husband, since men were notoriously shy of women who knew too much. 'Where,' inquired some of my friends sarcastically, 'will you find a colored man who has studied Greek?' They argued that I wouldn't be happy if I knew more than my husband." As black women's attendance surpassed black men's, they grew increasingly concerned with finding a husband of the same social stratum. Nationally and internationally, pundits claimed that too much education defeminized a woman. Professors warned black women away from difficult classes to "save them the trouble of hard work"; some black women, like Terrell, took this warning as a challenge to excel.[19]

Like Coppin, Terrell found hope in race reconciliation at Oberlin. She cited special friendships with both a white student and a black student and lamented: "it is unfortunate that the children of the two races early get the impression that each is the mortal enemy of the other. Few efforts are being made to teach them mutual forbearance and tolerance." Largely due to her light complexion and high social standing, she traversed racial and national barriers through diplomacy and travel in a way not all of her race could. Terrell served in the Aelioian women's club and twice represented the club in formal debates with the Ladies Literary Society, which Lucy Stanton led thirty years before. Terrell edited the college newspaper for a short time and was, according to her own account, very popular. She cited class as a larger factor than race in social relationships, writing: "my associates in college were, naturally, members of my own class. Until I reached the junior year I had only one colored classmate, and she lived at home. . . . Throughout the whole period in the Ladies Hall, never once did I feel that I was being discriminated against on account of my color."[20]

Terrell gave an uneven account of race relations at Oberlin, claiming full membership in that society but detailing numerous examples of racial slights, such as being snubbed as class poet for the Junior Exhibition: "There is no doubt that . . . the fact that I am colored prevented me from receiving the honor. . . . I know now better than I did then that 'blood is thicker than water' when several racial groups come together to elect a representative for the whole."[21]

Though she interpreted instances of racism in her life to be isolated occurrences, they were the norm for most black women, which she found when she left the shelter of Oberlin. As it had for Coppin, a critical moment of racial realization occurred when Terrell left Ohio: "While I was still in college I had the first bitter experience of inability to secure employment on account of my race, during a summer vacation which I was spending with my mother in New York City. . . . I thought I had secured employment three times, but three times I was doomed to disappointment." In one instance, the woman was surprised that Terrell was an educated black woman. Terrell was light-skinned and wanted to make sure that her potential employer was clear about her race: "if I had told her I was a gorilla in human form, she could not have been more greatly shocked. Never before in all her life had she come in contact with an educated colored girl, she said." Neither had most whites, which is why many found it difficult to believe that black women scholars actually existed.[22]

Terrell did not mention direct community service efforts at all during her college years. She was economically stable and did not have to work and seemingly considered her social status as her contribution to race uplift. She did teach after graduation but expressed exasperation at the workload and a desire to live a more "cultured" life instead. For Terrell, like very few black women of her day, college life was one of leisure. She did not, however, become purely a nonworking socialite as her father wished. She simply chose to work in the public sphere in unconventional ways.[23]

Zora Neale Hurston (1891–1960)

In *Dust Tracks on a Road* (1942), Zora Neale Hurston presented a fascinating rendition of life. She shared lessons learned as a daughter of Florida, as a chronicler of Creole and West Indian culture, and as a luminary turned persona non grata of the Harlem Renaissance's black intelligentsia. Hurston traced the adventures of her rocky upbringing in Eatonville, revealing an introspective childhood filled with tales of *Gulliver's Travels, Grimm's Fairy Tales,* and *Greek and Roman Myths.* She fondly recalled her college days at Morgan Academy in Baltimore, Maryland, where she completed high school requirements in 1918, and Howard University, where she attended from 1919 to 1924, earning an associate degree in 1920. She graduated from Barnard College with a B.A. in 1928 and published in a wide range of genres including short stories, novels, essays, and plays.

Her works ranged from "John Redding Goes to Sea" in *Stylus* (1921), "Spunk" in *Opportunity* (1925), and "How It Feels to Be Colored Me" in *World Tomorrow* (1928), to "Crazy for This Democracy" in *Negro Digest* (1945), and "What White Publishers Won't Print" in the *Saturday Evening Post* (1950).

Though she published a variety of nonfiction, she is most recognized for her novels, particularly *Their Eyes Were Watching God* (1937), which she claimed to have written in seven weeks while in Haiti. Though she conducted graduate research in the Department of Anthropology at Columbia University, she did not complete the degree.[24]

Hurston was a heralded member of Zeta Phi Beta Sorority and received a Guggenheim Award both in 1936 (to study West Indian Obeah practices) and in 1937 (for study in Haiti). She professed to love her work and described her life as having "touched the four corners of the horizon." She held controversial views about literature production but more so about political affairs. She rejected the 1954 *Brown* mandate to desegregate because she advocated the support of "self-association" that all-black schools afforded. She had been to all-white schools and apparently did not think they were better for black students than black schools. She passed away in January 1960 in Florida, where she had returned after leaving a New York life filled with hard times and heartbreak. Though she was penniless and living in a welfare home at the time of her death, over one hundred people paid tribute at her funeral. Hurston's stories have since garnered acclaim, thanks in large part to scholars like Alice Walker, Henry Louis Gates, and Maya Angelou, who resurrected her work, and to Oprah Winfrey, who produced the T.V.-movie version of *Their Eyes* in 2005.[25]

Hurston recalled liking geography and reading when she was young and, with her vivid imagination, "lived an exciting life unseen" growing up in Eatonville. Due to Hurston's mother's death, not getting along with her stepmother, and being passed around to siblings, she did not have a solid primary school experience and envied those who did: "when I saw more fortunate people of my own age on their way to and from school, I would cry inside and be depressed for days." After working various jobs, including as an assistant for a white actress, a hotel clerk, and a waitress, she landed in Baltimore. Tired of "nickeling and diming" to save for school, she enrolled in the high school department of Morgan College.[26]

Hurston enjoyed her work at Morgan but, like Terrell, admitted having creative differences with mathematics. She wrote: "my two years at Morgan went off very happily indeed. The atmosphere made me feel right. . . . The science courses were tremendously interesting to me. Perhaps it was because Professor Calloway was such an earnest teacher. I did not do well in mathematics. Why should A minus B? Who the devil was X anyway? I could not even imagine. I still do not know." She suspected Professor Johnson most likely gave her a *C* because she excelled in all other subjects. Apparently, Hurston never reconciled her differences with math: "I have been told that you can never factor A—B to the place where it comes out even. I wouldn't know because I never tried to find out."[27]

She initially planned to stay on at Morgan for college but met Mae Miller, the daughter of Howard mathematics and sociology professor Kelly Miller, who insisted that she come to Howard.[28] Enamored with the elite reputation of Howard, Hurston spoke adoringly of the institution and its professors:

> Now as everyone knows, Howard is the capstone Negro education in the world. There gather Negro money, beauty, and prestige. It is to the Negro what Harvard is to whites. They say the same thing about a Howard man that they do about Harvard—you can tell a Howard man as far as you can see him, but you can't tell him much. He listens to the doings of other Negro schools and their graduates with bored tolerance. Not only is the scholastic rating at Howard high, but tea is poured in the manner!"[29]

Given the socioeconomic status of Howard students, Hurston figured she could never fit in. Miller convinced her otherwise, and she moved during the summer to earn money for tuition.

Because of ranking and accreditation issues, Howard did not accept all of her credits from Morgan, and though she had financial difficulties, Dwight Holmes encouraged her to stay. Holmes, who taught at Morgan, moved to Howard to teach English, and Hurston had adored his classes. So she stayed. To Hurston, Howard was lavish. She described her first college assembly in terms of exaltation and greatness. She claimed, from that first day, her dedication to the university did not fade in the entire two years she was there, recalling: "when on Mondays we ended service by singing Alma Mater, I felt just as if it were the Star Spangled Banner. . . . My soul stood on tiptoe and stretched up to take in all it meant. So I was careful to do my class work and be worthy to stand there under the shadow of the hovering spirit of Howard. I felt the ladder under my feet."[30]

Hurston paid her school tuition with work as a manicurist at a barbershop owned by a black barber who took only white clients, many of whom were "bankers, Senators, Cabinet members, Congressmen, and Gentlemen of the Press." The barbershop provided a political education, and she claimed to be a confidante and a go-between for important men. She recalled the electric nature of the capital and witnessed firsthand black struggles for desegregation following the end of World War I. She credited Lorenzo Turner, Harvard graduate and head of the Howard English Department, with inspiring her to learn the work of literary giants. At Howard, Hurston studied under well-known professors Williams (Romance Languages), Davis (Greek and

German), and Alaine Locke, head of the nineteen-member Stylus literary society. Hurston began writing short stories and named the student newspaper the *Hill Top*. After earning her associate degree, she left Howard due to lack of funds.[31]

She lauded the sociologist Charles Johnson for establishing *Opportunity*, the cultural forum that called the Harlem Renaissance into being. Hurston initially moved to New York at the suggestion of Johnson. In 1925, she continued her course work at Barnard College and graduated in 1928. Upon entering Barnard, she made friends enough to proclaim, "I have no lurid tales to tell of race discrimination at Barnard" but she also admitted that because she was the college's only African American student, she became "Barnard's sacred black cow." She was encouraged to study fine arts, economics, and anthropology because of her prior work at Howard and soon fell in with professors Reichard, Benedict, and "King of Kings," Franz Boas.[32] Of Boas, she bragged:

> He is idolized by everybody who takes his orders. We all call him Papa, too. . . . Away from his office, Dr. Boas is full of youth and fun, and abhors dull, stodgy arguments. . . . As is well known, Dr. Franz Boas of the Department of Anthropology of Columbia University, is the greatest Anthropologist alive for two reasons. The first is his insatiable hunger for knowledge and then more knowledge; and the second is his genius for pure objectivity. He has no pet wishes to prove."[33]

After her graduation from Barnard, Boas arranged a fellowship for Hurston to collect folklore of the black South. Though Hurston did extensive graduate research with Boas at Columbia, she did not complete her graduate course work, the dissertation, or the defense. She did, however, give considerable attention to her research, recorded her reflections of academic life, and created powerful fictive narratives based on her ethnographic research in the African Diaspora.[34]

Anthropologist Gwendolyn Mikell rightly observed that because Hurston did not finish her degree, she is generally recognized for her literary production instead of for her formal research. This trend ignores her scholarly processes. "Research," Hurston explained in *Dust Tracks*, "is formalized curiosity." While collecting stories, she was conscious of her approach, recorded discrepancies with expected results, and formulated unique methodological strategies; she was well read, well trained, and focused; yet her writing was regarded as more hapless than scholarly.[35]

Regardless of how she revered Boas for his objectivity, her methodology for communicating with locals was what later scholars would call "subjective ethnography" and "reflexive" study. According to Hurston, the more a researcher related to the content of the study, the more accurate and rich the analysis. Conventional practice—scientific objectivity—ran counter to this approach. After gathering data in Florida, Haiti, and Jamaica, Hurston's excellent artistic product (most notably *Their Eyes*) proved the value of her scholarly process. After conducting field studies, Hurston returned to Columbia to begin her course work. In addition to working with Boas, she studied with Melville Herskovits. When she could not gain financial support for her practical approach to graduate studies, she left the university but continued to publish despite "losing interest" in obtaining the doctoral degree.[36]

Lena Beatrice Morton (1901–?)

Lena Morton's autobiography, *My First Sixty Years: Passion for Wisdom* (1965), tracked her family life with parents, grandparents, and a brother who were bound together as "hoops of steel." Morton's family moved from Kentucky to Ohio during the World War I northern migration so that Lena could attend an accredited high school, something she could not do in segregated Winchester or Lexington. Moving from a town of approximately eight thousand, she was "green as the blue grass of Kentucky" and experienced growing pains, but she soon adjusted to the big city of Cincinnati and fast-moving Woodward High School.[37]

As a child, Lena inwardly competed with older children in her Sunday school to excel in reading and outwardly competed academically with her brother, three years her senior. Her drive to learn resulted in quiet "intellectual victories," and her determination spurred her to apply to the University of Cincinnati (UC), despite the small number of African American students admitted. In her estimation, Woodward High School was "99.44 percent free of racial discrimination," but UC posed formidable racial barriers for her to overcome. Nonetheless, she earned the B.A. in 1923 and her M.A. in 1925, both from the University of Cincinnati.[38]

Against the advisement of the head of the English Department, Morton pursued doctoral studies in English and triumphantly earned the Ph.D. from Western Reserve in Cleveland, Ohio, in 1947. Desiring to explore the "Old World," she traveled in Europe during the summer of 1956, visiting London, Paris, Genoa, Rome, Pisa, Venice, Florence, Edinburgh, and Basel. She attended a summer session at the University of London, where she enrolled in "Literature and Art in England, 1750–1850." While a professor of English at Southern University in Louisiana, Morton enrolled in a summer semester at

Harvard, thus fulfilling her "three eminent goals"—to earn the Ph.D., study abroad, and study at the oldest university in the United States. By the time she took the Harvard course, she had already authored two books, *Negro Poetry in America* (1925) and *Farewell to the Public Schools—I'm Glad We Met* (1952), both of which she was pleased to find were housed, and utilized, at Harvard's Widener Library. Before penning her autobiography, she published *Man under Stress* (1960) and later *The Influence of the Sea upon English Poetry from the Anglo-Saxon to the Victorian Period* (1972), proving a sustained interest in English studies.

Morton's autobiography included pages from her academic diaries as well as original poems titled "Chase the Muse," "Admonition to America," "A Little Lower than the Angels," "To Teach or Not to Teach (Apologies to Shakespeare)," and "Courage for the Times," among others. The text also contained social commentary in which she took blacks and whites to task for behaviors that contributed to the "commotion in America" that racism caused. By the publication of *My First Sixty Years*, Morton had taught for four decades, including fifteen years at the college level, mainly at HBCUs. She was a member of Delta Sigma Theta Sorority, and, after holding a deanship at Lane College in Tennessee, she became a professor of English at Texas College and head of the Division of Humanities.[39]

There were many civil rights advances between the first attendees of Oberlin and the World War I–era college boom. In the face of black social advancement, however, Jim Crow policies intensified. Morton recollected the humiliation at the University of Cincinnati in her 1918 first-year English class:

> A goodly number of the professors followed the alphabetical arrangement in seating the white students but relegated the Negro students to the last row regardless of the literal sequence. . . . I was the only Negro member of the section. Without including me in the M's, the professor seated the white students alphabetically until she came to the last row. Here she placed me in the seat against the wall; then she left one seat vacant, and seated the remaining whites whose names were at the end of the alphabet. As I write this episode forty-six years later, I am able to record the incident with composure and good will. In 1918, as I sat there in the last row against the wall with an empty seat between my classmates and me, my freshman soul was utterly hurt. I stared at the cultured professor and pondered man's inhumanity to man.[40]

Though at the end of the semester Morton managed to "win over" the professor, who stopped her discriminatory seating practices, the account is nonetheless instructive about the daily humiliation visited upon black students. It is significant that the English professor was a woman. Often racism was defined in masculine terms, as "man's inhumanity to man." Though cruelty of white women to enslaved and segregated black women has been duly noted, Morton brings to light a salient example of the pervasiveness of modern white women's conformity to racism.

Athletic facilities, especially swimming pools, were hotbeds of racism. Morton recollected the humiliation of having to submit to racist school policy in order to graduate:

> Every student was required to take swimming before he received his degree. I had not taken it during my freshman year, because I resented the University's forcing its Negro female students to take swimming only on Friday afternoons after the white females had had their swimming lessons for the week. When the Negro swimmers were out, the water was changed and the pool was made fresh and ready for the Caucasian swimmers Monday morning.[41]

She waited until her final year to meet the requirement in hopes of avoiding the policy. The school threatened to withhold her degree if she did not capitulate. She obliged with no regrets because even though she lost the battle of the segregated class, she won the war of obtaining her college degree.

Morton continued her study and earned the Ph.D. in English from Western Reserve. There, she did not encounter the overt racism of her undergraduate years. Instead, she fell prey to the quiet discouragement disguised as "advisement" from the department chair. Morton recalled that when she stated her desire for admission to the graduate program, Dr. Foster answered:

> "Well, if you get a Ph.D. in English from Western Reserve, you will be the first Negro to do it." Then he rose from his seat and began pacing the floor of the office. "Miss Morton," he said, "I don't want to insult you, but we have Negroes to come up here year after year for the Ph.D. They start, but when we put the works to them, they balk. They can't hold out. They do one of two things: either they drop out altogether, or else they change fields and switch to some other area for their Ph.D. They can't get it in English." I enjoyed his performance, for he was grand as he pranced the room flooding it with his silver toned oratory, and awing my eyes with his venerable crown of silver hair.[42]

After Morton calmly responded, "I will hold out," Foster allowed her to enter the program. She performed well in her course work—even earning an "H" for high-distinction honors in his course. She recalled the sleepless night before her oral examination, though she did not provide readers an inside look at the dissertation defense itself.[43]

At the doctoral graduation ceremonies in 1947, Foster was the graduation speaker, and during the degree awards, he remained seated, but when Morton was hooded, "Dr. Finley Foster rose and graciously bowed to me. The audience gave a spontaneous blast of applause. . . . I was enraptured for the scholarly Caucasian who had so passionately told me that Negroes could not obtain the Ph.D. in English at Western Reserve was now bowing to me in recognition of that attainment." Although Morton claimed victory walking across the stage, the celebration belonged to a larger community. After commencement, she visited the Poro School of Beauty Art, where "Mrs. Ernestine Mahan transformed my ordinary curls into a crown of pompous waves." Morton attended an elaborate reception sponsored by her sorority. There, university officials, professors, family, and friends honored her and shared her joyful moment, which she distilled into a short story titled "The Perfect Evening."[44]

Morton's affinity for flowing narrative was especially rich when speaking of Europe. In 1956, when she studied at the University of London, she resided in Canterbury Hall, the international dorm. She was the only African American present but enjoyed relations with "Negroes" from Haiti and Africa. She was warmly received, but her classmates questioned her nationality (some mistook her for Spanish or Arabian) because educated black Americans were an anomaly.

Morton spoke in glowing terms of her European visit, where she "stood in the place where Milton, Wordsworth, Lord Byron, and Tennyson once pondered their studies." She praised the English as well-disciplined, polite, kind, unruffled, orderly, calm, and noble. She mentioned that Europeans, in turn, viewed Americans as loud, rude, arrogant, and uncivil. Later in the text, when recounting her experiences in teaching, she admonished Americans and African Americans for being loud, rude, undisciplined, and lacking in patience.[45]

In her writing, she espoused middle-class respectability and conservative definitions of proper behavior. Considering the publication date of 1965, she may have used respectability—and her personal claim as a well-mannered international student and citizen of the world—as a trope to bolster the advances black people were making at the time. She seemed to place a premium on civility and to immerse herself in "classical" studies as a means to refute black inferiority.

Rose Butler Browne (1897–1986)

Rose Butler was born "in the slums of South Boston, the eldest daughter and the third of seven children to bless the John Robinson Butler family." After growing up in Massachusetts, she finished high school at Rogers High School in Newport, Rhode Island. Browne's great-grandmother Charlotte—a woman who lived to be 107 years old whom Browne called the "High Priestess"—influenced her a great deal. Rose completed three years at Rhode Island Normal School in Providence to earn a degree and in 1921 graduated from the University of Rhode Island with an M.S. degree from the College of Engineering, specializing in entomology. After graduation, she moved to Virginia for her first teaching position at Virginia State College, which awarded its first four-year college-level degree in 1925 with her curricular assistance.[46]

In 1929, she married E. T. Browne, a local Baptist minister and principal of the elementary school, with whom she had her son, Emmett. Though Reverend Browne did not match Rose Butler in educational status, his stature as a minister and school principal placed them on an equal social plane, and she credited his support for her ability to pursue an advanced degree. While on leave from Virginia State College, she completed a comparative analysis of remedial reading techniques for primary levels. In June 1937, Harvard University awarded her a doctorate from the College of Education.

Browne had an extensive career as an elementary school teacher and professor; she taught at colleges including Virginia Normal and Industrial Institute, Virginia State College, West Virginia State College, Bluefield College in West Virginia, and North Carolina College in Durham. She worked with community agencies like the Girl Scouts, the PTA, the YWCA, and local churches and in 1953 became the first mid-Atlantic regional director for the Alpha Kappa Alpha Sorority. She consulted in textbook preparation and studied racial representation of African Americans in children's literature. In her autobiography, *Love My Children: An Autobiography, The Education of a Teacher* (1969), Browne presented her story in three parts, recounting her upbringing and graduate studies in New England, relaying her teaching experiences in the South, and outlining her recommendations for advancing educational opportunities for impoverished children.[47]

Lena Morton's proposal for the civilizing aspect of higher education was similar to Rose Browne's, which reflected the rising temperament of the 1950s and early 1960s: they both stressed the importance of modeled behavior. Yet, Browne's work differed from Morton's because she overtly stated her radical agenda: she proposed to use the cloak of conventional education not because it was intrinsically valuable, but because she could wield it to help black people. Browne did not glorify European culture or the "white" value system. The shift in expression of black identity from Morton's mid-1960s memoir to Browne's late 1960s memoir reflects the shift from civil rights to Black Power ideologies. Interestingly, Browne rejected an attempt to prove herself equal to the white standard; she claimed to be superior—at least in some academic terms—to her white male Harvard professors.

According to Browne, she grew up in a melting pot—Boston's South End—with "largely first-generation Irish, newly arrived Italians, newly arrived Russians, some German Jews, and some Negroes." Her parents were not educated beyond secondary school but encouraged her to excel. She attended predominantly white schools, where she described teachers who attempted to squelch the racial pride instilled at home by her great-grandmother, the "High Priestess." The local library program offered Rose an opportunity to develop her reading skills, and when her family moved to Newport, she took English, English history, Latin, and algebra in order to prepare for college. She described Rogers High School as "the joy of my life," even though she reported a caste system where, "outside of the academic contacts, the Jewish and Negro pupils had little or no social contact with other students."[48]

After obtaining a teaching certificate from Rhode Island Normal School, she enrolled in the University of Rhode Island College of Engineering, shunning the only alternate choice: home economics. Browne took general entomology, economic entomology, physics, and chemistry, describing them as "pure joy" and writing: "from my teachers in the engineering school I learned excellent work habits, personal standards of accuracy, and a perspective for evaluating relative values. The experience further confirmed my desire to teach." Browne identified two professors in particular who encouraged her. When in class she was mistaken about qualities of an insect and insisted she was right, she recalled how her professor handled the situation: he sat down with her, "in the kindest manner imaginable," and studied the insect under a microscope so she could see for herself that she was wrong. She was grateful that he did not resort to the public humiliation so often employed by less-skilled professors. She also appreciated studies with an English professor who "had a unique ability to get the most out of the subject material and at the same time stimulate her classes to original thinking and work." Browne recorded her master's program as a highway to learning, but she regarded her doctoral program at Harvard as a formidable roadblock.[49]

Browne sustained "nodding relationships" with students at Harvard during the phase of her course work in the College of Education's doctoral program. She even enjoyed a cordial and supportive relationship with her advisor. Until she appeared for an oral examination to defend her dissertation proposal, all went well. Having acquired a positive reputation as an effective teacher, Browne studied remedial reading to develop literacy programs for groups designated as "slow." She conducted her study with Irish and Italian elementary students in South Boston, but she was testing methods that she would employ with black students upon her return to Virginia.

During her course work, she collaborated with statistics and psychology professors to make sure her research design and methods were sound; she made the suggested proposal revisions given by those close to the project. Despite careful construction, the review committee arbitrarily proposed a third control group beyond the two required, which amounted to a considerable amount of extra work without a clear reason that she or her advisor could see. She charged: "the leverage they used to invalidate my work was really quite simple: impose impossible conditions on the research project. Then it might reasonably be assumed that Mrs. Browne, finding stipulated conditions impossible to attain, would quietly and peacefully go away." When she clarified their request with a hint of concern, the dean quipped, "Mrs. Browne, you know it does take something to get a doctorate at Harvard." Yes, she agreed, it did. So, she summarily rejected their proposal and told them that she would proceed with the study as written; if her findings or dissertation did not meet the final requirements, they could revisit the matter then.[50]

She did not back down because, according to her dissertation chair, advisory professors, reviewers from the Rockefeller Foundation, and the lab school officials, her research was a viable, valuable, and methodologically sound course of study. She stood on her principle, stating: "if I went down, and I certainly thought that I would, I knew it would be fighting. However, as a lady, I prefer a rapier to a club." According to her account of the remainder of the session with the review committee, she composed herself and gained strength from what she assumed was her great-grandmother's spirit. She then put the committee in check by reminding them of three things: first, her status as a Rockefeller Fellow; second, the General Education Board was not convinced that Harvard was the best place for her research because few scholars there were in tune with practical needs of black children; and third, Harvard's $12 million application to the Rockefeller Fund for the Growth Study might be jeopardized should she not finish her project or if she continued her research somewhere more open to reasonable requirements. Not surprisingly, the committee agreed to her proposal as originally stated, and

Browne's research, dissertation, and defense went forward without further incident.[51]

Browne possessed effective means of overcoming barriers to her work because she was an experienced schoolteacher and a college professor herself. She escaped racist bureaucracy because she had a good reputation, especially with the Rockefeller Foundation reviewers funding her literacy research, who were quite willing to support her. She prevailed because her work was cutting-edge and because Harvard was, after all, only Harvard.

Pauli Murray (1910–85)

Not all women enjoyed the leverage that Browne exercised in her doctoral program; some suffered unfathomable indignities with little or no recourse simply because they were black women. In 1938, Pauli Murray was rejected from the University of North Carolina because of her race; in 1944, she was denied admittance to Harvard Law School because of her gender. Though she graduated from Hunter College in 1933, was an outstanding student, and won a Rosenwald Fellowship, she was denied admittance specifically because she was black and a woman. But Murray was not to be stopped: she earned a bachelor of law from Howard in 1944, a master of law from Berkeley in 1947, and the doctorate from Yale in 1965. Murray's education, employment, activism, personal relationships, and spiritual development exemplified a complexity that defied the stereotype of a two-dimensional black woman.

Anna Pauline Murray was born in 1910 in Baltimore to Agnes Fitzgerald, a nurse, and William Murray, a high school teacher and principal from Maryland. William graduated from Howard's college preparatory department, and Pauli's mother, Agnes, attended St. Augustine's College in Raleigh and earned a nursing degree from Hampton University, where she met William in 1902. They married in 1903 and had six children. St. Augustine's, where Anna Cooper began her studies in the mid-1800s, was a long-standing hub for North Carolina elite, and Agnes's two sisters, Pauline and Sallie, both earned teaching degrees there. Pauli was among the first generations of black Americans whose parents had completed high school, so they reasonably expected her to attend college. Pauli's mother tragically passed away—pregnant with her seventh child—when Pauli was young, and her father suffered an emotional breakdown as a result. Her aunt Pauline then raised her and ensured that she was prepared for academic advancement despite family tragedy; relatives in Baltimore assisted in raising her five siblings.[52]

Being from a family of educators, Murray graduated from Hillside High School at the head of her class and moved to New York City and attended Hunter College. While financially struggling in New York, she was employed by the Work Projects Administration's (WPA) Remedial Reading Project. Her rejection from the all-white University of North Carolina spurred her involvement in the civil rights movement. With the support of the NAACP, Murray advocated desegregation of schools and public transportation. In 1941, she enrolled at the Howard law school and was an active member of the Howard chapter of the NAACP, which originated strategic sit-in protests around D.C. One year after arriving at Howard, she joined George Houser, James Farmer, and Bayard Rustin to form the Congress of Racial Equality (CORE). Murray later taught for sixteen months at the Ghana Law School in Accra.

In addition to her career as an activist and lawyer, Murray was a prolific poet, novelist, and essayist. *Dark Testament and Other Poems* (1970) chronicled her creative work beginning in 1943. Four other books—*States' Laws on Race and Color* (1951); *Proud Shoes: The Story of an American Family* (1956); *The Constitution and Government of Ghana* (1961); and *Song in a Weary Throat* (published posthumously in 1987)—represent her political, biographical, and autobiographical insights into an era of struggle, accomplishment, and hope.

In 1960, President Kennedy appointed Murray to the Committee on Civil and Political Rights, and in 1966, she was a founding member of the National Organization for Women (NOW). Like other black women activists, Murray was critical of male-dominated civil rights organizations and fought for equity based on both race and gender. While advocating change in the 1960s, Murray served as vice president and professor of political science at Benedict College and in the newly formed Afro-American Studies Department at Brandeis University.

At age sixty-two, Pauli Murray began study for holy orders at General Theological Seminary in New York and was ordained to the priesthood in 1977 as the first African American woman Episcopal priest. Before her retirement in 1984, she served as a priest in D.C. and Baltimore. Murray donated her personal papers to the Schlesinger Library at Radcliffe College. These materials are significant not only because they contain her memoirs and manuscripts but because the details of her family research uniquely document the lives of a middle-class African American family in the civil rights era.

Murray's story is also significant because of her complex representation of sexuality. By conventional nomenclature, she was a lesbian. Nevertheless, she did not identify with the term or, overtly, with the lesbian and gay movement that accompanied social movements of the 1960s and 1970s. Yet she openly shared her life with a woman, Maida Springer Kemp, despite her ordination as a priest. She was an unabashed feminist, and Murray's narrative serves as an example of the centrality of gender and sexuality in black women's lives. Such discussions have largely been silenced in black women's histories, often in order to combat the stereotypes of black hypersexuality that exist in the white popular imagination. Her story *Pauli Murray: Autobiography of a Black Activist, Feminist, Lawyer, Priest, and Poet* (1987) was published posthumously and demonstrated that above all, Murray was, by her own account, a poet on a pilgrimage.[53]

Black women who pursued advanced degrees did not always get hired as professors—even those who earned doctorates and amassed outstanding credentials. However, not all who earned a degree were enamored with the academy enough to want to work there permanently. Those who did earn a terminal degree and worked in higher education engaged in multifaceted careers and active lives outside of the Ivory Tower. They raised families, engaged in local, national, and international activism, and often sustained additional careers for which they were recognized. In short, they were well-rounded. Pauli Murray embodied this tradition.

In her autobiography, Murray recalled earning good grades in primary school, but she was precocious and had to acquire the taste for serious study. Fortunately, when she reached high school age, the segregated high school in Durham had just been rebuilt, and she was among the first class to enter a school with a new auditorium and gymnasium, cafeteria, library, science lab, playground and game field, and all-new sporting equipment. The school recruited recent graduates from Talladega College and Howard, Fisk, and Wilberforce universities to teach, so Murray blossomed in an atmosphere of newness and excitement that defied stereotypes of inferior black schools. She said of the teachers, "they were young and energetic, and they brought with them advanced ideas which helped to raise our sights." She kept busy managing the basketball team, editing the school newspaper, debating, and maintaining a Saturday newspaper route along with studies.[54]

Murray applied to Columbia University in New York because one of her favorite teachers attended Columbia College (in South Carolina) and Murray mistook one school for the other. Unaware of the confusion, Aunt Pauline took her niece to New York to make arrangements to apply. After finding that Columbia did not admit women, they inquired at Barnard. There, the registrar informed Murray that she was not qualified to apply with her current diploma but suggested she apply to Hunter. She recalled: "In my naïveté,

I did not know that [Hunter] was the largest women's college in the world, that it was dubbed 'the poor girl's Radcliffe,' and that its academic standards were so high it scooped off the top-level women students of New York City's high schools. I was soon jolted into reality." Murray did not qualify for entry at Hunter either, but she stayed with cousins in New York to take an additional year of high school and was then admitted.[55]

For Murray, the culture shock of moving from a southern black school to a northern white school was drastic. Adding to her distress, in order to meet Hunter's admissions requirements, she had to take a heavy course load on an accelerated schedule and decisively pass the New York school's exit examinations:

> When school opened . . . I was thrust into a strange world, the only colored person among four thousand students. My complexion and southern accent made me something of a curiosity, but I felt no hostility; in fact, the other students were very friendly, and my teachers seemed especially anxious to give me all the help possible. In spite of a pleasant atmosphere, however, I could not throw off the anxiety that dogged me during the first months. I had never competed with white children before, and however much I tried to suppress it, I could not overcome the nagging feeling of failure, which I felt would be charged not to circumstances but to inherent racial inferiority. My anxiety increased when I received my first school grades. Only a few months earlier, in Durham, I had been voted the most studious member of my class and had finished with top honors. Now I had dropped to a mortifying 65 in Latin, 77 in French, and, for me, only so-so marks in other subjects.[56]

Murray was dogged in the 1930s with the same insecurities Coppin had in the 1860s.

For the remainder of the year, Murray confined herself to her room to study. To exacerbate her alienation, she now had a very different family life. Her cousins were light-skinned, lived in an all-white neighborhood, and though they did not attempt to pass for white, they did not share the black pride that her Aunt Pauline, parents, and grandparents had instilled in her. Murray persevered to graduate from the northern high school, and in a chapter titled "Survival," she recounted that the trials of her Hunter years strikingly resembled these earlier difficulties.

While at Hunter, she had markedly different experiences from black college women in generations before. Murray worked as a waitress and then at a travel agency; she secretly married in her sophomore year (which lasted only a few months); she hitchhiked through New England; drove cross-country to California with a friend; and, when she got word that her aunt was ill, hopped freight trains for a dangerous but incident-free ten-day trip back to North Carolina. Murray recounted that during the Depression years, an estimated 200,000 to 300,000 homeless boys and "a few" girls between the ages of twelve and twenty hitchhiked and rode the railroad around the country in search of work. They faced armed guards, shanty homes, thievery, and hunger. Murray's adventures signaled a change from earlier college women's experiences, and though hers was not the norm, her intriguing account provided insight into major shifts in the modern world. Technology, economics, politics, and social mores delivered college experiences into the modern world, and black women changed with the times.[57]

Jobs were scarce during the Depression, especially for black women: some jobs advertised for "White Only," or "Light Colored Girls." Yet in a time of racial tension fueled by economic hardship, the only stark incident of racism that Murray experienced while in New York occurred in a Hunter classroom during a yearlong American history course:

> I was the only Negro in the class, and as far as my professor was concerned I did not exist. She was not openly insulting, but she never once suggested that colored people may have played a role in the nation's development other than as abject objects of the national controversy over slavery. Her treatment of slavery, the Civil War, and Reconstruction made me shrivel in my seat in the back row, feeling shame and resentment. I knew from my own family history that her presentation was one-sided but was too unsure of myself to challenge her in class. Unable to mount an effective protest against her bias, I performed so indifferently in the course that I got only passing grades in a subject in which I had always excelled. That ordeal, however, spurred me to become a passionate student of Negro history after leaving college.[58]

As Murray entered law school, she brought along the thick skin she had earned in New York to carry her through even tougher times.

Of her transition to Howard, Murray recalled: "the three years I spent at Howard thrust me into the rigidly segregated environment of wartime D.C. After the comparative freedom of New York, I found the racial segregation of the nation's capital so repugnant that I would have spent all my free time in the law library if I had been able to." At Howard, like Hurston decades before, Murray studied with major scholars in her field, civil rights law. William Hastie, Leon Ranson, George Hayes, George Johnson, William Ming, and James Nabrit all contributed to the broadening of the interpretation of liberty in the United States and greatly impacted Murray's work. She reported that Ranson, a man once knocked down the steps by a racist outside a courthouse (in the South) where he tried a case, prepared Howard students to "survive in no holds-barred legal combat." She reported: "he had great skill in forcing students to develop their arguments while remaining calm under harassment. Genial and kindly outside class hours, he could be ruthless in the classroom."[59]

Though her training on race activism was superb, it was at Howard that Murray learned lessons of gender and the law, which she labeled "Jane Crow." In the settings of all-women Hunter College and her work with the WPA, she encountered racialized hostilities, but "during my first year at Howard there were only two women in the law school student body, both of us in the first-year class. When the other woman dropped out before the end of the first term, I was left as the only female for the rest of the year, and I remained the only woman in my class for the entire three-year course." And in the 1940s, Howard Law School, like most in the country, had no women faculty.[60] She met the environment head-on:

> The men were not openly hostile; in fact, they were friendly. But I soon learned that women were often the objects of ridicule disguised as a joke. I was shocked on the first day of class when one of our professors said in his opening remarks that he really didn't know why women came to law school, but that since we were there the men would have to put up with us. His banter brought forth loud laughter from the male students. I was too humiliated to respond, but though the professor did not know it, he had just guaranteed that I would become the top student in his class.[61]

Murray's voice was seldom heard in class because her male colleagues talked over her, assuming she had nothing of import to say. She was barred from the legal fraternity and other areas of professional communication. She nonetheless earned respect through exemplary grades, graduated at the top of her class, and was deeply involved in controversial student activism on campus. Her bouts with racism and sexism were ever-present and multifaceted.

While at Berkeley, she continued to learn valuable lessons, especially outside of the classroom. As one of few black law students, she lived in the international house, and her two roommates provided an international perspective of World War II–era legal studies: one roommate had just been released after three years at a Japanese internment camp, and her other room-mate escaped Nazi Germany, where, she would later find, her family was decimated. They formed a panel, "showing the interrelatedness of minority problems and presenting facts and figures as part of our informal dialogue." This work would later be termed *consciousness raising* in the NOW organization, and she saw it as central to a complete education about the intersection of the humanities and legal studies. Unfortunately, like Browne before her, Murray experienced difficulty getting her thesis accepted.[62]

Murray wrote several drafts of her thesis, titled "The Right to Equal Opportunity in Employment," for her advisor, Barbara Armstrong. Murray recalled, "draft after draft of my thesis was rejected, and once she told me, 'We may be trying to make a second-rate lawyer out of a first-rate writer.'" Frustration mounted as her advisor grew increasingly dissatisfied, and "every conference with Mrs. Armstrong became an ordeal, and my anxiety increased as the work dragged on." The advisor eventually told Murray that she would have to stay through the summer to meet the requirement "to her satisfaction." But Murray was intent on not being kept behind:

> When Mrs. Armstrong got wind of my plan [to take a bar preparation course] she was furious. She called me into her office and told me bluntly she did not think I had the mental or physical capacity to both complete my paper and pass the bar examination. She went further and threatened to withhold approval of the thesis unless I cancelled the course. With my degree at stake, I was forced to accept her ultimatum, but . . . somehow I found the strength to complete the thesis and get her formal approval in time for it to be published as a leading article in the September issue of the *California Law Review*. I then astonished Mrs. Armstrong (and myself) by taking the three-day October bar exam and passing it.[63]

Murray's advisor, like so many before, underestimated black women's intelligence and capacity for academic excellence.

Between Berkeley and her 1965 Yale doctorate of law, Murray published books, worked in law firms, taught in Ghana, and heightened her political activism. As an adult known and respected for her work, her experience at Yale was much different from that of her undergraduate studies, though she experienced similar humiliation when she had difficulty finding housing in New Haven because of her race. She also had trouble securing a university teaching position because she held a more advanced degree than those who were interviewing her, and law schools in the United States would not have women law faculty until well into the 1970s. For Murray and her historic cohort, the "double bind" of race and sex greatly affected life choices in and beyond college.

Patterns and Changes

These collegiate memoirs tell of continuities in black women's experiences over time. In the classroom, black women fell in love with their studies and yet felt the sting of their perceived inferiority when attempting to form relationships with their classmates, professors, and the subjects themselves. Sometimes their insecurity came from within; sometimes their instructors attempted to convince them that they did not have the genes or the background to excel. Often, it seems, in the guise of protecting students from taking on more than they could handle, black women students were pressed down to a level below their potential. Too, they were assumed to be fundamentally wrong when their interpretation of a subject did not match the white male standard explanation. The students were humbled by advisors who pushed them to achieve higher levels of work and eternally grateful to those who supplied them with tools to advance.

Another interesting thread is that all of these women were international travelers. Some (Terrell, Browne, and Morton) went to Europe, but some (Coppin and Murray) went to Africa. This trend shows that black women's education took place within broader international contexts. While these women did express the marginality that Noble's data set identified, they nonetheless worked around those limitations in a way that supports an alternative negotiation thesis. In surprising ways, they were able to learn, grow, and write on their own terms.

On campus, these authors experienced a range of settings, but at PWIs, a sense of isolation and wariness was present most of the time, even if the environment was not overtly hostile. When one was the only black student in a high school of 4,000, singular in an entire college, or one of fewer than 50 black students on a campus of 1,500, difference was inevitable. Their commitment to engaging in that environment despite their isolation allowed them to prosper. For students at HBCUs, other variables such as skin color, family status, economic class, gender, or simple desire for privacy impacted them in significant ways. As will be seen in the next chapter, black women's college experiences were a constant exercise in making themselves seen and heard regardless of the institution type they attended.

For every triumph cited here, the academy crushed thousands of black women. Undoubtedly, some demonstrated an undying spirit independent of the lifeless value system of "higher" education and led full lives without conquering the college challenge. Many, however, left without their diploma, some not to return, and some never to recover.

For those who stayed, the college campus at once represented freedom and captivity: it was a shelter from dangers of the larger racist and sexist society but also a smothering microcosm of the intense conflicts inherent to the United States. The distinction between PWIs and HBCUs must be made for a fuller picture of the range of college experiences. To broaden the scope of the story given by the six writers above, examples of the larger range of black collegiate women are provided next.

"I Make Myself Heard"

Comparative Collegiate Experiences

Overall, black women's reflections on their collegiate days reveal a sense of appreciation for having access to higher education and a frustration at the social limitations they continued to face despite that access. As a result of their struggles, they demonstrated a dedication to advancing opportunities for others to attend college and secure lives of meaningful work.

Regardless of the inability of a college diploma to guarantee personal safety, economic prosperity, or social respect, students at PWIs and HBCUs alike were determined to excel. That black women attended college at all was remarkable; that they so carefully considered and recorded their experiences was a gift that pays tribute to the thousands of stories left untold.

Predominantly White Institutions (PWIs)

Though the 1954 and 1955 *Brown* rulings involved only elementary and high schools, the NAACP launched their initial fight for desegregated education at the college and professional level. However, long before the systematic dismantling of the *Plessy v. Ferguson* separate-but-equal doctrine began in the 1930s, some black students already attended majority white schools. Where black students did exist on white campuses, as evidenced in the memoirs discussed earlier, discrimination was commonplace, though not always overtly hostile. Black women who attended white schools wrote of prejudice in the curriculum, classroom, housing, campus, social clubs, and local towns. Whether from other students, faculty, administrators, or community residents, Black women faced insults, condescending attitudes, and demeaning requirements. When not directly assaulted, they were conspicuously invisible: shunned, ignored, treated as exotic, or silently despised. Though their quest to overcome was admirable, the famous Delany sisters spoke a truism in *Having Our Say: The Delany Sisters' First Hundred Years* (1994): Black women had to fight tooth and nail to have access to educational resources and, when admittance was allowed, had to work twice as hard to receive half the credit.[1]

In *There Was a Light: Autobiography of a University: Berkeley, 1868–1968*, Ida Jackson, a third-wave graduate, reported on her 1920s student life: "there were eight Negro women and nine Negro men enrolled on the Berkeley campus. Few of us knew each other before arriving there. Our isolation drew us together. The need for social life caused us to combine and organize the Braithwaite Club. All did not participate, as some did not wish to be identified as Negroes on campus." The pull toward group identification was strong because there were so few black students at PWIs, but the cost of being associated with the "Negro" group was perceived as worse than being black, so not all students participated in race-based social groups. Either way, being black at Berkeley was not easy. Jackson, like Morton at Cincinnati, experienced discrimination when she and a classmate were not allowed to enter the swimming facility at the Oakland YMCA with the white students. Though the San Francisco YMCA was open to African Americans, they could not afford the cost of travel or make it back to campus in time for other classes.[2]

Jackson, born one of eight children, attended high school in rural Mississippi, where she was inspired by her teachers who taught *As You Like It* in the eleventh grade and where she directed *Othello* as a senior class play. Yet, at Berkeley, she was not even recognized as a legitimate student: "one of the most difficult problems I faced was entering classes day after day, sitting beside students who acted as if my seat were unoccupied, showing no signs of recognition, never giving a smile or a nod." Though Jackson founded and became the first president of the 1921 Rho chapter of Alpha Kappa Alpha Sorority at Berkeley, that did not ameliorate the alienation she experienced on the larger campus and the lack of acknowledgment for African American students. When Jackson graduated with her B.A. in 1922, she lamented being ignored during graduation celebrations: "I participated in a few of the Senior Week activities, and although I walked alone, unnoticed by my fellow classmates, took part in the Senior Pilgrimage." Though the sorority took a group picture, it was excluded from the yearbook. Jackson advanced to graduate studies, taught in the California school system, and became a national president of her sorority. She was active in social causes ranging from summer school education in Mississippi to international disarmament, and Berkeley honored her in the 1990s by naming a new graduate residence hall for her. But in the 1920s, her academic and social success was hampered rather than bolstered by her experience at Berkeley.[3]

College, for young women, was a crucial time of transition from adolescence to womanhood; to attempt intellectual and social growth in a hostile environment clearly had lasting effects. Jane Bolin Offutt, one of two black freshman students admitted to Wellesley College in 1924, wrote of several racist incidents including cafeteria-seating snubs by southern students, rejection from a sorority supposedly interested in social problems, and an invitation to play an Aunt Jemima type—"bandana too!"—in a school play. In all, "there were a few sincere friendships developed in that beautiful, idyllic setting of the college, but, on the whole, I was ignored outside the classroom. I am saddened and maddened even nearly half a century later to recall many of my Wellesley experiences but my college days for the most part evoke sad and lonely personal memories." This was not surprising considering that even Booker T. Washington's daughter, Portia, was unwelcome at Wellesley when she attended during the 1901–2 school year and left because, among other problems, she failed to be included in classroom and campus activities.[4]

While black women's clubs were created for social reasons, a major function of the club was community development, which included support for college students. This support was vital because in addition to other campus pressures, housing was always an issue for black students at PWIs. For example, at the University of Iowa (UI), Black women students did not have access to campus housing. Their inability to secure such basic needs as food, clothing, and shelter often constituted part of their college experience. In 1915, the number of black women students at UI increased to seven, not all of whom could find the usual work as domestic servers in exchange for boarding. The young women petitioned the State Federation of Colored Women's clubs, and in 1917 a twelve-room home was purchased, renovated, and staffed by the organization. By 1929, it housed seventeen students and affected the campus ability to recruit and retain black students.[5]

The National Association of College Women also discussed the need for alumnae to assist with improving conditions for undergraduate students. The minutes from the 1928 convention proposed, "The question of the treatment of our girls in various colleges governed by the other racial group, the committee feels can best be handled by our making contacts with the alumnae of these colleges and interesting them." Identifying "the other" reveals race polarization and underscores awareness of the need to address black women's concerns on majority white campuses.[6]

A 1942 *Journal of Negro Education* article by Edythe Hargrave entitled "How I Feel as a Negro at a White College" outlined specific hardships that black students underwent in arenas where there was little support. Hargrave's experience as one of 20 black students at an unnamed college with 3,100 students meant that she too was barred from participation in sororities, assigned lower grades from professors, and subjected to cruelties passed off as jokes. White students often expressed disbelief or disapproval at her mere presence.

> I found that my biggest task was to accustom the students to my presence in the classroom. I found that entering a class for the first time, I met many surprised glances and looks of "Do colored students go here?" or frowns of disgust that said, "Here comes a nigger!" . . . I found that when I spoke the rooms would be in complete silence to see what the Negro girl was going to say. Well, honestly, my reaction was to show these people that I was a good student. The idea has obsessed me throughout my two years here. . . . So in the classroom I talk; I make myself heard.[7]

Hargrave indicated that prejudice was especially strong in physical education classes and in extracurricular life.

Beyond the poor treatment she received, Hargrave avoided some of her white friends who she felt treated her too nicely out of pity. She shunned some students because she felt they were condescending, especially one student who attempted to befriend her because she studied efficiently and he thought he could take advantage of her skills:

> I dodged a white boy that suddenly became my friend because I had my lesson prepared every day. It was much easier to ask the Negro girl after he once found she was capable; because then his white friends would never know just how inefficient he was. . . . I am much too smart to regard this as a distinction, however. I know when I am being used; I have spoken too many times and not been spoken to.[8]

Student life was a constant negotiation of roles and shifting identities; for black students, the usual trials that accompanied a reputation of being too smart or too dumb were exacerbated by race. And, on top of it all, sometimes just being a woman was dangerous, as seen by Adrienne Kennedy's work.

Kennedy, a first-year student at the Ohio State University (OSU) in 1949, was one of approximately 300 African American students on a campus of 27,000. She graduated in 1953, married, traveled widely, and authored over twenty plays by the 1990s. In a series titled *The Alexander Plays*, Kennedy wrote about life in the mentally and physically hostile environment of a newly desegregated campus. Though the plays were only semi-autobiographical, they presented a bifurcated character, torn by sexualized racism, self-doubt, and desire to tell a story that seemed too horrifying to tell. *The Ohio State Murders* documented the brutality black women faced in 1950s white academe. Kennedy's protagonist, Suzanne Alexander, was a fictional OSU student who suffered discrimination from students, administrators, and the English department, where she desperately wanted to learn to write. The character was tormented by a white male professor who was a sexual predator, and Kennedy's gifted storytelling detailed the snares that lay in wait for black students who attended white universities. The story brilliantly sketches the lingering psychological effects of those too-often tragic encounters.[9]

At PWIs, black students bore their race on their shoulders and had to "prove" themselves worthy to be enrolled. Regardless of an institution's location, size, or type, black students at PWIs had a rough journey to graduation. Very different roads existed for those at HBCUs.

Historically Black Colleges and Universities (HBCUs)

Physical facilities varied from campus to campus, but at HBCUs, students were often expected to work in the laundry, sewing room, garden, kitchen, dining hall, building development, or assist in other maintenance of the campus. With few exceptions, the bare minimum board was provided, and campuses hobbled along as cash poor as their students. In most cases during the early days of attainment, students supplied their own kerosene lamp oil, candles, bedding, or washbowls, and campus amenities were few. Before widespread electric lighting, indoor plumbing, or central heating, students studied, lived, and worked in coarse environments relatively void of all modern comforts, and curricular infrastructure was sometimes as feeble as the building funds. Black colleges were mostly run with minimal contributions from philanthropists or government funds, with significant financial backing of church bodies, and by sheer black communal willpower. Student desire to attend HBCUs compensated for deficiencies of material resources, but challenges were many.[10]

In a 1957 correspondence, Ruth Brown Hucles wrote about her experiences at Virginia State College in the late 1880s. She recalled the physical conditions of the college:

> There were 13 rooms on this floor, number thirteen being the bath room. But since there were no water connections this room was occupied by two girls. . . . The bath tub filled with quilts and blankets was converted into a studio couch. . . . Our rooms were furnished with iron cots and mattresses, a bare table and wash stand. . . . Our rooms were lighted with kerosene oil lamps since electric lights were unknown as well as electric cars. The building was heated by one large stove in the

hall and what a scramble there was on cold mornings to be the first to dress by the stove.[11]

To further complicate an already stressful student life and limited housing, campuses lacked adequate library or classroom space, which made studying difficult. Bethune-Cookman was an excellent example of a college that periodically struggled because its physical capacity was inadequate for the large numbers of interested students. Fund-raising efforts could not always keep pace with student needs, particularly during the Depression years.[12]

Not every black school or black student lacked resources. As there were class conflicts within a campus student body, so too were there conflicts and rivalries between schools. As Zora Neale Hurston's comments revealed, campuses like Howard and Fisk were treasure troves of physical, academic, and human resources compared to other HBCUs. Lillian Dunn Thomas, a 1935 Tennessee State College graduate recalled: "we thought the Fisk students thought they were better than us, you know. We had friends at Fisk, and they had friends at Tennessee State. There was a kind of rivalry with the games and things like that. I always thought that the Fisk girls really dressed well. We always thought they came from very rich homes." Like trends in the national scene, the accreditation ranking for HBCUs generally mirrored the socioeconomic status of their students. Still, with a few exceptions from the black upper crust, all students at HBCUs worked.[13]

At HBCUs, chapel was mandatory, and students labored to cultivate a spirit of holy service to mankind. Even in areas where students were well off, many schools required all students to work to instill respect for labor, uphold a sense of collective effort, and support social equality. At Atlanta University in 1900, Bazoline Usher recalled: "you did one hour's work a day. Everybody had a job, had something to do, everybody, regardless of what they paid. And those who were on full board had one hour and those who paid part time, did two hours. . . . Some of them took care of the teachers' rooms. . . . Some of them did hall duty, swept in the halls. Some of them waited tables. . . . Some of them really worked in laundry, and some of them worked in the kitchen preparing food."[14]

Those students who had no family support often lacked a basic level of housing, sustenance, or maintenance of personal appearance. Journalist Alice Dunnigan, a 1920s student at Kentucky State College (one of two HBCUs in the state), wrote in her autobiography:

My roommate had such a stove, so we bought a little frying pan. I could sometimes slip a potato or two from the pantry and we would have French fries in our room. . . . Sometimes I could sneak out a loaf of bread, taking it upstairs in my bosom. My friends and I were usually so hungry that we could consume the whole loaf of dry bread at one sitting. I had to make out with what I had because many times I didn't have three cents (the price of a postage stamp) to write a letter home to ask for additional spending change, even if I had a mind to.[15]

She could not afford to keep up with fashion but tried to maintain her beauty standard: "some of the girls sneaked tiny kerosene stoves into the dormitory for the purpose of heating straightening combs and curling irons. There were no electric curlers or combs in those times as far as we knew."[16] Not from a family of means, she worked harder than most for basic needs.

Dunnigan recalled her job in an understaffed dining hall where she set up tables, served classmates, cleared and cleaned plates, and worked under the pressure of a tough supervisor. She remembered the difficulty of the job because there were no electric dishwashers—"each dish had to be washed, rinsed and dried by hand then stacked on the table ready for the next meal"— and as hard as one worked, "there was no monetary reward."[17] In addition to harsh working conditions, Dunnigan reported: "I only received 'half-board.' That meant $7.50 was deducted from my board each month. No cash was involved, still I was happy. . . . My mother sent me ten dollars in November and the same amount each month after. That meant that I only had $2.50 a month for spending change. . . . Sometimes I was forced to wear stockings with runs as wide as two fingers before I could save enough to purchase a new pair."[18]

By her account, Dunnigan had three shifts a day in the dining hall, and just as she finished her last shift, she returned to her dormitory in time to hear her classmates singing, playing, and dancing on their study break. By the time she unwound and got into her homework, it was 10:00 p.m. and all lights had to be turned out, so she "found it necessary to lie flat on the floor and study by candlelight." If she was caught awake after lights out, she'd earn demerits. Even though she desired to earn a four-year degree, she did not have the finances to continue and had to leave after obtaining a teaching certificate. Many women did not pursue advanced studies because they simply needed to earn a living.[19]

The economic class of a student regularly determined her social standing on campus, making an already constrained social environment more unbearable. Dunnigan recalled:

Since the poor working student had neither money nor time to devote to social clubs or Greek-letter organizations, they missed out on most of the fun. Furthermore, working students were usually snubbed by the so-called high society. They were seldom, if ever, dated by the campus hierarchy so they had no chance of receiving invitations to the swank affairs. The working girls who worked in the dining room were slurringly referred to as "pantry rats."[20]

Though at some schools, like Atlanta University, modesty was promoted by enforcing a dress code that restricted jewelry, lace, and the type of dresses allowed, black female students found ways to alienate those felt to be undesirables based on narrow definitions of economic class.[21]

In order to moderate behavior and battle myths about "wild" or "uneducable" black women, regulations abounded. About her experiences at Tuskegee (1911–15), Hattie Kelly recalled: "Do you think we were free on this campus then to do what we wanted to do? Then you're wrong. I could take the strictness on the campus because I came from a home that was strict, but many girls could not. . . . Your room was inspected, your trunks inspected, your closets, your clothes, everything was inspected and you were given demerits if everything wasn't just right."

Some schools, like Tuskegee and Kentucky State, worked on the demerit system, threatening expulsion for too many infractions. Demerits were earned for any tiny mistake, no matter where on campus it took place. Classroom, dorm room, dining hall, study hall, and other public spaces were sites of potential reprimand by any school official. Social contact with boys was strictly regulated, and courting practices were often monitored by a go-between chaperone who could grant or deny permission to "keep company." House matrons and deans of women were often regarded as wardens.[22] Ruth Hucles, a student at Virginia State College, remembered:

Every evening from 4 to 5:30 was the hour [to draw water from the spring], and oh what a joy for this was an opportunity to meet the boys. They were allowed to fill the pitchers and escort the girls to the brow of the hill but no further for Miss Lucy Morse, our matron, was always standing there and smiling. . . . Very little recreation was provided as we were supposed to go to school to study and not to play. Cards and dancing were prohibited and athletic sports were not popular.[23]

Black women were under careful watch at every moment; the setting was rigidly constructed, and anyone out of line was immediately detained, questioned, and disciplined.

At those campuses where dances were allowed, formal behavior was expected, especially while dancing. Kelly explained:

and the men came into White hall for you and you'd walk over to the dining room; the dances were always held in the dining room. And we did dances like the Skating Schottische [and] the Waltz Oxford. Those kinds of dances were the kind of dances where you take hands and dance. . . . I could not dance [before] I came to Tuskegee. You see, good girls didn't dance. . . . Maybe city girls did, but you see, I was from a small town and we didn't go to dances. We had church parties and things.[24]

In many cases, formal invitations had to be offered for movies, lectures, concerts, or dances, and "a girl could not be escorted by a boy unless she received from him a formal invitation written in the third person on appropriate stationary, and properly answered, also in the third person, by the girl. . . . Invitations had to be delivered to the girls' dormitory. . . . Answers written in the same format were required from the invitee, either accepting, or expressing regrets." No unsupervised visits were tolerated, and punishment was harsh for those who broke the rules.[25]

Dunnigan almost got expelled when a young man, a friend and coworker, gave her a hug. Though the incident occurred while she was working in the dining hall in the middle of the day, and her other coworkers understood that Henry was part of her "play family" social structure, a teacher witnessed the interaction and reported her to the matron. Dunnigan agonized over the recollection:

> We were called on the carpet and chastised for such unbecoming conduct. We both explained the harmless incident but were not sure whether our explanation was accepted. . . . The matron sounded so villainous, making us feel like scum of the earth guilty of some heinous crime. She called all of the pantry girls in and questioned each separately about the incident. . . . I was questioned at length on whether Henry was my boyfriend. . . . I gave thanks to God that both Henry and I were finally cleared of any suspicious misconduct. So each of us got off with only five demerits.[26]

Dorm mothers, matrons, and deans of women were extreme caretakers, and "tough love" was standard operating procedure.

Black women had restrictions on both HBCU and PWI campuses. However, the quality and severity differed greatly. Black women's movement was restricted on PWI campuses through segregated dorms, classrooms, and dining halls. But on black campuses, the restricted movement was of a more intimate nature. The college staff and administrators took on a familial responsibility for the young women, which translated into intimidation, attempts to instill guilt or shame, and constant invasion of personal privacy. Though racism and sexism were pervasive on PWI campuses, the high expectations and standards of pure and perfect "ladylike" behavior that permeated HBCUs were an attempt to disprove popular "jezebel" sexual stereotypes and manufacture cultured, learned ladies.

Because local conditions were often hostile and students' safety could not be guaranteed, there were firm travel restrictions; students were rarely allowed off campus. Due to the added probability of sexual violence for women students, restrictions were harsher for women than for men. Kelly recalled: "It was very difficult to get an admit to leave the campus. . . . You couldn't go into town without a chaperone. . . . We couldn't go to chapel up on the street. The girls had to go down through the bottom to chapel and no boys spent any time over on the girls' lawn at all." Male students were allowed off campus only during approved hours. Female students, if off campus, had to be escorted, and Spelman women were easily spotted because they did not appear off campus without being extra sharply dressed . . . and always wearing gloves. Though PWIs had similar rules and regulations, officials at HBCUs applied the rules in a familial way that remained present long after "in loco parentis" at PWIs waned in the twentieth century.[27]

HBCU women were always under the watchful eye of someone; and that someone was most likely a dean, lady principal, or housemother. Despite the military-style restrictions, though, the dean of women was also a student advocate. Lucy Slowe's work with the National Association of Deans of Women and Advisors to Girls in Negro Schools was an effective attempt to standardize and modernize policies for young women at HBCUs and expand students' personal liberties. Regulations were made for students' protection because the real and perceived dangers of being a black woman in America were well founded.[28]

Slowe's research revealed that black women on college campuses lacked opportunity for self-direction because the campus rules were repressive. She argued that in modern society, women needed broader independence and self-governance because they would need to be citizens much as men were. If young women did not have more personal freedom, she argued, they would continue to see themselves as simply a counterpart of men rather than as whole individuals. For women at HBCUs and PWIs, the student experience was a negotiation of rules and opportunities, as well as a tension between individual expression and conformity to black women's popular group identity.[29]

General Feelings of Black Women Students

There is great variance in the memoirs of pre-*Brown* black collegiate women. Though experiences at PWIs and HBCUs differed, three overarching themes emerge from the collective narrative: appreciation, frustration, and dedication.

APPRECIATION

Each woman presented here, regardless of institution type, era, or level of degree attainment, expressed overwhelming appreciation for the opportunity to attend college. Coppin claimed: "my obligation to the dear people of Oberlin can never be measured in words. . . . I have the kindest remembrance of the dear ones who were my classmates. I can never forget the courtesies of the three Wright brothers . . . the Chamberland girls, and others, who seemed determined that I should carry away from Oberlin nothing but most pleasant memories of my life there."[30]

Three decades later, Terrell wrote: "I do not see how any student could have enjoyed the activities of college life more than I did. Learning my lessons as well as I could was a sort of indoor sport with me. I had my troubles and trials, of course, because occasionally I broke the rules by going skating without permission, for instance, or breaking the study-hour rule, or sitting up after ten o'clock, but that was all included in the course, I thought." She described her desire for a degree as an obsession and, because she wanted it so badly, begged God, "earnestly not to let me die before Commencement." She graduated and counted herself most fortunate because of the opportunity.[31]

Even Dunnigan, who labored so hard but left without her B.A., remained grateful to have attended: "all of this campus life was great fun for me. It was an exciting, interesting, wonderful experience. There were continuous activities, never a dull moment. The year was chugged full of all kinds of adventures, many pleasant and some heartrending. The latter was chiefly due to the poverty which I was forced to endure, going week after week without a single penny and many times hungry." After leaving Kentucky, Dunnigan's hardships were not over. She struggled to find employment but did not lose hope, stating, "my mother's favorite phrase echoed in my mind: 'Where there's a will, there's a way!'" Her way was mired with obstacles, but her gratitude for college was nonetheless evident.[32]

Most authors used words like joy, pleasure, or happiness to express their feelings about the learning process. Through constant pressures of psychological warfare, intellectual strain, public humiliation, or physical duress, they appreciated the exercise of learning enough to power onward.

FRUSTRATION

Even where there was tremendous willpower, black women expressed aggravation with the barriers they encountered and the insults leveled by those who sought to stunt their growth. Terrell vigilantly defended black women's rights to pursue college. In a 1901 *New York City Independent* article, she claimed:

> in order to prove the utter worthlessness and total depravity of colored girls, it is boldly asserted by the author of *The American Negro* [W. H. Thomas] that under the best educational influences they are not susceptible to improvement. Educate a colored girl and a white girl together, he says, and when they are twenty years old the colored girl will be either a physical wreck or a giggling idiot, while her white companion will have become an intelligent, cultured, chaste young woman. It would be interesting to know where the author of this book made his observations, or from what source he obtained his information. . . . I am also personally acquainted with colored women who have graduated from Ann Arbor University, Cornell, and the Chicago University, from Oberlin, Radcliffe, Smith, Wellesley, Vassar and other institutions throughout the North, South, East, and West, and not one of them is either a giggling idiot or a physical wreck. On the contrary, they are a company of useful, cultured women who would be a blessing and credit to any race.[33]

She then referenced her five years as superintendent in the D.C. school system and refuted the author's claim that black children were uneducable and more base or dull than other children.

Many black alumnae refused to abandon their beloved alma mater, even when they had been greatly mistreated. Morton wrote that despite the humiliation that she experienced at University of Cincinnati, she honored and adored her alma mater. Though she clearly was disturbed by her negative experiences, her attitude about the school experience remained positive. Some, like Jane Offutt of Wellesley and Ida Jackson of Berkeley, became disillusioned and resentful toward their schools despite their love for college life.

Sarah and Bessie Delany's best-selling autobiography revealed many themes present in the other narratives. Both sisters graduated from St. Augustine's, in North Carolina—and they remembered Anna Cooper's positive impact on the campus. Sadie went on to earn a B.S. from Columbia Teacher's College in 1920, and Bessie (who could not attend New York University's all-male program), graduated from Columbia University with a Doctor of Dental Surgery degree in 1923. Both told of incidents of race hatred, including receiving lower grades than earned, public humiliation by professors, and one of Bessie's white colleagues stealing dental supplies from the school and trying to frame her for it. Though Bessie appreciated access to advanced studies in Jazz Age New York, the daily challenges—on and off campus—soured her experience greatly: "I suppose I should be grateful to Columbia, that at that time they let in colored people. Well, I'm not. They let me in but then beat me down for being there! I don't know how I got through that place, except when I was young nothing could hold me back."[34]

Offutt, a 1928 graduate of Wellesley, was appointed a judge in New York City in 1939—one of the first African American woman judges in the United States. She did this despite the vote of no confidence by her Wellesley guidance counselor who attempted to dissuade her from pursuing a law degree. She recalled that the woman "threw up her hands in disbelief and told me there was little opportunity for women in law and absolutely none for a 'colored' one. Surely I should consider teaching." Decades before Murray did, Offutt graduated from Yale Law School, and, although she received much recognition in her judgeship appointment, she bitterly recalled that, with the exception of a few close classmates, no one from the school acknowledged her groundbreaking success.[35]

Jackson, the 1922 Berkeley graduate, expressed anger that education did not guarantee success for African Americans:

> Many of my early teachers, both Negro and white, preached the same doctrine: "Get the type of education the white man gets, behave as the more refined white man behaves and the Negro will be accepted as an American citizen; then the opportunities for advancement will appear for the Negro, according to his skills, education, and talents." In my experience and that of many other Negroes, this has proved to be a mirage—to date.[36]

The myth of meritocracy in the United States was evident when black women graduated from college, tried to earn an honest living, and develop an honorable reputation but repeatedly were rebuffed by the racist dominant group.

Given the difficulties they faced, depression was not unknown to black women students. While at Oberlin, Terrell encountered a woman who sustained family losses, and coupled with the college pressure, became depressed and committed suicide. In a harrowing conversation before her demise, the woman suggested that Terrell laugh while she could, before life "turned against" her. Outside of the free-spirited adventure that college offered her, Terrell admitted, "many a time since that Sunday evening prayer meeting I have tried to laugh when the sorrows and cares of life have pressed hard upon me, and couldn't."[37]

Coppin expressed outrage that academic preparation did not ensure social justice for black people. When Octavius Catto, one of the ICY's longstanding dedicated teachers, was murdered while trying to exercise his newly won right to vote, the silence of the Quaker Board of Managers showed that even a black person with high educational attainment who demonstrated service to community, model morality, and responsible citizenship could not warrant protection from a racist, violent America. Dominant white society proved unwilling to demonstrate the basic virtues of democracy, diplomacy, or good character that it adamantly denied black Americans were capable of.

Ida Jackson's father barely escaped a lynching because he had stood up for his land rights in court against a white man. Though he persevered and provided a sound home for his family, that threat of violence impacted Jackson's understanding of what it meant for her to be upwardly mobile. Though Murray's parents both were college educated, that did not eliminate problems. After her mother died, her father quickly deteriorated emotionally, and he was placed in a mental institution. Years later, when Murray was in college, she learned that because he resisted racist treatment, her father was taken to the basement and beaten to death by a part-time attendant. Black women's cultural identity deeply affected their college experience; when they took one step forward, the surrounding violence dragged them and their families two steps back. Those who pursued a college education hoped for increased social standing, or at least safety, yet they were well aware that degree attainment guaranteed neither.[38]

DEDICATION

Despite their frustration, these remarkable authors expressed a dedication to excel and to assist others. Browne felt compelled to attain the terminal degree at the most esteemed college in the United States because she needed to be better equipped to educate African American children in the South, whom she adamantly called "her children." She refuted the popular notion that "Negroes who received an education beyond the average level of attainment . . . stopped work to parade their intelligence before their admirers."

Rather, she declared: "I wanted this education not in order to make a million and drive a Cadillac, but to prepare myself to help my children. They
needed me, and I desired to feed my ego on this sense of accomplishment
as I worked with the future generations of my people." Generations of black
college women embodied "lifting as we climb" long before the NACW adopted the motto as their guiding principle.[39]

At HBCUs, service was part of the campus climate. Atlanta University
President Horace Bumstead congratulated students for volunteering with
temperance advocacy, domestic services, nursing care, and teaching elementary and Sunday schools. In the 1930s, Spelman women participated in projects that sought "a clean-up of unsightly spots, the elimination of billboards,
the creation of parks, the beautification of public places, and the general
improvement of outward conditions. Along with this would go, of course,
the betterment of child life, of schools, of social and recreational facilities,
and of social conditions generally."[40] In a 1938 article on Bennett College, it
was noted that students had enhanced Greensboro by serving in theaters, a
college choir, a nursery school and parent education center, and a homemak-
ing institute. Historian Cynthia Neverdon-Morton tracked women students'
social service efforts at HBCUs in Virginia, Alabama, Georgia, Tennessee,
and Maryland, and showed how their gender roles heavily influenced their
racial politics and vice versa.[41]

Shaw also outlined service-based learning programs at HBCUs. Some of
these included Hampton ("Training in Community Work" program and the
Circle of the Kings Daughters); Hartshorn Memorial College (Rachel Harts-
horn Educational and Missionary Society and Moarshorn Home Workers);
Fisk (the Department of Science programs "People's College" and "Children's
Institute"); Tuskegee ("Rising Star Model School," "Tuskegee Mother's Club,"
"Rural Extension Program," and "Tuskegee Health Center"); and Atlanta
University ("Gate City Free Kindergarten Association" and the Department
of Sociology's "lab work" requirements).[42]

Beyond student service, one graduate of Virginia State College gave her
life to the school and exemplified the complete allegiance to institutions that
many demonstrated toward HBCUs:

after working as teacher 2½ years, State College adopted me into its
official family as the wife of the Treasurer and Business manager. Our
wedding reception was held in this chapel with the entire student body
present. My work continued here for nineteen years after, for although
not on the pay roll, the welfare of the State College was always upper-

most in the minds and hearts of its former graduates. . . . These are the traditions of service we are called upon to maintain.[43]

Black women students and innumerable staff members offered dedicated service that built legacies.

Many endlessly labored to build HBCUs in reciprocal support of surrounding communities to create launching pads for black leaders. Scores of black women offered labor as secretaries, physical plant workers, and matrons far beyond any pay they collected. A sense of duty dedicated them to serve their institutions whether they attended classes at the college or not.

·   ·   ·

Generations of black women insisted they could think for themselves and create their personal or professional lives in their own image. As seen at both PWIs and HBCUs, a central aspect of this image was commitment to community development and passing on the torch of opportunity. Black women's effort to make themselves heard and to tell their own stories would carry them to advanced studies and, ultimately, creation of a new academic knowledge base through attainment of the doctorate of philosophy.

6

"The Third Step"

Doctoral Degrees, 1921–1954

Progress toward building a critical mass of undergraduate degree holders moved at a tortoise's pace for black women; their attainment of graduate degrees proceeded at an even slower snail's pace. The first and second waves of undergraduate studies illustrated a compelling ebb and flow of knowledge consumption. In the third wave of attainment, black women's graduate research reflected an equally compelling story of intellectual production.

Progression to the Doctorate

In *The Negro College Graduate*, Johnson calculated that by 1933, 75 doctorates had been awarded to black men and 10 to black women. By 1936, African Americans had earned 1,555 M.A.s, and 153 Ph.D.s. But here, as before, the quantitative historical record is not consistent. In *Holders of Doctorates among Negroes*, Harold Greene calculated only 296 M.A.s had been awarded to African Americans. Again, the discrepancy arose from the number of institutions counted. While Johnson's number reflected all known counted degrees, Greene's number reflected degrees awarded from only fifty colleges classified as "eminent" top-ranked universities. While each calculation represents the researcher's unique perspective, both numbers indicate the relatively low participation of blacks in graduate education. In all, African Americans were far behind in degree attainment: It was estimated that by 1876, 25 PWIs had already awarded 44 Ph.D.s, putting black scholars six decades behind in doctoral degree attainment.[1]

By Greene's account of the 381 known doctoral degrees awarded to African Americans by 1943, only 48 had been awarded to women.[2] Here, the estimates of black doctorates were problematic for different reasons than in previous studies. Whereas earlier researchers faced the difficulty of finding black scholars in PWIs that did not record race or those in which black or mixed-race students passed for white, Greene had trouble differentiating between black scholars and scholars of black studies. An amusing example is Herbert Aptheker, whom Greene mistakenly counted as an African Ameri-

Figure 7. Dr. Eva Beatrice Dykes. Courtesy of Moreland-Spingarn Research Center.

Figure 8. Dr. Georgiana Simpson. Courtesy of Moreland-Spingarn Research Center.

Figure 9. Dr. Sadie Tanner Mossell Alexander. Courtesy of University of Pennsylvania Archives.

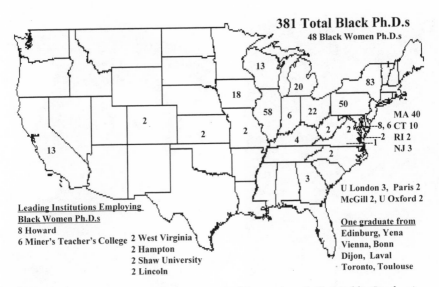

381 Total Black Ph.D.s
48 Black Women Ph.D.s

13

20

83

18

58   6   22

50

2

MA 40
8, 6 CT 10
2   RI 2
NJ 3

2

2

2

2

4

13

3

2

U London 3, Paris 2
McGill 2, U Oxford 2

Leading Institutions Employing
Black Women Ph.D.s
8 Howard
6 Miner's Teacher's College   2 West Virginia
2 Hampton
2 Shaw University
2 Lincoln

One graduate from
Edinburg, Yena
Vienna, Bonn
Dijon, Laval
Toronto, Toulouse

Map 5. Greene, *Doctorates among American Negroes* (1946). Created by Stephanie Y. Evans.

can Ph.D. because Aptheker's dissertation topic, slave revolts, addressed black history. Again, accurate numbers of graduates remained elusive. Gender also posed a problem with precision in the historic record. Some scholars were listed by initials only, and scholars with names like Allison Davis might easily be mistaken for a woman by those unfamiliar with past naming patters.[3]

Topping the list of doctoral degree–granting institutions for African Americans by the 1930s were University of Chicago (40 graduates); Columbia (35); University of Pennsylvania (28); Cornell (25); Harvard (25); and Yale (10). Radcliffe had awarded only three degrees. Most degree earners lived in Washington, D.C. In the 1940s, 85 black doctorate awardees (22 percent) lived in D.C.; Howard alone employed 70, including 8 women. An additional 6 of the 48 black women Ph.D. earners taught at Miner's Teacher's College; overall, one-quarter of all black women doctorates resided in the nation's capital after graduation.[4]

Explaining the narrow opportunity for black women to be properly prepared for graduate study, historian Linda Perkins reported:

Of the top five institutions that had awarded baccalaureate degrees to the black Ph.D.s, two were male institutions—Lincoln University in Pennsylvania and Morehouse College in Atlanta, Georgia. The other three—Howard, Fisk, and Virginia Union—were institutions with strong liberal arts and professional schools that enrolled large numbers of men. None of the teacher-training institutions or black state land-grant colleges, where women were heavily concentrated, ranked among even the top twenty baccalaureate-producing institutions. Overwhelmingly, the black women who received doctorates were graduates of white undergraduate institutions where they had taken liberal arts courses compatible with graduate training.[5]

Of the first four black women Ph.D. earners, only one, Eva Dykes, attended an HBCU, and she had to repeat her entire undergraduate degree when she attended a PWI for graduate school.

Because of the heavy recruitment of women to the teaching profession, there was little or no support for advanced study. By 1930, there were 45,672 black women teachers compared to only 8,767 black men teachers, and few women attempted to attend graduate school. Similarly, black women's opportunity in educational leadership was abysmal: one in five black women were elementary school principals, and only one in fifteen were high school principals; the only black woman president of an accredited college before 1954 was Mary Bethune, though Elizabeth Wright in South Carolina and Mary Branch in Texas had headed schools. Access to higher levels of college education determined leadership positions, and black women were systematically barred from obtaining the requisite degrees, restricting them to lower rungs of administration. As black women pushed the envelope of scholarly achievement, they met resistance: problems with thesis committees; responsibilities for raising families or taking care of relatives; participation in necessary but time-consuming civil and human rights activism; trying to improve the working conditions for the majority of black women (who were employed in low-skill, exploitative, and dangerous work); and studying while under stress in a tragically oppressive academy hindered growth.[6]

Breaking down Barriers, Climbing over Walls

Oberlin African American alumni records reflect 16 master's degrees awarded by 1899, including three to women: Anna Julia Cooper, Mary Church Terrell, and Ida Hunt. Cooper and Terrell conducted additional study after their B.A., and, though the degrees were deemed honorary, they were awarded their M.A. degrees together in 1888, the first known black women with master's degrees. Black women's graduate student numbers did not increase beyond single digits until after World War I.

Like Rose Browne, Berkeley graduate Ida Jackson provided key testament to the difficulties black women graduate students faced: "I had been interested in the reports of the Alpha Army Tests and the then widely accepted notion that the Negro's highest mental age was 15. Bare cases indicated that there was development beyond that. Intelligence tests were the criteria for the Alpha Army Test results and became the criteria for judging the educability of the Negro." Jackson's research challenged established racist pseudoscience, but her findings did not sit well with all of her committee members. Though her thesis committee chair offered her great support, the two psychologists appointed to her committee would not sign off on her thesis, "The Development of Negro Children in Relation to Education," because she cited the influence of environmental factors on children's learning, which undermined the declaration of African American biological inferiority. The Berkeley Graduate Council had to bypass the committee and give approval in order for Jackson to graduate. While it was apparently difficult for black women to get into graduate school, it often proved more difficult to get out.[7]

Black collegiate women were adept at teaching and effective at serving their institutions and communities. Teaching and service fell in line with the acceptable vocations for black women and did not challenge established gender roles. Scholarly research, however, was considered out of the purview of black women's reasonable aspirations or perceived capabilities. Patricia Mazon asserted that the German university—the model for research institutions—revolved around an idea of citizenship that was inherently male. In *Gender and the Modern Research University: The Admission of Women to German Higher Education, 1865–1914*, she argued that academies universally geared their curricula for a student imagined as male, middle-class, and nationalist. In *A Room of One's Own* (1929), Virginia Woolf revealed how women writers were denied development of their genius by lack of financial support, a denial of private space, and an inability to secure ample solitude. Women were daughters, sisters, mothers, wives, and keepers of communal responsibilities: a room of one's own was a selfish indulgence. Woolf argued that for writers, "a lock on the door means the power to think for oneself." This was doubly so for women interested in pursuing advanced study and exponentially so for black women in graduate school.[8]

Despite service responsibilities, black women did seek time and space to study. However, they would not find comfort in the seclusion of a solitary room. On predominantly white and male campuses and in graduate programs, they were already isolated—usually the only one of their kind. Consequently, they sought sisterhood and community. Unfortunately, their sense of community often conflicted with their need to study. To balance individual and community identities, they completed graduate studies by producing scholarly research that situated them as members of both black communities and campus communities. They took private time to produce scholarship reflecting discipline and advanced skills development, but research was produced for the common good. By theorizing humanity and researching themes central to justice, they sought to simultaneously uplift the black race, improve women's status, and add to human knowledge.

Constructing the Doctorate

As previously stated, graduate studies began in the United States as master's of arts degrees in 1831: between the Civil War and World War I, some colleges developed into universities. While the undergraduate degree was a product of England, the doctorate was German by design. In 1810, Johann Fichte established the first doctoral program at the University of Berlin. The University of Göttingen awarded the first doctorate of philosophy, in 1817, to Edward Everett. Yale awarded the first three American Ph.D.s in 1861, and the first African American man to earn the doctorate, Patrick Healy, did so abroad in Louvain, Belgium, in 1865. Edward Bouchet was the first African American male to earn a doctorate stateside, from Yale in 1876, and in 1877, Boston University awarded the degree to Helen Magill White. The first American white woman to earn the doctorate abroad, Rowena Mann, did so in 1904, from the University of Jena.[9]

Some academics who critically commented on the early American Ph.D.s noted that as the degree proliferated, "the work represented by these degrees was of uneven quality. . . . But the degrees meant that a notion of serious study beyond the B.A. was being widely established."[10] As late as 1884, with a faculty of 189, Harvard had but 19 professors with doctorates, and Michigan with a faculty of 88, had only 6: these low numbers led to the proliferation of the honorary degree, most popular before 1910. Universities scrambled to rapidly increase the percentage of "doctors," much to the chagrin of old-fashioned scholars like Harvard philosopher William James, who argued that the degree meant nothing because it did not indicate effective teaching. In 1903, James called the doctoral degree "an octopus, 'a mere advertising resource, a manner of throwing dust in the Public's eye,' 'a grotesque tendency,' 'the Mandarin disease,' 'a sham, a bauble, a dodge whereby to decorate the catalogues of schools and colleges.'"[11]

The Ph.D. eventually became the coin of the academic realm. "Research, teaching, and service" replaced "the head, the heart, and the hand" as the mantra of higher education, and eventually the measure of worth in academe devolved to the one-dimensional scope of, simply, "publish or perish." University professors and distinguished institutions like Johns Hopkins captured the public imagination by deeming themselves the only credible interpreters of culture and the public good. Rudolph noted: "The new university, in other words, found its purpose in knowledge, in the world of the intellect. It is the universities which edit, interpret, translate and reiterate the acquisitions of former generations both of literature and science." Amidst these developments, the relationship between black women and advanced study expanded in remarkable ways.[12]

Black Women's Intellectual Production

Before the establishment of the United States as a nation, black women contributed to the public narrative. Writers emerged as exemplars of black women's dedication to learning and literature production. Lucy Terry (1746), Phillis Wheatley (1773), Mary Prince (1831), Maria Stewart (1832), Elleanor Eldridge (1838), Ann Plato (1841), Zilpha Elaw (1846), Hanna Craft (ca. 1850), Frances E. W. Harper (1851), and Harriet Jacobs (1861) are but a few of the early black women poets, dramatists, novelists, elocutionists, activists, and autobiographers who inserted themselves in the social contract as civic participants by penning their own stories. They did not need to obtain a degree to write. Their production, in any genre, contained an element of research, creative narrative, and critical social science worthy of acclaim if not degree. Yet, American society did not acknowledge these scholars as "educated."[13]

Black women's publications were often tools of advocacy, belying a struggle between scholarship, art, and activism—a debate unresolved even in current discourse. Ida Wells's late nineteenth-century investigations and publication of *Southern Horrors: Lynch Law in All Its Phases* in 1892 and *A Red Record* in 1895 mirrored Frances Harper's critical advocacy in the early nineteenth century. Public lectures traversed spaces of protest and poetry. Black women's contributions to publications such as the *Colored American, Colored Women's Magazine*, and *Crisis* consistently blurred the line between research and advocacy.

An important inauguration of black women's history developed early: Black women moved from telling their own personal stories to telling the stories of other black women. *The Negro Trail Blazers of California* (Beasley, 1919), *Homespun Heroines and Other Women of Distinction* (Brown, 1926), *Women Builders* (Daniel, 1931), and *Lifting as They Climb* (Davis, 1933) set the tone for modern-day black women historians and indicated the different story that materializes when a subjugated people records its own history.

The First Black Women Ph.D.s

The first three black women who earned doctoral degrees all did so in 1921. Their fields varied—English philology, German, and economics—but their findings all exemplified complex negotiations of their identities as both black women and scholars.[14] As with previous writers, collegiate black women injected their cultural mores into disciplinary epistemology and contributed sophisticated, practical knowledge.[15]

Before 1954, the majority of women pursuing doctorates, what Anna Cooper called the "third step," did so in education:

Education	17
Languages	12
Social science	6
Psychology	3
Biology	3
Home economics	2
Music education	1
Library science	1
Geology	1

It is interesting, then, that none of the three 1921 scholars earned their degrees in education. This was because the field of education was in early stages of development: Harvard granted the nation's first Ph.D. in education in 1920.[16]

The first three black women doctorates—Eva B. Dykes, Georgiana R. Simpson, and Sadie T. Mossell Alexander—wrote dissertations that varied greatly in discipline, length, content, and structure. Their approaches and conclusions both complemented and contradicted each other. Each manuscript held broader implications for African Americans and women. Expanded opportunity created by World War I explains the granting of three degrees in the same year. The phenomenon of three degrees being granted in one year at different institutions and in different disciplines allows fascinating comparisons.

Dykes, in English philology, wrote an in-depth analysis tracing English writer Alexander Pope's (1688–1744) rise and fall in popularity in the United

States. Simpson, in Germanics, explored philosopher Johann von Herder's (1744–1803) interpretations of *das Volk* (the people) as both a national and racial category. In economics, Alexander queried the financial systems of one hundred black participants in the northern, urban Great Migration to find the status of the black family and made suggestions on how they might secure a better fiscal future. Each scholar sought to interpret some aspect of African American and women's experience, though in markedly different ways.[17]

EVA DYKES

Eva Dykes was born in 1893 in D.C. and in 1910 graduated from M Street High School, where she had been a student of Anna Cooper. Dykes earned a B.A., summa cum laude, from Howard in 1914. Radcliffe did not recognize the Howard degree, so when she moved to Massachusetts, she repeated her undergraduate studies to earn a B.A. (1917), then advanced to an M.A. (1918) and Ph.D. (1921). It was not uncommon for transferring students at elite schools to repeat course work; at the time, Harvard did not even accept degrees granted from Boston College. Radcliffe had graduated its first black woman student, Alberta Schott, in 1898 and was relatively liberal regarding its admission of black students. Radcliffe led the Seven Sister colleges, but even that degree did not guarantee economic or job security. After graduation, Carter G. Woodson advised Eva Dykes to move west, where more opportunities were available, suggesting: "You should leave Washington as soon as possible that you may find an opportunity for development. . . . If you can secure a useful position at Howard University, you may be able to do some good: but even there you will find many handicaps." She did not follow his advice. Dykes stayed in D.C. to teach at her alma mater (then renamed Dunbar High School) from 1921 to 1929 and then taught at Howard until 1944, when she accepted a position at Oakwood College in Huntsville, Alabama. She was inducted into Phi Beta Kappa in 1940 and published *The Negro in English Romantic Thought or A Study for the Sympathy of the Oppressed* (1942). She retired from Oakwood in 1968 but continued to work there until 1973. The Oakwood library was named in her honor, and she passed away in Huntsville in 1986.[18]

Of the first dissertations, Dykes's was the most abstract. Not once in 644 pages did she mention the status of African American women as such. Nor did she use her findings about Pope to state how his work exemplified a sympathetic position to those Africans enslaved during the tenure of his popularity. She simply did literary and linguistic analysis. First, Dykes identified characteristics of Pope's writing style, form, and voice. She then placed

Pope in his European context, detailing his stature as a writer and esteemed reputation as a translator in England. She argued that by tracing personal letters, New England newspapers, magazines, travel diaries, or popular and obscure poetry, one could clearly recognize that Pope's influence in the emerging United States was far wider than had been previously acknowledged. Many—including Benjamin Franklin, Thomas Jefferson, and Noah Webster, poets and journalists alike—quoted, cited, or copied Pope, though after the early 1800s, they did not overtly credit him.[19]

Dykes laid out the social and historical context in which Pope lived and wrote, but fully two-thirds of her dissertation consisted of a close linguistic reading. She drew parallels between Pope and his emulators, analyzing his use of the heroic couplet, satire, and his inventive "paraphrasical form," which stated things simply, yet creatively. She supported her thesis with dense grammatical evidence that outlined American poets' conscious and unconscious replications and parodies of Pope's form, sentiment, and diction. She worked through his translations of the *Iliad* and the *Odyssey* but spent most of her time tracing moral and existentialist themes and weighing pieces like "Essay on Man" and "Essay on Self Knowledge."[20]

She made a case for analyzing authors in their own historical context and for recognizing the evolution of Pope's writing over time. She disputed former critics' narrow reading of Pope and highlighted the complexities of the movement from Awakening to Enlightenment, through romanticism and naturalism that were essential to understanding how Pope wrote and how his work was used in eras of competing ideologies. She indicated that in the Revolutionary era, American identity formation was a death knell to all things English, including English literature. She concluded that though American literature evolved swiftly with a style of its own, it did not cease to pay homage, even if only silently, to the voice and form that Pope perfected.[21]

On the surface, this research had nothing to do with black women's issues. Dykes did some gender analysis but only in order to explain Pope's popularity with all American readers, including women. She estimated that Pope was so popular that even "young ladies who wished to make an impression in company were advised to 'get by heart' some lines of Pope or [John] Dryden to show that they 'have read these fine bards.'" Though she recognized that Phillis Wheatley was influenced by Pope's style, Dykes did not draw attention to Wheatley as an enslaved African poet; she simply included Wheatley as one who wrote in Pope's literary tradition.

I suspect that Dykes focused on Pope because he was a moral idealist who demonstrated a modicum of humanity toward Africans during a time when human love, kindness, and spirituality were ignored, scorned, or punished. Given his humanist philosophical framework, he represented a literary and idealistic paradigm worthy of study. Her interest in Pope was definitely tied to her race and gender because he furthered high ideals of love and ethical social behavior in the face of worldwide African enslavement and increasingly oppressive European imperialism.

Yet, for Dykes, spirituality was a more important factor than either race or gender. She left her teaching position at Howard because she was deeply dedicated to her religion. In 1944, she accepted a position at Oakwood College and for four decades contributed much to that college's institutional growth because not only was it an HBCU, but it was a Seventh-day Adventist college as well. Thus, for her, being a "race woman" was not more important than being a religious woman. She was also a sorority member and among the first fifteen inductees into the newly formed Delta Sigma Theta Sorority at Howard, which demonstrated a commitment to club work that paralleled her spiritual devotion.[22]

Eva Dykes was a meticulous scholar. Her work demonstrated that black women academics have the ability to produce "abstract," "scientific," and "objective" research in the most obscure scholarly aspects of an arcane discipline. This, however, did not mean that she ignored her identity but simply that she subdued it in her graduate research, which changed later in her career. In *The Negro in English Romantic Thought* (1942), her research became expressly about race and gender. Here, she directly connected literature to activist traditions. She dedicated an entire chapter to women abolitionists, allowing her personal standpoint a more prominent role in her publications. Though her doctoral scholarship may not have spoken directly to her cultural identity, the work still had relevance for African American women, and Dykes clearly built her scholarly work on her black, religious womanhood.[23]

GEORGIANA SIMPSON

Like Dykes, Georgiana Simpson was born in D.C., in 1866, and attended Miner Normal School under the instruction of renowned educator Lucy Moten. Simpson earned her B.A. from the University of Chicago, completing her work while teaching elementary school. Chicago was a progressive institution, and Simpson worked in the midst of scholars such as Robert Parks, Allison Davis, Charles Johnson, and St. Claire Drake, though her work focused on classic Germanics, not social science, and her Chicago records indicated no study with those scholars.

Simpson completed summer studies at Harvard, did postdoctoral work in Germany, and pursued advanced study in French. After Chicago, she returned to D.C. and taught at Dunbar High School until 1931, then at Howard from 1931 to 1939, and was an esteemed member of Alpha Kappa Alpha Sorority. She was fifty-five when she earned her doctorate, unlike Dykes and Alexander, who were both in their twenties. As a seasoned scholar and professor, Simpson contributed much to research and teaching in D.C., and after leaving Howard, she worked with Anna Cooper at the Frelinghuysen University in the Department of Foreign Languages. Simpson died in a tragic accident at her home in 1944.[24]

Simpson's dissertation, "Herder's Conception of 'das Volk,'" was—like Dykes's work—an analysis of language and ideas. The noticeable difference was that instead of focusing on linguistics, Simpson dove directly into philosophy. Simpson's analysis of Herder rested on the contentious role of *das Volk*. She explored themes such as Romantic notions of "low" common culture and the alleged innate creativity of the masses, and she investigated claims of "primitive" artistic ability. Simpson outlined Herder's argument that common people were the highest representation of freedom, art, and culture; and she explained ideas that "common" expressions reflected basic utterances that were closer to nature than those of the aristocratic "cultured" class.

She began the fifty-nine-page dissertation by exploring definitions of "the people" and displayed her mastery in language, especially Old English, Old German, Latin, and Greek as she provided an etymology of *Volk*. She analyzed power dynamics between social classes, delineating the two senses in which Herder used the term *Volk*: (1) a nation as a group bound by blood or race, and (2) a nation that does not suffer what he considered the "deteriorating" effects of "civilization." She translated his characterization of individual and group identities and demonstrated how he favored less processed "primitive" dance, community stories, literature, and music as "pure" exotic expression. She then contextualized Herder's work within eighteenth-century English, French, Spanish, and German philosophy. She used Rousseau's social contract to connect Herder's individual and group identity to the state. She concluded by showing how Herder's conception of *das Volk* was instructive because he recognized the power, potential, and beauty of the masses—the common people—who, in his estimation, were closer than the ruling class to spontaneous and compassionate humanity. Simpson claimed that Herder celebrated the common people; she thereby vindicated her own race and gender, which were both portrayed (usually in a disparaging manner) as closer to nature than the more "civil" white and male citizens.[25]

Simpson's thesis, though providing a more benign view of "the folk" than was sometimes offered, nevertheless fell prey to the "noble savage" portrayal that was rampant in Romantic paternalistic scholarship. She presented a complicated and calculated view of the "lower classes." However, her analysis, extolling the virtues of the masses, ran contrary to Sadie Alexander's work. Unlike Simpson, Alexander did not see virtue in commonness and claimed that the masses, particularly the black World War I–era migrants, had no admirable culture. Unlike Herder, Alexander argued that common folk needed to be "uplifted" by exposure to high culture.[26]

Where Simpson's dissertation treated the theoretical realm of philosophy, Alexander's dealt with the practical world of economics. Alexander's voice was one of an objective researcher, and in keeping with disciplinary expectations, she identified herself as the "investigator." Though very different, both Simpson and Alexander wrote dissertations to vindicate black people.

SADIE ALEXANDER

Born in 1898 and raised in Philadelphia, Sadie Tanner Mossell, like Dykes, graduated from M Street High School in D.C. and was influenced by Anna Cooper. She earned her B.A. in economics from the University of Pennsylvania in 1918 and her M.A. in the same discipline one year later. After earning her doctorate from Pennsylvania in 1921, she, like Lucy Sessions in the 1850s, found barriers to adequate employment. So, she pursued a law degree, graduating from the University of Pennsylvania in 1927, in order to work in a field commensurate with her education. She too was a member of Phi Beta Kappa, inducted in 1970. Like Terrell and Anderson, she married within her educational class: a Harvard-trained lawyer. In 1925, she cofounded the National Bar Association, the professional organization for black lawyers, and in 1927 Alexander became national secretary. While she earned her graduate and professional degrees, she became the first national president of Delta Sigma Theta Sorority (1919–23) and later served as the organization's legal advisor for three decades. Alexander was recognized with many honors, including five honorary degrees and an appointment by President Truman. She died in 1989, over sixty years after earning her Ph.D.[27]

For her doctoral research, Alexander studied the financial situations of post–World War I African American migrants, the majority of whom were economically and educationally deprived. To translate economic deprivation into cultural depravation revealed controlling mores cast on black Americans. Yet, Alexander's dissertation was less a condemnation of the black lower class than an economic analysis of what would be required for them to gain real economic stability. She advocated means to achieve social respectability in a northern city that, despite the wartime industrial boom, offered limited mobility for black workers. Alexander was cognizant of unique class conflicts that migration caused. When 400,000 black people moved north between 1916 and 1918, there were both *interracial* and *intraracial* antagonisms. In a fifty-page dissertation, Alexander revealed the findings of her interviews with one hundred families in the Twenty-ninth Ward of Philadelphia.[28]

As scholar Julianne Malveaux has pointed out, Alexander's methodology, "a cross-sectional consumption survey," complicated racial analysis by investigating consumer, expenditure, and income data, which revealed a range of economic realities within the black northern urban experience and exposed class schisms within black communities. Malveaux offers one of the few analyses of a black woman's scholarship from a disciplinary perspective. She argues that, because of racism and sexism, leading academic economists failed to sufficiently support Alexander's transition into a top-level analyst and problem solver. If economists had paid attention to Alexander's case study and had granted her the support that Du Bois, Johnson, and other male academics enjoyed, she surely would have extended her efficacy and offered much-needed solutions to widespread social ills of the day. I submit that, when considering the gendered nature of Alexander's economic analysis, which included variables like rent and electricity but also women-driven expenditures like church tithes, it is obvious that she built on and departed from the sociological understanding that Du Bois demonstrated in his 1899 *The Philadelphia Negro*. Where Du Bois took a macrolevel institutional approach, Alexander provided the microlevel individual family-unit point of view.[29]

The convergence and divergence in conclusions between the scholarly inquiries of Dykes, Simpson, and Alexander reflect larger disagreements on the meaning, significance, and purpose of higher education. America was not in agreement on what college should prepare one to do or be. For African American women, the clash of values inherent in their roles as activist and as researcher demonstrated these tensions in academic integration.

With varying explicitness, black women scholars addressed issues facing black women. Particularly, their research addressed ideas of morality, power, and autonomy, all inherent in black women's struggle to gain access to higher education and to maintain their cultural identity in light of their scholarly ambitions. Nowhere was this more apparent than in Anna Cooper's 1925 dissertation, "L'attitude de la France a l'egard de l'esclavage: Pedant la Revolution," written for her University of Paris doctorate. Though Cooper's educational philosophies will be explored in the next section, it is appropriate here to focus on her academic experiences and doctoral research.[30]

Anna Cooper's "Third Step" to Doctoral Studies

Interestingly, Cooper felt very differently than Terrell and Hurston did about mathematics, writing that she "craved and clamored for" differential calculus. Her undergraduate major in mathematics eventually gave way to graduate studies in language, but Cooper expressed "sheer joy" in the process of lifelong learning, and math and Latin remained her passions, even as French and history became her academic specialization. In addition to her 1892 *Voice* and 1925 dissertation, Cooper translated *Le Pelerinage de Charlemagne* (1925). She worked on the epic poem about the ninth-century ruler Charlemagne (742?–814), converting the text from Old French to Middle French as a proposed doctoral thesis. She finished the piece at the same time as completing her dissertation, not for Sorbonne credit but rather for her own scholarly ambition.

Her purpose for translating the text, she asserted, was to pay homage to the Oberlin tutors who had taught her French and "to do a favor to American students by facilitating the study of an important and rather rare text." The rendition was deemed a substantial scholarly contribution and received positive reviews in Paris. Nevertheless, Cooper had difficulty getting a press to publish the work in the United States because university officials nationwide denied significance to work by black women—while recognizing its scholarly value, they chose not to support it. In historical perspective, Charlemagne was at once a champion of common education and a ruthless imperialist. He serves as an ironic metaphor for rulers in the empire of American higher education who encouraged Cooper to learn the French language but refused to grant her legitimacy in their kingdom.[31]

Though not much was made of Cooper's doctoral accomplishment in terms of pay increase, promotion, or scholarly credibility, she was widely supported in D.C., and was part of a thriving scholarly community. Cooper was not alone in the benefit she received from the international post–World War I education boom: in 1925, the year she graduated from the Sorbonne, Mercer Cook, John Matheus, and Jessie Fauset were all studying in France. Cooper's memoir of her graduate studies abroad tells how the "third step" came at the end of a long but fruitful journey. She discussed her school experiences with triumphant imagery. Her recollections of Oberlin were similar to Coppin's and Terrell's in that she noted initial resistance to her advanced workload but otherwise had fond memories. Where her autobiographical reflection differed from the others was in the significance that she assigned to her dissertation defense.[32]

Cooper began her study abroad in 1911 and worked four summers in Paris before completing her research at the Guilde International, Bibliothèque Militaire, and the French National Archives. Under threat of losing her position at Dunbar, she completed the dissertation manuscript in time for defense and, when she arrived in Paris, "burned out a devastating number of candles" making extensive adjustments and corrections to her manuscript. She wrote the dissertation in French, but her American-manufactured typewriter did not have French accents, so she punctuated the entire copy by hand. She worked in less than ideal conditions: electricity was not installed in the apartment she rented in France, so she had neither adequate heat nor light. She also made it through the bureaucratic university process even though her communication with Sorbonne administrators and committee took place in French.

Cooper clearly fused her personal experience with her education: the first word of her dissertation, written in French, was *Esclavage*. Slavery. She argued that the cause of France's downfall was greed, then presented clashing ideologies between the "Friends of the Blacks" and the power mongers who advocated enslavement during the revolutionary era of Haiti and France. Cooper's personal history as someone enslaved certainly influenced her scholarly interest in international power struggles over race, economic development, and attitudes influencing dehumanization of Africans in the Diaspora; something that clearly made her committee uncomfortable.[33]

To top all, she faced a formidable final battle because one of her committee members forcefully opposed her thesis and her philosophical framework. For her dissertation defense, she quickly had to decide what to change, what to keep, and how to rationalize her findings to a native French-speaking senior scholar with whom she fundamentally disagreed:

> I had but one short week to think it through. Besides and more emphatically I was frankly afraid of Bouglé. My French ear seemed duller than ever when he spoke and my tongue stupidly stuck in my throat. Madame told me that he was Breton which explained his variation from the more accustomed Parisian. But to make matters worse, I found myself on the opposite side in some pronouncements from his own thesis in *Égalité*, and when I gave out my opinion to Madame she said: "That will not help you. Bouglé is atheist."[34]

Cooper was on opposite sides of the table from her committee members in both social standing and in thought.

Underneath Cooper's controversial content about French slaveholders and abolitionists, her philosophical framework directly challenged Bouglé's: he claimed that the rights of man were an invention of Nordic man and therefore granted by man; she countered that the rights of man were granted by God and could be neither granted nor taken away by mere humans. On March 23, 1925, she successfully defended, in French, the dissertation that she had written and championed her beliefs of freedom, race, nationality, and Divine origins of human rights.

When Cooper reflected on her defense twenty years later, she remembered the process fondly, despite the tension and ideological dispute. In "The Third Step" (1945), she recounted:

> As I entered for the first time the awesome portals of the *Salle du Doctorate* I was met by an elderly personage in black gown who addressed me as Mademoiselle and inquired what college was designated by my Master's hood of crimson and gold. He conducted me to a table at front on which a carafe of water, a goblet and a bowl of sugar for what purpose I was too painfully preoccupied to try to guess. I think I recall a painting of the great Cardinal and blurs of others high on the walls but too remote in consciousness to leave any impression today.[35]

Cooper noted the novelty of being called "Mademoiselle" because she was sixty-six at the time, hardly what she considered to be a "young lady," which the term denoted. After discussion with her committee and defense of her thesis ensued, the chairman advised textual changes and challenged her view about the participation of the mulattoes of Haiti. He argued that they did not feel nearly the solidarity with the blacks that she supposed and that the three classes—black, mulatto, and white—were more complex than she represented. She noted his objection and made the required changes in her manuscript. Overall, she recalled benefiting greatly from the process:

> To me this discussion was both significant and informative. I realized, not unpleasantly that a *soutenance* was not a test [or] "exam" to be prepared for by cramming and cribbing the night before and brazened through by bluff and bluster the morning after by way of securing a "passing" mark. . . . Rather and most emphatically a *soutenance* "sustaining," supporting, defending if need be, an original intellectual effort that has already been passed on by competent judges as worthy a place in the treasure house of thought, affords for the public a unique

opportunity to listen in on this measuring of one's thought by the yard stick of great thinkers, both giving and receiving inspiration and stimulus from the contact.[36]

Cooper wrote that, though Bouglé took exception to her activist tone—which he called "partisan pleading"—she passed her defense with his grudging approval and apparent respect.

Stepping It Up—Those Who Followed

After Dykes, Simpson, Alexander, and Cooper, Zora Hurston emerged to push the boundaries of acceptable graduate research practice in academe in the 1930s. Hurston employed "ethnographic subjectivity," which challenged objective and positivist stances by traditional researchers. Hurston pushed even the most progressive anthropologists during her graduate studies at Columbia. She left in frustration, without the doctorate, and was not recognized for her genius until long after her passing. Stories of scholarly rejection like Hurston's are accompanied by countless instances of denied admittance, like Pauli Murray's.

As previously discussed, Murray's applications to the University of North Carolina and Harvard's law school were rejected because of her race and gender. Even in the post–World War II era, examples of discrimination abounded: best known were Ada Sipuel's suit against the University of Oklahoma State School of Law (1948) and Autherine Lucy's suit against the University of Alabama Graduate School (1952). These were just two of the most visible examples of the near-insurmountable legal bureaucracy, institutionalized hatred, and white mob violence that prevented black women from engaging in advanced studies.[37]

Despite the multitude of challenges, there were over 60 doctoral degrees awarded to black women between 1921 and 1954. Before *Brown*, black women earned the doctorate in English (Cromwell), dental surgery (Watkins), education (McAlister), psychology (Howard), nutrition (Kittrell), history (Wright), library science (Gleason), zoology (Young), anatomy (Lloyd), government and international relations (Tate), geology (Thomas), theater (Cooke), chemistry (Daly), mathematics (Brown and Granville), and musicology (McGinty). These hidden accomplishments were astounding considering the barriers present for black women scholars. Yet, the vast array of fields in which they distinguished themselves shows the wide range of interests black women had and that their intellectual abilities traversed the academic map.[38]

In addition to Sadie Alexander, Mary Terrell and Mary Bethune received honorary doctorates: Terrell from Oberlin, Wilberforce, and Howard; Bethune from Bennett, West Virginia State, Rollins College in Florida, and Benedict College in South Carolina. Though the recipients clearly warranted recognition, honorary degrees were far less common for black women than for others. This was not surprising considering that those who did earn degrees by completing graduation requirements were often ignored or held in low regard despite their attainment.[39]

August Meier once observed that, "like [Horace Mann] Bond, Marion M. Thompson Wright (1904–62), the first black woman historian to make a contribution to the field of Afro-American history, did her dissertation on the history of education." Given the direct relation of educational attainment to improved social status, it stands to reason that, when given the opportunity, scholars aspired to understand and influence issues in the field of education. Wright, herself a teacher, graduated from Howard and Columbia Teacher's College. She researched seventeenth- and eighteenth-century ideals in her dissertation, "The Education of Negroes in New Jersey" (1941). She argued that—given the imbalance in access—if Dewey's ideal education for democracy was to be realized, discrimination in American educational systems would first have to be addressed and eliminated.[40]

Education mattered, and African Americans sought to make it work for them, regardless of the various methods employed to attain it. The doctorate, in the right hands, became a tool for racial justice and equal human rights. When black women gained access to graduate degrees, they infiltrated the academy in hopes of redefining scholarship and rechanneling resources of educational institutions to benefit the historically disenfranchised.

From Lucy Stanton to Pauli Murray, this educational history broadens understanding of past trials and triumphs of collegians in the United States. Part 2 will demonstrate that black women academicians significantly altered definitions of research, teaching, and service.

PART 2

Intellectual Legacy

Research

"The Yard Stick of Great Thinkers"

*History affords abundant evidence that civilization has advanced in direct
ratio to the efficacy with which the thought of the thinkers has been translated
into the language of the workers.*

Mary McLeod Bethune, Hampton University, 1934

Research, teaching, and service are the core of higher education. Each area
raises questions of interest about scholarly agenda, curricular focus, pedagogical practice, and responsibilities to communities. Though black wom-
en's access to formal education was limited, their scholarship was present
in America from the 1700s, when Lucy Terry and Phillis Wheatley first put
ink to parchment. Black women's contribution to civilization, as Bethune
affirmed above, has at every stage of degree attainment effectively linked
thought to action.[1]

Cooper's and Bethune's ideas of research, knowledge creation, and
meaning making were very much informed by their cultural identities, but
nuances emerged. For example, though both women heavily referenced
religion in their work, they did so in noticeably different ways: Cooper's approach was rational—arguing the logic of faith in God—and Bethune's was
metaphysical, claiming to have visions and powers from her ancestors. They
both, nonetheless, located religion as central to education and moral education as central to democracy. They expressed ideas in different ways and did
so within a community of black women who engaged in rigorous study for
both personal and collective growth.

Cooper's Critique of Pure Reason

Much of Cooper's *Voice* addressed the position of women in American society. Cooper was at once a historian, philosopher, sociologist, and poet. Her
unfailing belief in the Divine informed her philosophical research premise.
She believed that in order to fulfill our purpose—to be "good"—we must
work by faith. For her, both the origin and purpose of research was Christian

Figure 10. Dr. Anna Julia Cooper.
Courtesy of Moreland-Spingarn
Research Center.

Figure 11. Dr. Mary McLeod
Bethune. Courtesy of Bethune-
Cookman College Archives.

education. In her dissertation, she suggested that humans have a "singing something" that connects them with the universe and compels them toward good. This assertion challenged Bouglé's argument that human rights are based on European ideas of equality and are created by humans. Researcher Karen Baker-Fletcher convincingly argues that Cooper wrote from a spiritual center, challenging the prevailing values of individualism, objectivity, and atheism so widespread in European higher education.[2]

Cooper noted that Bouglé was dissatisfied with her dissertation because he would have preferred her research to engage issues of slavery from a more distanced viewpoint. As a former slave, she apparently, in his opinion, was too close to the topic for a clear view. Cooper, on the other hand, asserted that the calculated distance that most researchers maintained from their work was a root cause of immoral thought, scholarship, and action. In her essay "The Gain from Belief," Cooper contrasted the philosophical thought of David Hume, Francois Voltaire, Auguste Comte, and John Stuart Mill in an effort to discern where each had gone wrong by not paying due homage to God as the alpha and omega of thought and inquiry. For her, "objective" research was not the best approach, and distance from moral evaluation of thought resulted in faulty or self-indulgent scholarship. However, she did later absolve Voltaire because of his opposition to the African slave trade. According to Cooper, what scholars should pursue is simple: scholarship based on Christian principles. In her mind, judging research by Christian principles saved a researcher from the "abyss" of relativism that blocked one from right judgment.[3]

Cooper expressed pleasure in the scholarly process. Learning was a joy, and gaining knowledge was an interactive as much as a reflective exercise. Throughout her writings, Cooper discussed the imperative, life-giving force that academic study offered women. When discussing her own satisfaction at being able to engage challenging texts to which she was introduced while at Oberlin, she wrote:

> I grant you that intellectual development, with the self-reliance and capacity for earning a livelihood which it gives, renders woman less dependent on the marriage relation for physical support (which, by the way, does not always accompany it). Neither is she compelled to look to sexual love as the one sensation capable of giving tone and relish, movement and vim to the life she leads. Her horizon is extended. . . . She can commune with Socrates about the *daimon* [divine guidance] he knew and to which she too can bear witness; she can revel in the majesty of Dante, the sweetness of Virgil, the simplicity of Homer, and

the strength of Milton. She can listen to the pulsing heart throbs of passionate Sappho's engaged soul. . . . Here, at last, can be communication without suspicion; Friendship without misunderstanding; Love without jealousy.[4]

This interpretation of reading the classics, in her essay titled "Higher Education of Women" (1890–91), demonstrated Cooper's appreciation for literature but also revealed her dedication to making sure that women, especially black women, were afforded the luxury of literature appreciation and contemplative reading.

Remarkably, Cooper's musing, clearly written to demonstrate that black women too have the ability to understand and engage literature, predated W.E.B. Du Bois's essay "Of the Training of Black Men" in his *Souls of Black Folk* (1903), where he wrote: "I sit with Shakespeare and he winces not. Across the color line I move arm in arm with Balzac and Dumas, where smiling men and welcoming women glide in gilded halls. From out of the caves of evening that swing between the strong-limbed earth and the tracery of the stars, I summon Aristotle and Aurelius and what soul I will and they come all graciously with no scorn or condescension." Both authors mastered the Romantic language prevalent among the college-bred class in the early twentieth century and made the case for African American intellectual capacity; however, in this instance, Cooper's Romantic expression of scholarly appreciation came a decade before Du Bois's. Also of interest, as a woman scholar, she recognized the woman poet Sappho as a great writer, unlike the men scholars, who generally referenced only male writers.[5]

Cooper asserted that learning is a collective enterprise. Study was not something that took place only in libraries, and research was not confined to laboratories. She enjoyed the "Friday Night Art Club" on Corcoran and Seventeenth Street on Sundays in D.C. In her last major publication, "Early Years in Washington" (1951), she reminisced about the evenings spent in D.C.'s social world, writing about the pleasure of the shared intellectual company: "I wish I could find in the English language a word to express the rest, the stimulating, eager sense of pleasurable growth of those days. . . . The word study (Latin: *studere*) connotes zealous striving. . . . But here was just growth for the sheer joy of growing." While the ultimate goal of education was to address social justice issues, there was certainly room for indulgent and joyful learning.

As evidence of her passion for diligent learning, she recalled her desire to study calculus while at Oberlin:

In the old college days my record was far from guiltless of faculty head-
aches for guiding professors, by reason of my insatiable craving for
"more." Faculty business was interrupted to consider the case "of one
'Miss' Cooper, who asks permission to carry four subjects when three
is the limit under the rules." On one such occasion, when differential
calculus was the fourth pleaded for . . . Mrs. J . . . informed the faculty
in her deep sonorous voice that the only explanation she could offer
for the phenomenon was, "Calculus is hard, and Mrs. Cooper likes to
tackle hard things."[6]

Cooper slyly concluded, "and I did enjoy my math." This, in particular, was a
political statement since (according to Thomas Jefferson and the like) African Americans were not supposed to be able to master advanced mathematics, much less enjoy it.[7]

Building on the claims of Maria Stewart, Frances Harper, and Sojourner
Truth, Cooper articulated the "particularity" of black women's position.
She challenged black women's subjugation and argued for powers of self-
definition and self-determination. In "The Status of Women in America"
(1892), she wrote:

The colored woman of today occupies, one may say, a unique position
in this country. In a period itself transitional and unsettled, her status
seems one of the least ascertainable and definitive of all the forces
which make for our civilization. She is confronted by both a woman
question and a race problem, and is yet an unknown or an unacknowl-
edged factor in both.[8]

This essay, as well as "Our Raison d'Être" (1892), "Womanhood: A Vital Element in the Regeneration and Progress of the Race" (1886), "The Higher
Education of Women" (1890–91), and "Woman vs. the Indian" (1891–92),
revealed Cooper's dedication to understanding black women's position and
to adding "this little voice to the chorus." She spoke often and wrote about
the black men's resistance to recognizing black women's roles and leadership
in uplifting the race. She bristled, "it seems hardly a gracious thing to say,
but it strikes me as true, that while our men seem thoroughly abreast of the
times in almost every other subject, when they strike the woman question
they drop back into sixteenth century logic."[9]

Because black women occupied this "unique" space, Cooper argued, they
possessed a heightened capacity to challenge racial and gendered disparities: "Delicately sensitive at every pore to social atmospheric conditions,

her calorimeter may well be studied in the interest of accuracy and fairness in diagnosing what is often conceded to be a 'puzzling' case." To judge the trueness of American democracy or figure the viability of a proposed solution, ask a black woman. As university research became increasingly used to rationalize and maintain social inequity, Cooper argued for a subjective and critical approach, from the perspective of the marginalized, to measure the relevance and reliability of knowledge claims. Cooper's research on black women in higher education was especially valuable in assessing democracy in the United States at the turn of the twentieth century.[10]

In "The Higher Education of Women," she traced, and refuted, reasons given to excuse the lack of educational opportunity afforded women. After outlining barriers to attainment for [white] American women, she lamented, "now I would that my task end here" and then outlined additional barriers that women of color faced. She demonstrated a clear research agenda that was based on assessing the growth and opportunities for black women and began work that was followed by scholars like Slowe, Cuthbert, Noble, and Player.[11]

Cooper claimed that intellect is gendered, but her claims were not simplistic arguments of biological determinism. True, she argued that men possessed greater reason and women greater sympathy, but she linked this to the pervasiveness of gender roles in socialization rather than to biological destiny. As a result of the reinforcement of these dispositions, Cooper argued that men could possess great passion and compassion, but that they learned it from women. Women could articulate ideas of brute strength, but they were simply mimicking dominant sentiment—speaking in a "false tongue and parroting men" versus speaking with their "true heart." It was in this line of thinking where she concluded that women—particularly black women—possessed a greater capacity for social justice work.[12]

Despite her belief in women's gentility, Cooper fought against claims that scholarly inquiry was unwomanly. Arguments advanced by the likes of Silvain Marechal's "Shall Women Learn the Alphabet?" (1801) warned that educating women would result in a lag in productive "women's work," leaving homes in ruins and societies in chaos. Cooper countered this view with the assertion that everyone should be educated, no matter what station, vocation, or gender. She criticized women who downplayed their intelligence in order to placate men and rebuked the popular preference for marriage over educational attainment that many women chose or felt pressured to choose. Cooper assessed women's access to education, recorded barriers, and challenged African American communities to support "not the boys less, but the girls more," in order to enable women to reach their highest academic potential.[13]

Cooper did not equate excellence with pedantry and especially challenged stagnant teacher education at the university level. In "The Humor of Teaching" (1930), she critiqued popular teacher education research methods, educators who subscribed to bandwagon mentality, Johnny-come-lately theoretical approaches, and the "dry as dust abstractions" that drove out the creative thinking process that research and teaching were supposed to encourage. She dismissed professors' "mental gymnastics embalmed in an outworn college curriculum that have no discoverable connection with the practical life interests of the student." She fought abstract, automated instruction, arguing, "there is a need of ripe scholarship among teachers themselves, specifically the frivolous fledglings just out of college and serving an indeterminate sentence to teach on their way to something hoped for." Her frustration was with teachers who ingested curricular materials without digesting them; the result was half-baked scholarship and piecemeal teaching. She traced rotten pedagogy to the college professor: "many fellows come hungering and thirsting to college as to an interpreter and unfolder of life, a warm touch of an understanding friend—but too often in place of the Bread of Life they get a stone."[14]

Teachers, particularly those in segregated schools, were forced to follow pedagogical fads without regard for the applicability of the work to their students. She charged:

> Segregated teachers are largely book-fed. What is worse, they believe what is in the books. . . . They race to summer schools and institutes, to lecture courses and evening classes to "keep up" with their work and perhaps earn a much needed promotion. All of which is most commendable and highly necessary. But the lectures and summer courses are unavoidably sketchy and packed in under pressure. They read, mark, learn, but there is no time to "inwardly digest". . . . She is determined there shall be no flies on her teaching—and there aren't except that she gives herself no joy in the act and loses entirely all sense of humor in the process. Thus saith the book—and that puts the inviolable closure on all further debate.[15]

Cooper identified institutional pressure as a problem for professors who were force-fed bad pedagogy.

Though the college accreditation movement of the first two decades of the twentieth century allowed for the standardization of learning objectives and evaluation, that standard, in Cooper's estimation, was not always conducive to critical learning. Specifically, she thought the movement from liberal thought to standardized testing was a move in the wrong direction: "We have been so ridden with tests and measurements, so leashed and spurred for percentages and retardations that the machinery has run away with the mass production and quite a way back bumped off the driver."[16] She insisted on critical thought and expected innovation from professors responsible for teacher training or researchers whose findings influenced academic standards.

Cooper's critical assessment of white males was especially bold for her time. Despite the trappings of her classical writing style, she demonstrated race pride. While some suggested that African Americans would do well to emulate whites, Cooper rejected the Eurocentric ideal. She denied that to love learning was to strive to be white and considered herself a scholar capable of academic rigor and scientific inquiry but one who put race and gender at the center of her analysis in a manner that challenged traditional academic paradigms. She also adamantly rebuked the male dominance of social and political science, musing:

> How like Longfellow's *Iagoo*, we Westerners are, to be sure! In the few hundred years . . . we have had to strut across our allotted territory and bask in the afternoon sun, we imagine we have exhausted the possibilities of humanity. Verily, we are the people, and after us there is none other. Our God is power; strength, our standard of excellence, inherited from barbarian ancestors through a long line of male progenitors, the Law Salic permitting no feminine modifications.[17]

She dared to refute "whiteness" as a panacea:

> If Alexander wants to be a god, let him; but don't have Alexander hawking his patent plan for universal deification. If all could or would follow Alexander's plan, just the niche in the divine cosmos meant for man would be vacant. And we think that men have a part to play in this great drama no less than gods, and so if a few are determined to be white—amen, so be it; but don't let them argue as if there were no part to be played by black men and black women, and as if to become white were the sole specific panacea for all the ills that flesh is heir to—the universal solvent for all America's irritations.[18]

The above critical appraisal of American racial politics in "Has America a Race Problem? If So, How Can It Best Be Solved?" (1892) was controversial then and remains so now. It revealed how African Americans advocated for progressive politics and access to higher education and how their demands did not necessarily convey assimilationist desires.

Conversely, she disagreed with accommodationist strategies that accepted racial segregation. She was indeed a Pan-Africanist but not a separatist.[19] She professed that the "philosophic mind" sees that all human beings are tied by fate, so one should identify their own interest as being in line with that of all of humanity:

> The philosophic mind sees that its own rights are the rights of humanity. . . . It is not the intelligent woman vs. the ignorant woman; nor the white woman vs. the black, the brown, and the red,—it is not even the cause of woman vs. man. Nay, 'tis woman's strongest vindication for speaking that the world needs to hear her voice. . . . Her wrongs are thus indissolubly linked with all undefended woe, all helpless suffering, and the plenitude of her "rights" will mean the final triumph of all right over might, the supremacy of the moral forces of reason and justice and love in the government of the nation.[20]

In Cooper's view, each group should have pride but should see their fate intertwined with all others; all should work for the harmony that separatism, or sexism, would not produce.

In assessing which knowledge claims were valid, Cooper valued plurality and asserted that African American voices were essential to accurate representation of their intellectual abilities. She, like Eva Dykes, traced sympathetic portrayals of African Americans in literature but also challenged black authors to move beyond what she viewed as demeaning and base portrayals of black life or simplistic "thumbnail sketches" invoked by preachers. In 1892, she placed *Uncle Tom's Cabin* in the realm of propaganda rather than literature, as James Baldwin would do sixty years later. She held true to this standard, and wrote heavy-handed critiques of both Richard Wright and Langston Hughes. She faulted them for presenting unrefined black characters as "authentic." In their introductory essay to her collected work, Lemert and Bhan depicted Cooper as "somewhat of a moralistic crank." However, I interpret her resistance to "low culture" as more nuanced than "moralistic." On one hand, Cooper positioned blackness as contrasting favorably to whiteness; on the other, she rejected "common" black culture and advocated upper-class aesthetics of creative production. Her "crankiness" in defining qualities of black life was a complex dance involving standpoint, language, and audience that reflected dilemmas inherent in black art from the advent

of ragtime music through the 1960s black arts movement to the 1990s explosion of rap and hip hop culture. Her critique was an important example of
the enduring conflict over defining the black aesthetic.[21]

In addition to her critical approach to educational, economic, political,
and literary research, Cooper deconstructed popular culture with linguistic
analysis. For instance, she offered a biting review of the 1930s radio show
Amos and Andy. In "The Negro Dialect," Cooper asserted that the language,
popularized by white minstrels in "satires" on African American life and
dialect was both culturally and linguistically inaccurate:

> "Andy's" "sitchation" runs true to phonic form, preserving the tonic syl-
> lable and all of the sound that is essitonal to carrying the sense (as any
> winged word should); the "u" never having been seen or consciously
> stressed is of course entirely negligible. The same analysis applies to
> "regusted" which has nothing whatever in common with the Irish "rr"
> in its first syllable, being hardly more than the movable "nu" in Greek
> or the "eh-reh" so often in hesitating for a word.[22]

She also discredited racist attacks on black entertainers that were constructed to portray black people as ignorant:

> By the same reasoning "am dat," ascribed to Paul Robeson by the press
> and vouched for by Mr. Hannen Swaffer, must go. . . . It is as artisti-
> cally impossible to Robeson. . . . His genius leans to flowing sounds,
> easy liaisons, more French than German, a prevalence of vowels, semi
> vowels, and liquids. He might say: "whea dat" or "Wheah's dat," or even
> "whah dat hankycher"—but never, never, I pledge you my word, will
> you hear a Negro, not drilled into it for stage effect, utter of his own
> accord: "Where am dat kandkerchief" [*sic*]. It is simply impossible.[23]

Cooper took critical writing seriously—especially writing that affected the
image or opportunities of black people. But her ideas of producing and judging texts were mired in the ideological conflicts of competing social classes.
Despite these complications, Cooper's writing remained grounded by ideas
of self-definition, moral accountability, and innovation that grew from love
of learning and freedom that only education offered.

Cooper wrote of research, particularly in reference to her doctoral work,
as "measuring one's thought by the yard stick of great thinkers," but she
measured ideas in a way that challenged the canonical ideas of those "greats."
She also took note of exemplars in the developing U.S. educational system
and measured them by her criteria. She was aware of popular educational
theorists as well as historical research produced on a wide range of topics,

and her views changed over time. For example, she recognized Booker T. Washington in 1892 for the solid gains made at Tuskegee, but by 1938, she published a scathing critique of his educational policies in the NAACP's *Crisis*. Cooper also engaged with W.E.B. Du Bois as a scholar. When Claude Bowers penned the *Tragic Era* in 1929, which depicted Reconstruction as a black reign of terror for the country in general and for whites in particular, Cooper wrote a personal letter imploring Du Bois to offer a response. In 1935, his *Black Reconstruction* suggested an alternative view of the important period. She critiqued Washington as "a colored leader of white American thought" and encouraged Du Bois to produce research that depicted African Americans as more than scoundrels and loafers, even as she contributed her own work.[24]

As significant as John Dewey was to become in the world of higher education, it is noteworthy that Cooper's 1892 publication predated Dewey's most famous works. She did not mention Dewey in her manuscript, probably because the University of Chicago was founded that same year and Dewey was still at the University of Minnesota, as yet unknown in the national arena. Cooper did, however, make reference to Jane Addams's work at Hull House (founded 1889) in Chicago. Significantly, Cooper lauded other black women educators whom she considered exemplars, including Sarah Early, Hallie Brown, and Fanny Coppin.[25]

In her thought and practice, she charged all people, regardless of their level of education, with working toward social justice. The goal of research was not simply publication:

> For, after all, Social Justice, the desired goal, is not to be reached through any panacea by mass production. . . . As I see it then, the patient persistence of the individual, working as Browning has it, "mouth wise and pen-wise" in whatever station and with whatever talent God has given, in truth and loyalty to serve the whole, will come as near as any other to proving worthwhile.[26]

Each person was to ask and answer academic questions based on a moral understanding of social responsibility.

Bethune—Investigation, Interpretation, and Inspiration

During Jim Crow, most whites thought that educating black people was folly. From her personal experience, Bethune was conscious of the loss of self that lack of education meant. When reflecting on her denied access to education as a child, she wrote: "I could feel in my soul and my mind the realization of the dense darkness and ignorance that I found in myself . . . with the seeming absence of remedy." She lamented that a result of long-standing repression was that black children often lost their sense of aspiration. Education, she argued, must be widely available and must be a tool of encouragement, particularly for those historically denied admittance to formal training. In her thought and work, Bethune was aware of the complex and central role that cultural identity played in one's educational attainment.[27]

Bethune asserted that, in addition to critiquing dominant culture, African Americans must cultivate knowledge of their own heritage. From 1936 to 1951, Bethune was president of the ASNLH. In her 1938 presidential address to the organization, "Clarifying Our Vision with the Facts," Bethune continued Woodson's mission to "scientifically" study black history and present the facts for assessment in the arena of all cultures. She began the speech with a story of Henri Chrisophe, a Haitian revolutionary, and of his desire for black people to have a written account of their culture. She then emphasized the imperative for researchers to recount black history:

> Through accurate research and investigation, we serve so to supplement, correct, re-orient and annotate the story of world progress as to enhance the standing of our group in the eyes of all men. . . . We must tell the story with continually accruing detail from the cradle to the grave. From the mother's knee and the fireside of the home, through the nursery, the kindergarten and the grade school, high school, college, and university,—through the technical journals, studies and bulletins of the Association,—through newspaper, storybook and pictures, we must tell the thrilling story.[28]

Bethune echoed Cooper's pride in being black and articulated a clear and powerful denunciation of whiteness as an ideal.

She reminded educators they must teach African American intellectual achievement. After outlining the statistics and accomplishments of blacks in education, she offered:

> It is the duty of our Association to tell the glorious story of our past and of our marvelous achievement in American life over almost insuperable obstacles. From this history, our youth will gain confidence, self-reliance and courage. We shall thereby raise their mental horizon and give them a base from which to reach out higher and higher into the realm of achievement. And as we look about us today, we know that they must have this courage and self-reliance. We are beset on every side with heart-rending and fearsome difficulties.[29]

Through her demand for recognition of African Americans in history, she implored members of the NACW to keep excellent records: "We must create a literature," she claimed. She advocated collecting, documenting, and referencing black accomplishments as a corrective to the dominant white national narrative.[30]

Bethune outlined three responsibilities of colleges: investigation, interpretation, and inspiration. She lectured that education, particularly higher education, was the largest business enterprise because it dealt with the three main concerns of a society: science, democracy, and religion. She stressed that scientific, technological, and political instruction was incomplete without religious training: it was unreasonable to expect citizens to behave morally if moral training was not a central focus of the educational system at all levels. Bethune patiently explained the difference between knowing and understanding: one could know the technicalities of a subject but, without moral training, not understand the implications, significance, or applications of that subject. One must have both theoretical and practical training, but social uplift was the main evaluative measure.[31]

In her organizational addresses of the 1930s and 1940s, Bethune argued that education was a key component in fulfilling democratic promises—particularly for African Americans. For her part, she worked to develop institutional access to compensate for prior discrepancies, especially in Florida. Not only did she establish her school for girls in Daytona, but she consistently increased the quality and level of study until it gained full accreditation and "A" rating as a college.

Higher education, as a means of political and economic access, had top priority on her agenda even before Bethune-Cookman was a full-fledged college. She identified graduate school as an area in much need of development for African Americans, explaining, "we tried to get the authorities to see the importance of giving special opportunities to Negroes in the upper tiers of training in order that we might get the master's degrees and doctors' degrees necessary for persons to head up our schools." In 1935, the first year she was in a position to allocate resources as the director of the NYA in the Roosevelt administration, she requested—some might argue she demanded—$100,000 to direct toward graduate training. Of course, she received it. From those funds, she immediately wrote checks for $20,000 to Howard and $16,000–$18,000 to Atlanta University; she funded graduate education at Fisk and advanced study at Tuskegee. Clearly, she supported access to education at the primary and secondary levels, but she also advocated increased access to graduate training.[32]

Like Cooper, Bethune treated education as both an individual and collective endeavor. She wanted students to be allowed to "follow inner urges" and choose a course of study of personal interest but also saw the value of creating a community of scholars and instructing students to meet the real needs of society. While students should be trained in any field for which they are naturally inclined or develop a desire to learn, teachers and colleges should offer instruction that encourages social responsibility.[33]

For Bethune, learning was linked to God. She gained strength, faith, belief, and determination from her mother's example of spiritual connectedness and integrated the concept of meditation in her informal and formal learning. She built her school on faith and seeded spirituality and religious training into the soil of the campus. She saw herself as teaching the whole person and refrained from compartmentalizing learning as disciplinary approaches tended to do. She wrote, "we think education is as much for the sake of character as for knowledge." Though "character education" fueled major philosophical and pedagogical debates from the seventeenth to the twentieth centuries and evolved in meaning, Bethune saw the idea of liberal disciplines, vocation training, and religious instruction as inherently intertwined.[34]

Bethune referred to the horrors brought on by the atomic age and argued that by adhering to principles such as the Golden Rule, world citizens could overcome monstrosities like atom bombs that worldly education had created. The origin and outcome, the end and the means of education should be centered on biblical lessons. As she educated others for service to the world, she herself served in local, national, and international communities according to her beliefs.[35]

Cooper's and Bethune's definitions of research were in stark contrast to larger academic developments at PWIs. At institutions run by the "authorities," publication gained primacy, and the joy of advanced inquiry, the mutual benefit of shared scholarship, or the application of research findings for the public good were soon squelched by raw competition, the demand to produce, and "intellectual property" squabbles.

Ascendance of Research in Academic Institutions

The surest way to ameliorate oppressive conditions, according to Bethune and Cooper, was a combination of direct agitation, institution building, and scholarly analysis of the issues that affected public policy. Surely then, learning and teaching at PWIs had its place in black liberation movements. The design of university systems, however, did not support black women's agenda. One major problem was the changing definition of the professor's role and an increased focus on "objective" published research.

In 1915, John Dewey led the American Association of University Professors (AAUP) in penning a treatise that outlined the rights of college faculty. Professors desired free speech and self-governance for research, free rein for teaching, and freedom from administrators or trustee board interference in the educational process. Autonomy was central to the AAUP's professional ideals. At most institutions, tenure became a concern for professors who wanted autonomy.[36]

From the first decade of the twentieth century, research and academic study at PWIs grew increasingly divorced from working toward the common good and became more wedded to rationalizing and perpetuating unequal social conditions or war-focused political agendas. Though there were pockets of progressive politics, as a whole, the American education system perpetuated social inequality. The professor became an expert rather than a public servant. For example, the University of Chicago was among the first to evaluate research above teaching, but the practice of granting tenure based on publication eventually became standard. Ironically, Chicago was one of the few major institutions that admitted black graduate students, and the Sociology Department was on the cutting edge of the field. Yet, mainstream academe, even Chicago, remained grounded in the manufacture model of scholarship. Publishing—raw production—trumped scholarship focused on effective social justice and outweighed teaching as a measure of faculty worth. In addition, massive publishing, seen as "overwhelming scientific evidence," became an important means by which privileged white Americans maintained dominance.[37]

According to Bethune, the university should serve as a place where investigators, interpreters, and inspirers reside. This was not far from standard definitions, but how black and white educators saw those activities was quite different. Rudolph maintains that the "'acquisition, conservation, refinement and distribution of knowledge' were services that the emerging university rendered to the society at large. . . . It is the universities which edit, interpret, translate and reiterate the acquisitions of former generations both of literature and science."[38] The power of university researchers to produce knowledge that rationalized racism and sexism increased with the legitimacy accorded university systems.

Further, the establishment of hierarchies between academic institutions mirrored social hierarchies. In the battle for primacy, universities sought to distinguish themselves by membership in the Ivy League or by imitating institutions considered to be in that elite network. One way of ensuring perpetual standing was to garner both public and private funds but abrogate public accountability. Like big business ventures, public funds provided elite schools with subsidies from which private parties profited, despite the public labor that produced the wealth. Or most institutions, like Brown University, were enriched by blood money from the African slave trade and centuries of unpaid or underpaid black labor.[39]

Within individual institutions, hierarchies developed through competitiveness between disciplines. Departmentalization and disciplinary specialization gave way to professional organizations that established stylized guidelines for publication. By doing so, organizations claimed the final word in evaluating scholarship. The American Philological Association was the first such modern organization, founded in 1869. Then came the American Chemical Society (1877), the Modern Language Association (1883), the American Historical Association (1884), the American Economic Association (1885), the American Mathematical Society, and the Geological Society of America (1888). When publishing became the measure of academic worth, the ability to publish was strictly regulated by what the insiders of the racist, sexist, and classist organizations deemed worthy to print.[40]

Each disciplinary faction fought to "prove" its academic worth when placed against other fields. All scholarly fields, however, subscribed to the tenet of black inferiority. By the 1930s, researchers had created "psychometrics" and "eugenics," which, no matter how injurious to humankind, were institutionally protected. The incorporation of statistical and quantitative methods used "science" to make race calculable and to substantiate claims of white supremacy numerically and "logically." True, racists in the humanities also claimed superiority based on dichotomies of "civilization" and "primitiveness" and concluded that African Americans were not cultured enough to correctly understand, interpret, or produce great art (as evidenced by the resistance Lena Morton encountered in her effort to undertake a Ph.D. program in English). But disciplinary bifurcation gave way to battles between sciences and humanities in which natural and physical scientists' claims of "objective" research captured the academic high ground.

Ultimately, scientific research claimed victory in the battle between long-standing Awakening and Enlightenment debates: science became more valued than humanities—in both monetary and intangible terms. Thus science became the most prevalent rationalization for social and institutional inequalities. To some degree, African Americans would eventually be credited with producing cultural work, a "subjective" scholarly process, but it would still invariably be denied that they had capacity to conduct scientific research, an "objective" scholarly process.

African American women educators produced valuable ideas about education, but because they were barred from the upper echelons of higher education, membership in professional societies, and admittance into publishing houses, their ideas were not widely dispersed. Even when mainstream academics acknowledged black women's ideas as interesting, their work failed the "rigor" test of objectivity, and they were seen mainly as "teachers," who were seen as less valuable than "researchers." Teachers instructed, researchers published. With few exceptions, "peer-reviewed" publication became the measure of academic worth:

> publication, indeed, became a guiding interest of the new academician. Each book, each article, was a notch pegged on the way to promotion. . . . This de-emphasis of the teaching role of the American professor . . . was soon recognized as a necessary concomitant of the university idea. . . . University rivalry required that each university be certain that its professors were better than its rivals, and one way of making that clear was by coming in ahead in the somewhat informal annual page count in which universities indulged. It made it clear who was to be promoted, when, and why. . . . "Publish or Perish," the slogan became. . . . By 1898 the number of copies of University of Chicago journals printed in a year totaled 150,000. . . . By 1904 Columbia professors were churning out 35 serial publications. The consequence of these massive journal performances was to lead many universities to the conclusion that respectability required its own set of journals; this conclusion led to a great deal of publication that was not exactly of high quality.[41]

It was in this context, then, that John Dewey—the most highly regarded educational philosopher of the twentieth century—grew to be so highly regarded; he was well published. The epitome of productivity, his written works comprise thirty-seven volumes. Dewey and others published large bodies of work because they had the time, resources, institutional support, and professional reputations to do so. By the time Dewey gained widespread acclaim, the first black women had just been allowed access to the Ph.D. Though many black women wrote and independently published research before Dewey, they remained obscure because they lacked institutional access and support.

Black Women's Critical, Creative, and Scholarly Production

Black women did write, and specifically, they wrote about knowledge creation, production, and application. Both Cooper and Bethune offered useful approaches to understanding education, but neither held the academic sway extended to Dewey, Washington, and Du Bois or the resources afforded institutional leaders like Charles Johnson.

It is not for lack of general public recognition that these women are so rarely referenced in scholarly work. In their day, they were national and international figures. During her time in Roosevelt's "Black Cabinet," Bethune wielded as much influence as Washington had before her. Also, while Cooper was studying for the doctorate in France, many people knew of her: in her memoir she recalled how, after having her doctoral prospectus approved, a reporter from the Paris edition of the *Chicago Tribune* approached her for an interview. Both women were known in their time, but academe has been slow to recognize and canonize this body of knowledge because, in many circles, "dry as dust abstractions" still prevail.[42]

Black women's critical contribution to formal inquiry was filled with their wit, candor, and keen eye for redefining popular knowledge. Thousands of unknown women wrote in black newspapers, journals, and magazines. These contributions, some in periodicals like the NACW's *Women's Era* and NCNW's *Aframerican Women's Journal*, or in publications like the *Journal of Negro Education*, comprise a body of information that warrants consideration. While white male politicians and educators established institutions of higher education in the United States and espoused philosophies of equality, many were, in essence, slaveholders, rapists, and warmongers. Likewise, their claims to academic and social superiority by use of "objective science" fell flat; they gained power by violence and coercion, not by intellectual prowess. Also, many white inventors held patents for work engineered by black workers. Cooper was especially adept at pointing out the hypocrisy in white academic knowledge claims, but it was through letters, not science, that she offered an alternative view. Cooper valued performing arts, and while a teacher at Dunbar, she directed plays and sponsored piano recitals in her home to enrich the community and her students. As she partook of literature, she too contributed to the world of arts and letters.[43]

Cooper's enduring intellectual capacity was demonstrated by her collection of handwritten poems produced well past her ninetieth birthday. One poem, "They Also," revealed her understanding that one must progress beyond academic pedigree. To be a person worthy of admiration, one must be right in thought *and* action:

They Also
I wanted just to be useful,—
I could not express it in song,
But my heart yearned to lift in life's struggle
Some need of humanity's throng.

I had not the gold nor the silver,
Nor houses nor lands in my store;
E'en the poorest thought scorn of my pittance
And flung it unglad at my door.

So I toiled along earning my ration,
I would not repine for Earth's pelf,-
When lo, from afar, the faint whisper:
"You have lifted by being Yourself!"[44]

Thus, Cooper might argue, scholars must lift society by lifting barriers to equality, not merely by objectively discussing the hypothetical merits of equality or constructing abstract games of logic never to be applied for the common good. She "measured her thoughts by the yard stick of great thinkers," and often she found them wanting. According to Bethune and Cooper's criteria, if research findings do not result in a more equal society, and researchers themselves do not actively work toward that equality, then academic degrees, journal publications, book manuscripts, and professional acclaim simply are not of any real value, scholarly or otherwise.

8

Teaching

"That Which Relieves Their Hunger"

*The hungry cannot listen well to any teaching but that
which relieves their hunger.*

Mary McLeod Bethune, on visiting Liberia, 1952

In 1865, the Bureau of Refugees, Freedmen, and Abandoned Lands (commonly known as the Freedmen's Bureau) was housed in the War Department, just as the Bureau of Indian Affairs was in the 1820s. Educating black people was not initially a priority of the Freedmen's Bureau; it was organized for the managing of property and the maintenance of social order during a time of national upheaval. When the education of freedmen did become an issue for the postbellum federal government, the systems were built on pre-existing systems or were mainly sustained by black people's efforts to educate themselves. Most white missionaries who taught assumed black biological inferiority. Those few who did advocate African American education presupposed a moral, intellectual, or cultural absence within black families and communities. Government and philanthropic education often attempted to get the "Negroes" to accept their lower status in society while educating them enough to be materially useful. But not all teachers instructed from such a narrow primer.[1]

Between the Civil War and World War I, teacher education provided the major thrust for a higher education population explosion: the people were hungry for knowledge, and a teaching force needed to be trained. Most American colleges and universities of this era became teacher-training institutions, generally "producing more teachers than anything else." African American colleges were no exception to this trend. Black women were seldom offered administrative or prime teaching positions, routinely taught more students for less pay, and struggled to overcome external and internal badges of inferiority. But they moved with the rest of the country in a surge of educational development. Black women dedicated their lives to teaching; Cooper and Bethune detailed their pedagogies, leaving a guide to teaching relevant to institutions interested in developing socially engaged and civic-minded campuses.[2]

Cooper—Teaching beyond Books

Cooper argued that schools in general and teachers in particular were parts of communities and were therefore responsible to parents and families. In her estimation, before pointing to parental shortcoming as an explanation of students' maladaptive school behavior, school administrators and teachers needed to consider the larger social climate that impacted parental choices and options. Instead of blaming parents, teachers needed to hold themselves accountable for assisting students in any way possible and for gathering relevant information that might assist in fairly assessing and appropriately facilitating the students' development. Though the efficacy of teachers largely depended on institutional support, legal constraints, and physical resources, Cooper's insight was instructive because she saw herself as a community servant who was not bound by school grounds or college campus.

Historians have documented the increase in the number of lynchings between Emancipation and World War I and the great toll they took on black families, particularly in the South. When Cooper volunteered to teach in West Virginia at the war's end, she encountered a black family devastated by the murder of the father. While tutoring the children of the Berry family, she noticed that they were quiet and withdrawn. In "Sketches from a Teacher's Notebook: Loss of Speech through Isolation" (1923?), Cooper described what took place when she visited the family. The mother was at first reluctant to talk to Cooper.[3]

It was not until I had left W—that I understood the tragedy of Mrs. Berry's grim struggle with life. Her husband, an innocent man, had been torn from her arms by an infuriated mob and brutally murdered-lynched. The town realized its mistakes afterwards when the true culprit confessed but it was too late to bind up that broken family, and the humble drama of that obscure black woman like a wounded animal with her cubs literally digging herself in and then at bay dumbly turning to face—*America*—her "head bloody but unbowed." I swear the pathos and inexorable fatefulness of that titanic struggle—an inescapable one in the clash of American forces, is worthy of an Epic for its heroic grandeur and unconquerable grit. And I wondered what our brand of education, what our smug injunction that the home "is expected" to cooperate with the school will find or create for the help and guidance of such a home.[4]

By this time in her life, Cooper had held a college degree for forty years and had over fifty years of experience as a teacher. She took personally her duty to communicate with family members because she wanted to understand how most effectively to assist students.

Cooper maintained that it was the lack of institutional responsibility at the primary and secondary levels that impacted students' access, will, and preparedness to advance to postsecondary education. However, it was not the schools themselves that were to blame; rather, what severely impacted students' abilities to learn was a combination of the inequities of the larger social order in conjunction with schools that were divorced from surrounding communities. Schools placed the burden on parents to become involved, yet rarely did teachers and school officials offer the type of engaged, aware participation that they demanded from parents.

Cooper's memoirs as a teacher provided testament to her understanding of how neither experience nor education must be confined to the classroom. In "What Are We Worth?" (1892) and "On Education" (1930s?), she advocated "learning by doing," but she did not limit one to learning by doing alone. Regardless of birth status, social status, or desired vocation, each person should have the right to quality schooling that challenged the mind as much as the body. Admittedly, she argued, postsecondary liberal education was a leisurely activity; however, everyone was deserving of such leisure if he or she so desired. Basic literacy, moral instruction, science and mathematics, and a broad range of humanities courses should be available in all schools, beginning at the primary level, in order to provide the foundation that was needed should students choose to pursue liberal arts in college. Beyond educating people—particularly African Americans and women—to be "hands," education needed to train students to think critically and creatively.[5]

Born enslaved in the last of days of slavery, Cooper knew what it was like to be denied free movement, to have limited access to resources, and to be expected to work without financial gain or social progress. In "What Are We Worth?" her evaluation of industrial education and African Americans' collective contribution to America's political economy, she asserted a need for general education for workers beyond vocational specialization. To her, learning only to carry out physical tasks was incomplete education.[6]

White teachers often got hired before black teachers, even in segregated schools; black students and community members experienced difficulties relating to white instructors teaching a white curriculum. Some black parents felt that segregated schools were acceptable as long as black teachers were hired. However, Cooper argued against racial segregation in the schools and asserted that teachers in segregated schools—regardless of race—often wittingly or unwittingly instilled ideas of racial inferiority in the students. Cooper noticed the damage that segregation caused in black schools: "Segregation in education puts an undreamed of handicap on the student in the colored college from the all-unsuspecting teacher himself." Though she would not claim that HBCUs were inherently inferior, and she proudly became head of an all-black community college herself, she understood that it was important to have the option to attend an HBCU but believed that not having access to one's chosen institution because of legal segregation was wrong.[7]

Cooper had been teaching for ten years when *Plessy v. Ferguson* solidified segregation in 1896; she was still teaching in 1954 when the Supreme Court ruled on *Brown*. Though she critiqued much about black-led education, she challenged the perception that black schools needed to prove themselves worthy by emulating white structure and curriculum. In some cases, HBCUs developed an inferiority complex: the black "subjects" sought to be more "royal" than the white "king" by imposing standards that PWIs often themselves did not meet. For Cooper, white was not always right. Though she taught European literature, she interpreted the text through African culture. For example, in 1920, when she directed *A Midsummer Night's Dream* as a play for the dramatic reading class at Dunbar, she staged the production with Egyptian as well as Greek settings. Though she was conservative in her cultural aesthetic (rejecting broader expressions of blackness and embracing European "classics"), for her, black culture permeated all culture.[8]

Cooper critiqued quantitative measures as the sole indication of educative value, and she challenged standardized "objective" testing as the primary means of assessing student learning or teaching efficacy, scoffing: "I wonder that a robot has not been invented to make the assignments, give the objective tests, mark the scores and—chloroform all teachers who dared to bring original thought to the specific problems and needs of their pupils. But ideas are as potent today as they were 2,000 years ago." For her, all dimensions of higher education, from classroom testing to university accreditation processes, were infested with the automation of educational bureaucracy.[9]

Though she did teach and chair a department of romance languages at the college level and presided over a small community college, most of Cooper's teaching was at the secondary level. Her focus remained squarely on liberal arts, particularly the humanities, but her teaching was most certainly grounded in practical application and experiential approaches to those subjects.

Bethune—Training Citizens

Bethune was more an administrator than a classroom teacher; however, she made B-CC, the surrounding Daytona community, and Washington, D.C., into her classroom. She knew that learning equated to freedom and did not miss any opportunity to teach a lesson that might mean the difference between poverty and prosperity for black students. That the ignorance of her childhood was followed by her educational success in adolescence provided the impetus for her role as an educator. She felt that her role as a teacher was to "meet the pressing needs" of those in her community. She taught thrift, accountability to community, and self-determination as core principles for students of all ages. Her parents had been enslaved most of their lives, so Bethune intimately knew poverty, hunger, and want. Yet her grandmother provided strong moral guidance, and her parents were proud and resourceful people—as landowners, they were prosperous by South Carolina standards. Clearly she was also familiar with determination, compassion, and accomplishment in the face of adversity.[10]

Bethune's insistence on character education stemmed from personal experiences with selfish, rude, and privileged children. She reflected on her experience as a child relegated to the corn and cotton fields and recalled being painfully aware of the difference of a life of hard labor and one of opportunity to expand one's mind:

> I could see little white boys and girls going to school every day, learning to read and write; living in comfortable homes with all types of opportunities for growth and service and to be surrounded as I was with no opportunity for school life, no chances to grow.[11]

She was aware of the discrepancy in resources and critical incidents that spurred her to dedicate her life to learning. In the 1940 interview with Charles Johnson in which she told the story of a white child who yelled at her and said she had no right to read, Bethune expressed determination to turn her own pain into opportunity for others.[12]

The range of subjects at B-CC revealed education as a creative as well as an economic endeavor. At B-CC, there were crafts and fine arts classes, commercial dietetics, physical education, and music instruction, in addition to the secretarial, nursing, and domestic science courses. Though Bethune readily followed Washington's industrial model, she also worked with Frances Keyser, head of curriculum development, to expand the college beyond purely vocational instruction. One student who was enrolled at B-CC in 1915 recollected: "with Mrs. Bethune, there were just no short cuts, and another part of the character training, shall I call it, would be through the phrases that she would use, like 'whatever you do, do it to the best of your ability.' . . . [and] 'In whatever you do, strive to be an artist.' Wasn't that a concept?" Bethune personified the values taught at black colleges: basic communal ethics, creativity, and spirituality.[13]

Black history was of central importance to Bethune. In "Clarifying Our Vision with the Facts," she argued the significance of knowing and teaching African American history in addition to European history. She gave specific examples of culturally appropriate curricula:

When they learn the fairy tales of mythical king and queen and princess, we must let them hear, too, of the Pharaohs and African kings and brilliant pageantry of the Valley of the Nile; when they learn of Caesar and his legions, we must teach them of Hannibal and his Africans; when they learn of Shakespeare and Goethe, we must teach them of Pushkin and Dumas. When they read of Columbus, we must introduce the Africans who touched the shores of America before Europeans emerged from savagery; when they are thrilled by Nathan Hale, baring his breast and crying: "I have but one life to give for my country," we must make their hearts leap to see Crispus Attucks stand and fall for liberty on Boston Common with the red blood of freedom streaming down his breast. With the *Tragic Era* we give them *Black Reconstruction*; with Edison, we give them Jan Matzeliger; with John Dewey, we place Booker T. Washington; above the folk-music of the cowboy and the hill-billy, we place the spiritual and the "blues"; when they boast of Maxfield Parrish, we show them E. Simms Campbell. Whatever man has done, we have done—and often better. As we tell this story, as we present to the world the facts, our pride in racial achievement grows, and our respect in the eyes of all men heightens.[14]

This speech reveals a side of Bethune not commonly recognized; though she was a skilled diplomat and held conservative views on some issues, she also demystified and directly challenged white power.

Bethune saw women as central to education, taught as a community-based activity, and believed that universal education was the foundation of a strong democracy. Bethune held that women's training was necessary for both public and private service. She saw mothers—as centers of the home—

as forming the first line of "good citizenship." She wanted teachers to take vows to teach democracy in schools but also in their own homes at their "hearthstones."[15]

As an educator, Bethune incorporated the Daytona community into her teaching practices. In 1915, during her unending efforts to grow the school, she invited the mayor and city council members to "inspect" the campus. After the visit, she published an open invitation to city residents in the *Daytona Morning Journal* to visit and take part in school activities. This was her constant effort to garner support, and she wrote that the school should benefit the local community as much as the community supported the school.[16]

She felt her role was to educate community members—black and white—as much as to educate her campus-based students. Toward that end, she successfully held integrated meetings at the high tide of segregation and utilized school resources to teach community members who fell outside the traditional definition of college student. In her *Twenty-fifth Annual Report of the President* (1926), she reported:

the confidence of our community is being very appreciably strengthened. Through Sunday afternoon community meetings a bond is established that definitely cements the friendship and interest of tourists and residents. The attendance at these meeting[s] all during the year attests to the appreciation and interest of the entertainment of this unique, colorful gathering.[17]

In addition to seeing the community as partners in learning, she often utilized community members as teaching assistants to enhance the learning of students enrolled at the college.

As a teacher, Bethune partnered with her community; as an administrator, she provided structural support for all teachers to engage in the surrounding community for the betterment of all. In her frequent reports to benefactors, Bethune documented innumerable interactions with various representatives of local, state, national, and international society. She was a genius at networking and a talented organizer with a gift for creating—and maintaining—relationships on a micro, macro, and global level. When she ascended to her federal post, she continued to build on a national level, but long before her appointment in the 1930s, she saw the importance of local collaborative efforts to improve African American education.

In her 1924 presidential address to the National Association of Teachers in Colored Schools, Bethune advocated improved teaching networks:

Fellow teachers, this is no time to parley or hesitate. The gauntlet is down, the challenge is out. It is ours to meet in the might of our organized strength, and through this organization make known our educational needs and rights, and contend for every educational privilege, vouchsafed to our children as the coming citizens of a free democracy.[18]

Whereas Cooper argued that access to education was a human right, Bethune would employ the language of democracy and citizenship to claim African American rights to access. Though the reasoning was very different, the conclusions were the same: African Americans, and particularly black women, had a right to educational opportunity far beyond what they had been afforded.

Though B-CC evolved into a coeducational institution, Bethune's primary focus was the education of young black women. Her same-sex education experience at Scotia Seminary and training with Laney exercised a lasting positive influence; even after B-CC became coeducational, she once attempted to return to an all-women's institution. In her estimation, the aim of her work was to "uplift Negro girls spiritually, morally, intellectually, and industrially . . . [and] to develop Christian character."[19] In her essay "A Philosophy of Education for Negro Girls" (1926), she stated:

> for the past seventy years the Negro has experienced various degrees
> of freedom. . . . A great deal of this new freedom rests upon the type
> of education which the Negro woman will receive. Early emancipa-
> tion did not concern itself with giving advantages to Negro girls. The
> domestic realm was her field and no one sought to remove her. Even
> here, she was not given special training for her tasks. Only those with
> extraordinary talents were able to break the shackles of bondage. . . .
> Very early in my life, I saw the vision of what our women might con-
> tribute to the growth and development of the race—if they were given
> a certain type of intellectual training. I longed to see women, Negro
> women, hold in their hands diplomas which bespoke achievement.[20]

Bethune worked within a network of dedicated black women educators. Though she focused on private sphere and vocational education, she recognized public accomplishments as well. She hailed the achievements of her contemporaries:

> has the Negro girl proved herself worthy of the intellectual advantages
> which have been given her? What is your answer when I tell you that

. . . such are Nannie Burroughs, Charlotte Hawkins Brown; they are proprietors of business, we recall Madame Walker and Annie Malone; they are doing excellent work in the field of Medicine, Literary Art, Painting and Music. Of that large group let us mention Mary Church Terrell and Jessie Fauset; Hazel Harrison, Caterina Jarboro and Marian Anderson as beacon lights. One very outstanding woman is a banker. Others are leaders in Politics.[21]

Bethune not only recorded the "talented tenth" but acknowledged the contribution of the masses of black women who were, just one generation out of enslavement, making strides toward participating in democracy their own ways:

in the rank of average training we witness strivings of Negro women in the school rooms of counties and cities pouring out their own ambitions to see them achieved in the lives of the next generation. The educated Negro girl has lifted the standard of the Negro home so that the present generation is better born and therefore has the promise of a better future.[22]

Bethune's view of struggle was of particular interest. In "A Philosophy of Education for Negro Girls" (1920), she argued that black women should be prepared for struggle since the world weighed harsher on them than most others:

Negro women have always known struggle. This heritage is just as much to be desired as any other. Our girls should be taught to appreciate and welcome it. . . . Every Negro girl should pray for that pioneering spirit. Let her Arithmetic, History, Economics, and what not, be taught with the zeal of struggle; the determination to win by mettle and fairness and pluck. For such she needs after she leaves the school of life and enters life's school.[23]

This question of noble struggle is significant; one might ask, should this be a universal principle of education? Should all students aspire to struggle? Did black women's historical struggles make them especially equipped? Regardless of the answers, Bethune knew that her standpoint did not allow any other option but to prepare black women for inevitable hardships they would face in earning their degrees and after graduation.

Bethune was the ultimate example of black women's capacity to build institutions. B-CC did not receive senior college status until 1945, but within its first ten years, the school had instructed thousands of girls in academic subjects (English, science, algebra, geometry, black history, and music) and vocational subjects (sewing, cooking, weaving, dairy agriculture, and gardening) at the high school level. Higher education for blacks in Florida was virtually nonexistent. Though three other HBCUs existed (Florida A&M, Florida Memorial, and Edward Waters College), by 1910 Florida had not produced one African American woman college graduate. The major state school, the University of Florida, remained staunchly segregated until the 1960s. By building her school into a college, Bethune provided academic hope for black girls in an otherwise barren swampland.[24]

Black Women Teachers and Institutional Leadership

Cooper and Bethune taught, led schools, and developed ideas with historical understanding of the central role black women played in education; they were simply carrying forward a well-established tradition. A century before their leadership, as evidenced in the first wave of attainment, black women nationwide opened schools to educate black people. Women dominated the profession of teaching in the United States—74 percent; the percentage of African American women teachers was even higher than the national average—76 percent. By 1930, black women in the teaching profession outnumbered men by a ratio of over five to one. Though in later years the majority of these teachers were trained at HBCUs, the first generation of teachers graduated from PWIs.[25]

Many followed the lead of mid-nineteenth-century women and, after attending college, headed their own schools. Fanny Coppin headed the Institute for Colored Youth (ICY) in Philadelphia, and Mary Patterson became the principal at the Colored High School in Washington, D.C. Lucy Laney in Georgia, Elizabeth Wright in South Carolina, and Mary Bethune in Florida were joined by Charlotte Hawkins Brown in North Carolina and Nannie Helen Burroughs in D.C. in developing schools to advance black women's education. The curriculum varied, but scholars of all ages who attended schools like those highlighted here increased their chance to attend college and educate successive generations.[26]

Fanny Coppin cultivated ICY as a fertile ground of academic excellence but especially focused on teacher training. She created a normal school training course that included theory of teaching, school management, and methods training; students in the Preparatory Department later reorganized the course as a school mainstay. Under Coppin's leadership, ICY benefited from distinguished staff, including Richard Greener, a Harvard graduate (who also taught in D.C.) and Edward Bouchet, a Yale graduate who returned to New Haven to earn a doctorate in 1876. ICY also played a central role in the surrounding community.

Though praised for earning an early B.A., Oberlin graduate Mary Jane Patterson (1840–94) is not widely recognized as the foremother of the African American educated class. Patterson did not publish journal articles or books, but from 1871 to 1884 she built a significant foundation that became a cornerstone of multigenerational black scholarly development. As Terrell pointed out in a 1917 journal article, it was Patterson who transformed the black school in D.C. from a preparatory school to an academically advanced high school. Though Harvard graduate Richard Greener headed the school during the 1872 school year, Patterson guided the school for over a decade. The high school became M Street School (1889) and then Dunbar High School (1916), an epicenter of black genius that successfully prepared black students for top-ranked national and international universities. Thirty years after Patterson (1901–6), Cooper became principal and upheld the academic focus that Patterson had established early on. Patterson is largely responsible for a school that later produced Allison Davis (anthropologist), Charles Drew (M.D.), and the highest number of black doctorate earners before 1954.[27]

Similar to her northern counterparts, Lucy Laney (1854–1933) insisted on taking a more challenging course of study than was traditionally offered to women. Laney graduated from Lewis School in Macon, Georgia, and was one of the 27 women of the first 89 students who entered the AMA's Atlanta University. While Patterson and Coppin became principals of existing schools, Laney founded her own in 1886, which became Haines Normal and Industrial Institute, affiliated with the Presbyterian Church. Laney developed Haines into a leading preparatory high school in the South that attracted well-trained, dedicated teachers, most notably Mary Bethune, who in turn developed a school of her own. Laney, also part of the black women's club and educators' network, worked closely with Terrell and Cooper. Though she never married or bore children, she birthed a school that is still operating today and, like Bethune, she rests eternal on the campus she built.[28]

Elizabeth Evelyn Wright (1872–1906) was born in Talbotton, Georgia— the seventh of twenty-one children. Wright opened a school in the South that evolved, against all odds, into a college. Voorhees College in Denmark, South Carolina, became a haven for opportunity despite white southerners' opposition to black schools. Wright, an 1894 graduate of Tuskegee, started four schools in different locations: they were either burned down or she was driven out by hostile whites. In April 1897, she started a school with fourteen students above the local general store that grew and stood the test of time. Sadly, six months after Wright married Martin Menafee, the school bookkeeper, she died at the age of thirty-four. Voorhees Industrial School became affiliated with the Episcopal Church in 1929 and earned college rating in 1964. Fortunately, the school continues to educate students and "make a way" for those who are dedicated to learning.[29]

Charlotte Hawkins Brown (1883–1961) opened Alice Freeman Palmer Memorial Institute in 1902 and served as its president for fifty years. Brown was born in North Carolina, but her family became part of the post-Reconstruction migration, and she was raised in Massachusetts. After graduating from high school in Cambridge, Hawkins returned to North Carolina to teach at an AMA school. Though the association closed that school and many others a year later, Hawkins remained and built an institute for the youth of Sedalia. In keeping with the strict social guidelines she articulated in *The Correct Thing to Do, to Say, to Wear* (1941), Hawkins interviewed and handpicked her student body, which never grew above two hundred per year, and trained them to be respectable, responsible, and proper citizens. Though the school closed in 1971, a decade after her death, it provided a valuable training ground and positive influence for thousands of young men and women—including her niece, Natalie Cole.[30]

Black women's effective teaching inspired generations of dedicated school leaders. Nannie Helen Burroughs (1879–1961) was born in Virginia and attended high school at the M Street School, where Mary Terrell and Anna Cooper had great influence on her intellectual growth and leadership skills development. Burroughs founded the Women's Convention (WC), the auxiliary group to the National Baptist Convention, and with the support of the WC, opened the National Training School for Women and Girls (1909). The junior and high school became famous for "the three B's: Bible, bath, and broom," and served more than two thousand young women in the first twenty-five years. Burroughs's work in D.C. mirrored efforts of thousands of other dedicated teachers and community leaders who passed on lessons of thrift, spirituality, and empowerment that overcame barriers to black achievement.[31]

Comparative Educational Philosophies

Fanny Coppin and Rose Browne, two of the scholars who wrote autobiographies discussed earlier, provided valuable insights about early teacher training. Coppin's *Hints on Teaching* (the text accompanying the 1913 *Reminiscences of School Life*), was especially relevant in defining groundbreaking pedagogical methods. Her recommendations for teaching included a rejec-

tion of corporal punishment, which was still common at the time, and a rec-
ommendation of kinesthetic methods for teaching geography. Of additional
interest was the notion that students should be held to high standards but
also given the tools with which to meet those standards.

Coppin wrote of the nerve-wracking pressure to reconcile her professors'
high standards and low expectations while at Oberlin. When she became
a teacher, she maintained high standards for her black students and, unlike many teachers of her day, assumed that all students, with the proper
support, could achieve high-quality academic work. She was selective with
promotion, and although she practiced character education, she did not en-
dorse social promotion.

Coppin studied political economy and noted with great resentment the
racism present in the trade unions in the late nineteenth century. Unlike
those who proclaimed fundamental tension between industrial and liberal
education, Coppin recognized the compatibility of higher learning and work.
Like Cooper, she asserted the need of the working class to be educated; this
was controversial because many thought that maids and janitors should be
workers, not learners. She advocated special training of those who went into
industrial services and did not consider domestic service or manual labor at
all "unskilled." Her own status as an enslaved youth and adolescent domestic
servant influenced her perception of the ways labor can be used as a replace-
ment for educational opportunity.[32]

Like Bethune, Coppin did not believe that high academic training auto-
matically equated to high moral training, and she assumed that both were
needed to qualify a person as truly educated. Moreover, formal school or
college training provided no guarantee of a person's intelligence. She wrote,
"unfortunately book learning is respectable, and there is so much of it all
about us, that it is apt to crowd out the prosy process of thinking, compar-
ing, reasoning, to which our wisest efforts should be directed." Too often, attainment of an institutional degree acted as a poor substitute for wisdom. In
addition, she admonished those who lacked common decency, writing that
"good manners will often take people where neither money nor education
will take them," and that, "however brilliant a person may be intellectually,
however skillful . . . [it does not eliminate the need for] character, kindness,
and love."[33]

Students needed to learn lessons applicable outside of the classroom and
be active in their learning process. In the chapter "Methods of Instruction,"
she wrote: "I am always sorry to hear that such and such a person is going
to school to be educated. This is a great mistake. If the person is to get the

benefit of what we call education, he must educate himself, under the direction of the teacher."[34] And later:

> we want to lift education out of the slough of the passive voice. Little Mary goes to school to be educated, and her brother John goes to the high school for the same purpose. It is too often the case that the passive voice has the right of way, whereas in the very beginning we should call into active service all the faculties of mind and body.[35]

Her philosophy of teaching pre-dated both Woodson's notion of "miseducation" (1933) and Paulo Freire's oft-cited treatise against the passive "banking method" of teaching (*Pedagogy of the Oppressed*, 1970).

Coppin's text illustrates intersections between African American women's educational philosophies and work by educators like John Dewey. For instance, some similarities can be seen in two of Dewey's seminal works, *Democracy and Education: An Introduction to the Philosophy of Education* (1916) and *Experience and Education* (1938).

Dewey wrote, "in education, the currency of these externally imposed aims is responsible for the emphasis put upon the notion of preparation for a remote future and for rendering the work of both teacher and pupil mechanical and slavish." Later, he noted: "the trouble with traditional education was not that educators took upon themselves the responsibility for providing an environment. The trouble was that they did not consider the other factor in creating an experience; namely, the powers and purposes of those taught." Further: "there is, I think, no point in the philosophy of progressive education which is sounder than its emphasis upon the importance of the participation of the learner in the formation of the purposes which direct his activities in the learning process." Here, obvious parallels exist between Dewey's and Coppin's perceptions of student-centered curriculum, self-reflective pedagogy, and active learning; however, it must be noted that Coppin published her book three and twenty-five years, respectively, before Dewey's oft-cited texts.[36]

Rose Butler Browne also provided historical perspective on teaching, recording her reminiscences half a century after Coppin, with similar observations. Browne, who began teaching while enrolled in Rhode Island Normal School, recollected:

> In my classes were slow readers and children with special learning needs, and hovering nearby was the irate parent who simply knew that his or her child was not getting the needed attention. Obviously, if I

was to survive at the Coggeshall School, things had to be done differently. So I did them differently. Instead of singing the scale—do, re, me, fa, sol, la, ti, do, re—we learned rhythm by stepping to the music of the waltz. . . . By trying to show a practical motive for learning a given subject, I soon had most of the children reasonably happy and productive. Most of all, my children knew they had a teacher who loved them and wanted to help them.[37]

Browne, like Coppin, loved her work and her students. Though she expressed ample frustration and certainly did not "like" every student, she understood she was to be guided by duty and appreciation for all humankind. She also understood that dedication to her students was not enough to guarantee her adequacy as a teacher. She worked closely with parents to improve their ability to assess their child's progress and held herself to the same high standards she expected of her students. Kinesthetic techniques like those described above demonstrated her ability to teach to the students' needs rather than by rigid pedantic methods that often alienated students with different learning styles. Children designated as "slow" could often perform to standard when engaged teachers, appropriate instruction, and patience were made available.

Though response to her teaching and administrative style was positive, she noted, "If I, a Negro, wanted to get ahead in my chosen profession, my credentials would have to be better than those of most white applicants." With this realization in mind, she attained her master's degree and then pursued a degree at Harvard. She acknowledged the inescapable hierarchy of degree attainment and used it to her advantage: though she could not escape the condition of her racial stigma, she could at least acquire a tool to aid her cause. She wrote: "Although some civil rights activists believe I went to Harvard to crack a hateful segregation barrier, the truth is I sought an education so superior that it could never be referred to as a Negro education. I wanted to start any future educational conference with my credentials unquestioned." It was ironic that in order to improve schooling for southern underclass blacks, some needed a northern, upper-class, "white" diploma.[38]

Black Women Professors

A survey entitled "The First Black Faculty Members at the Nation's Flagship State Universities" revealed that for the first black women college graduates, there were no faculty positions available. Sarah Woodson Early was among the first black women to teach at the college level (Wilberforce, Ohio, 1859), and after her there came a few notable faculty such as Josephine Silone Yates, who taught at Lincoln Institute in Missouri (1880–89) and headed the Department of Natural Sciences. There were forty-eight black women who earned Ph.D.s by 1938; at least fifteen worked in D.C. (the majority at Howard). There were also adjunct faculty like Dorothy Height, who taught religion at Columbia while in a master's program at New York University. Height, a member of Delta Sigma Theta Sorority, also taught internationally, for a semester at University of Delhi, India, in 1952. Though a few black women earned faculty positions before *Brown*, a critical mass of black women college professors was nonexistent until the 1960s.[39]

In the 1920s, after the first solid generation of college graduates gained teaching certificates, black high schools were more likely to have well-qualified black teachers. Because of Jim Crow policies, black high school teachers often held a master's degree—or occasionally a doctorate.

For those who had college or graduate degrees and did not want to teach at elementary or secondary schools, the dean of women's position at the college level enabled them to utilize their advanced skills. By the 1920s, the position uniformly required a B.A. so deans modeled the advanced learning that they encouraged in students. The dean of women position was not purely administrative; the academic function was important as well. As stated by administrators at Virginia Normal and Industrial Institute, a dean of women's (or lady principal's) "relation to the educational policy of the school can be made concrete by actual membership upon and participation with committees. The dean needs to be well informed on such subjects as ethics, psychology, and sociology. She needs to be able to appreciate individual differences and to have knowledge of intelligence tests and their application." The reference to academic subjects is telling: the dean of women had to be aware of relevant theories in order to be effective in practice.[40]

For those black women who eventually became university professors, the glass ceiling for pay and promotion was unreasonably low, which is what prompted Woodson to urge Dykes to move west toward richer prospects. But Dykes stayed in D.C., and after she earned her Ph.D., she taught at Howard. Woodson was right. Despite her doctoral degree, she was denied pay raises and promotions because of her gender. Men's higher pay was justified as a "family wage," but women were caretakers, and their role as providers was evident, even if conveniently ignored.[41]

But some black women professors, like Mary Branch, did pursue job opportunities in the West. Tillotson in Austin, Texas—now Huston-Tillotson College—was initially a woman's institution, founded in 1877 by the AMA;

it turned coeducational in 1935. Branch was heavily recruited to assume the presidency in 1930 and remained head administrator there until her death in 1944. She graduated from Virginia State College and earned a Ph.B. and a master's degree from the University of Chicago. She earned credits toward her doctorate, but her work schedule prevented her from finishing the degree.

When Branch took the lead of Tillotson, the college was in financial and physical disarray. By 1935, student enrollment had jumped from 69 to 500 and the library holdings had grown from 2,000 to 21,000 volumes. She solidified the curriculum and received an "A" rating from the Southern Association of Colleges and Secondary Schools. Like Bethune, Branch did heavy local outreach and was the president of the Austin NAACP chapter.[42]

Black women in universities before 1954 rarely had the chance to be professors in the contemporary sense of the word. Even when they earned the doctorate and worked at a university, they not only advanced research and pedagogy but were administrators, counselors, and community organizers. Exemplars in this category include Merz Tate, a 1941 Harvard graduate who taught at Howard for twenty-five years and who effectively moved institutions and international relations toward equal distribution of resources. They were, above all, dedicated teachers and public servants. In contrast, for the dominant culture, doctorates were less training for pedagogy than a ticket to a professorship in which teaching was of least concern.

The Faculty Club

As research became the dominant institutional ideal, "scientific" training entranced college professors. Faculty trained students in scientific research while divorcing—in the name of "reason"—the moral implications of their research findings. Students were not required to grapple with the potential ramifications of their experiments, which involved them in the same cognitive dissonance, rationalization, and hypocrisy present in the construction of U.S. society. Professionalization of this sort rapidly transformed the professorate into an insulated group of nonteachers who apparently neither realized nor cared that lecturing was not necessarily teaching.[43]

As the faculty changed, "the American faculty club [developed into] merely one more occupational variation of the gentleman's club—the manufacturer's club, the banker's club, the broker's club. There in an atmosphere of sociability the organization could be advanced; there something of that old-time casual spirit and sheer good fun might be recaptured." This club was for comfort, shared agenda, and validation of self-designated experts;

outsiders need not apply. But as more graduate degrees were earned, the faculty changed, engendering internal rifts. Initially, college faculty were clergymen or trained in theology: "of 130 members of the Union College faculty between 1795 and 1884, 55 were clergymen. Two thirds of the professors at Dartmouth between 1828 and 1862 had had theological training. The faculty at Lafayette was composed entirely of clergymen in 1841, and in 1868 at Princeton on a faculty of 10, there were 7 Presbyterian ministers." These professors, though religious, did not always deny the value of science, nor did they see scientific objectivity as incongruent with religion. For them, natural and physical sciences proved God's existence: "the evangelical saw science as a useful tool in demonstrating the wondrous ways of God." In the modern American university, however, professors' training was secular. Religion was ghettoized. The faculty club suffered bitter division in the move to centralize power in indisputable knowledge claims outside the purview of God.[44]

With enhanced graduate studies, teaching assistants became a source of cheap labor that even further removed the professor from teaching duties. Intended to be an apprentice system, exploitation of graduate teaching assistants became commonplace as professors assumed the role of revered untouchables—aloof geniuses not to be questioned or bothered to explain things to simpleminded undergraduates. Adjunct faculty, often those who could not or did not care to compete in the publication race, were another exploitable source of labor in the university.[45]

As trustees became more important for securing funds to increase physical grounds or purchase prestigious scholars, they gained more power. A struggle between faculty and trustees ensued, as exemplified by the 1915 AAUP declaration. The question of faculty rights and responsibilities was embedded in the tenure system; how was the professor to be evaluated? Though research, teaching, and service were the three pillars of academies, teaching at PWIs became irrelevant, service to campus was deemed optional, and service to community was seen as a waste of energy, discouraged at best.[46]

In the mainstream university, course work became a means for students to achieve a financial end: college students sought a diploma so they could earn more money. Education, far from being spiritual, moral, or intellectual striving, became a twisted dance of supply, demand, and business cost/benefit analysis. Students were concerned mainly with the expedience of the bottom line, and "grades" replaced learning. In this environment, some black women continued their dedication to old-fashioned ideals of service, community, and family—which resulted in their further marginalization in the academy. When the doctorate in education was developed, black women flocked to graduate schools in that field. Even those who did not pursue advanced degrees continued to populate teacher certification programs, and teaching remained the overwhelming professional choice of women in general and black women in particular.[47]

Teaching—A Most Noble Profession

Collins clarifies that not all African American women were teachers or aspired to selflessly serve their communities:

> Neither Black feminist thought as a critical social theory nor Black feminist practice can be static. . . . stressing the importance of Black women's centrality to Black feminist thought does not mean that all African-American women desire, are positioned, or are qualified to exert this type of intellectual leadership.[48]

Thus, it is important to track historic patterns of black women educators but also to understand that these patterns were not universal or without exception. Not all black women taught, and of those who did, not all were gregarious, professional, or effective. Some, like Frances Harper, Ida Wells, Mary Terrell, and Charlotte Grimké, taught only briefly and excused themselves early, admitting their inability or unwillingness to give what teaching required. They uplifted in other ways.

Of those in the historical record who did teach and administrate by profession, I have observed the following consistencies: (1) black women overcame many barriers and participated in a broad range of formal and informal, academic and intellectual pursuits; (2) black women linked educational attainment to the practice of community service; and (3) though black women articulated various individual ideologies regarding the methods, goals, and outcomes of education, as a group they maintained an epistemological standpoint that assumed a connection between educational attainment and social responsibility. Their teaching, regardless of era, level, or venue, reflected perseverance, diversity of interest, community service, and social justice epistemology.

What is of great interest to present-day scholars is the rich appearance of the collective tapestry woven from these women's ideas. As educators, African American women employed creative teaching methods, expanded learning beyond the classroom, and often disavowed curricular texts if the ideas ran counter to their lived experience. They held high standards of academic excellence but also held high standards for democratic participation—unequivocally pointing out a lag in the Eurocentric classroom, the boardroom, or the courtroom.

Collins contends that black women have no greater capacity or responsibility for human empowerment than does any other race or gender. She offers a range of approaches to black feminist thinking, not asserting that black women were a monolithic group poised to save the world but rather arguing that researching black women's history of oppression and resistance offers hints on how to eradicate social, political, and economic inequalities, writing: "the words and actions of these diverse black women intellectuals may address markedly different audiences. Yet in their commitment to black women's empowerment within a context of social justice, they advance the strikingly similar theme of the oneness of all human life." Unlike many professional university faculty in the twenty-first century, many black women felt a duty to instruct well and regarded directing the learning process as an honor. The educational process could not be removed from community engagement, and they felt the need to teach by example as well as by instruction.[49]

Feminization of the teaching profession, characterized by low pay, was mirrored in the white American population, thus education has been predominantly a woman's issue, although the administration of higher education has been male-dominated since its inception. The higher the level of education, the fewer women were allowed to participate. Education was not the only occupation in which this phenomenon occurred: women were cooks, men were chefs; women were nurses, men were doctors; women were teachers, men were professors. This held true across racial lines.[50]

Though Cooper reached the height of degree attainment and unquestionably outclassed most (past or present) who considered themselves "academics," she identified herself as a teacher, not a professor. She wrote the poem "No Flowers Please"—at the age of eighty-two—asking that, when she passed away, no one take up a collection plate. Rather, she requested:

No flowers please, just the smell of sweet understanding
The knowing look that sees Beyond and says gently and kindly
"Somebody's Teacher is on Vacation now.
Resting for the Fall Opening."[51]

Though distinguished and ever-scholarly, she deemed teaching as a noble calling and criticized the professors who neither took the time nor had the patience to learn to teach their students well.

9

Service

"A Beneficent Force"

The only sane education, therefore is that which conserves the very lowest
stratum [and] according to his capacity ... converts [each] into a beneficent
force in service of the world.
Anna Julia Cooper, Howard University, 1930

Despite the various means of learning, black women educators' articulation of the function of education was tied directly to community service.
However, they did not all have the same definition of service. There was
general belief in an innate and reciprocal relationship between education,
community service, and social justice. "Social justice" was characterized by
both human and civil rights: this included increased access to resources like
health care and land, improved quality of life through freedom from mental
or physical violence, freedom from labor or cultural exploitation, and equal
opportunity to excel politically, economically, and intellectually. These ideals were present in mainstream American higher education but faltered in
the face of personal gain or race privilege. Though they varied in tone, the
voices of black women educational leaders identified a link between education and advocacy.[1]

Cooper–Service for Social Justice

For Cooper, earning an education was a form of service, and those who had
the privilege of formal learning owed their gains to the community. Cooper's definition was directly tied to her conceptualization of race and gender
identity. Her idea of service was far more profound than current definitions
of campus-based committee work. She insisted that educators engaged in
community service work for the purpose of social justice. Social change was
not specific enough; justice was the goal of philanthropic projects, and education played a central role in advancing the nation toward social equality.
Without eliminating the inequities that caused the need for "service," altru-
istic service alone was ineffective.

Cooper's idea of justice was based in freedom. She interpreted "freedom" in a way that encompassed all human beings. In "Woman versus the Indian," she wrote an open rebuttal of Reverend Anne Shaw, a speaker at an 1891 meeting of the National Women's Council. Though Shaw protested individual prejudices against black women in employment, she summarily disparaged Native Americans by advocating that white women demand civil rights before "the Indians" were allowed to claim theirs. Cooper saw this argument—employed by white women against black men during the suffrage battle of the 1870s—as divisive, racist, antihumanist, and anti-Christian:

> woman should not, even by inference, or for the sake of argument, seem to disparage what is weak. For woman's cause is the cause of the weak; and when all the weak shall have received their due consideration, then woman will have her "rights," and the Indian will have his rights, and the Negro will have his rights, and all the strong will have learned at last to deal justly, to love mercy, and to walk humbly; and our fair land will have been taught the secret of universal courtesy which is after all nothing but the art, the science, and the religion of regarding one's neighbor as one's self, and to do for him as we would, were conditions swapped, that he do for us. . . . All prejudices, whether of race, sect, or sex, class pride and caste distinctions are the belittling inheritance and badge of snobs and prigs.[2]

Freedom, as Cooper saw it, was a universal responsibility of each to all. Her concept of equality was not compartmentalized or subject to special conditions, and equality was a uniting cause rather than divisive. Though she did participate in uplift movements, she understood that the basis of such work was not a singular group's position but rather that all those who were oppressed should fight for equality in solidarity with other disenfranchised groups.

She wrote that insofar as we see our fate as human beings tied together, to that extent shall we succeed in uplifting all of humanity: if we do not all gain social stability, none of us will. Ultimately, all excel or none do. Though Cooper asserted that black women, by virtue of their compounded subjugated circumstance as African Americans and as women, possessed unique insight into social solutions, she held everyone responsible for community building and collective empowerment.[3] In "What Are We Worth?" she demanded that all citizens give in greater measure than they receive:

> The question must in the first place be an individual one for every man of whatever race: Am I giving to the world an equivalent of what it has

given and is giving to me? Have I a margin on the outside of consumption for surplus production? We owe it to the world to give out at least as much as we have taken in, but if we aim to be accounted a positive value we must leave it a little richer than we found it.[4]

Everyone owes according to his or her capacity to give, and everyone owes more than is received.

Cooper did not envision service as an easy or utopian concept; service was beyond simple measure. In a 1930 response to a survey by Charles Johnson, she declared:

> my "racial philosophy" is not far removed from my general philosophy of life: that the greatest happiness comes from altruistic service and this is in reach of all whatever race and condition. The "Service" meant here is not a pious idea of being used; any sort of exploitation whether active or passive is to my mind hateful. Nor is the "Happiness" a mere bit of Pollyanna stuff.[5]

Cooper's comments revealed a conviction of the need for service that transcends the sentimental or romantic. Rather than mindless kindness, she insisted that service be political. Her sense of service provided insight into her lifelong dedication to the "education of a neglected people."[6]

However, despite her rejection of romantic approaches to service, she accorded women a particular role in service to society. She argued that women constituted a societal "moral police" because they possessed a "feminine flavor" that provided special influence. Southern white women, Cooper claimed, were to be held responsible for the brute actions of southern white men; though it was the men who were ignoble, it was the influence of southern women, as "ladies," that would—or should—keep their men in check. Women had to be honest about calling honor into question when men behaved dishonorably. Cooper gave full credence to a gendered sense of moral responsibility because often it was the southern white ladies themselves who claimed a higher sense of morality—she simply was holding those accountable who made the claim. She herself played on her identity as a "southern woman" and thought her role as a black woman required her to be above reproach in order to be a moral compass for all black people. She argued that only women could say "when and where I enter, the whole race enters with me," and thereby challenged black male definitions of leadership. She carried her argument to an extreme and suggested that only women could perform the greatest of all social service—abolish capitalism.[7]

Cooper's critique of economic class systems, along with racial and gendered caste systems, provided a complex base from which to understand the need of all citizens to have access to food, clothing, shelter, employment, and education. In "The Social Settlement: What It Is and What It Does" (1913), she argued that African American communities needed basic services, like access to clean water, and that there should be churches rather than bars in neighborhoods. Cooper was well aware of the role settlement houses played in community building and the vital role that college students played in the settlement movement. As Rudolph explained:

> a characteristic collegiate expression of Progressivism, especially in urban institutions, was the college settlement house, an institution which enabled young men and women to combine the old Christian purpose of the colleges with the new efforts to cope with the breakdown of American promise in the cities.

Settlement work began at Oxford and Cambridge, England, in the 1860s. In the United States, Smith College developed a house in 1887, and then New York, Philadelphia, Boston, and Chicago followed. Settlement house events included "lectures on scientific subjects by university professors, dispensaries, diet counseling, libraries, English classes, co-operative coal clubs, studies in American history, and citizenship clubs," among other activities.[8]

Rudolph underscored that though the settlements were linked to colleges, they were founded by college students, not professors or administrators. Students pledged:

> "We believe," said the creed, "in self-sacrifice for the good of all the people.... We want to be good citizens.... [We want to make Chicago a place where] government may be pure, her officers honest, and every corner of her territory a place fit to grow the best men and women, who shall rule over her."[9]

This pledge by Chicago students, like similar proclamations on the national level, advocated social service for the good of all people, but what "all people" meant, in essence, was all white people. Cooper asserted that only when settlement house workers eliminated racial prejudices could they really offer services that were truly effective and noteworthy:

> Paradoxically enough, the very period of the world that witnesses the most widespread activity in uplift movements and intensest devotion to social service finds in America the hard wall of race prejudice against Negroes most emphatically bolted and barred. This is perhaps because the transfer of narrow minds from individual selfishness to

group selfishness covers with the glamour of religious consecration the sordid meanness of one race towards another.[10]

In spite of such critiques, Cooper lauded the social settlement movement and mentioned Jane Addams and Hull House in Chicago as exemplars of potential community-university collaboration.

Cooper wrote of great possibilities for those involved in this movement: "The Social Settlement, with its home life, its neighborhood visiting, its clubs, classes and personal service, is endeavoring to bring higher ideals of life and character to many who are largely cut off from good influences and opportunities; to stimulate ambitions, raise moral standards, strengthen character and develop capacity for self-help." She was in line with Progressive ideals and supported the suffrage, temperance, and settlement house work, but she charged that those ideals of service were empty without actual justice for all, regardless of race or gender.[11]

Bethune's Will and Testament of Service

Bethune affirmed that community service and social responsibility were core tenets of higher education. She saw service as care for one's community and modeled herself after Miss Wilson, one of her early teachers, who demonstrated "patience, tenderness, and kindness." For Bethune, everyone had a communal responsibility, but it was the charge of the middle class to uplift the underprivileged and disenfranchised masses. Bethune "resigned" herself to service and committed herself with missionary zeal to those people and institutions in need of assistance.[12]

While Bethune was a beneficiary of much philanthropy, she also passed on resources to organizations she worked with. In a 1923 letter to Ms. Payne and Ms. Jackson, matrons of a local girls' home she helped manage, she wrote, "as long as I have a penny, I am willing to share it with you." Bethune's policy of sharing resources exemplified the communal foundations of the black women's club movement—a dedication to collective struggle and collective gain. When she founded the Home for Delinquent Girls in Ocala (1921), she held all of Florida accountable for the girls' well-being and felt quite justified in soliciting support from Florida residents far and wide.[13]

As with all college presidents, Bethune understood the importance of raising funds for institutional development and sustainability. She linked advancement in higher education to larger social issues; she also wrote as a southern woman to southern white women (of YWCA and similar organizations) about the need to join forces for mutual benefit. Bethune and members of the Southeastern Federation of Colored Women's Clubs published an article in the *Southeastern Herald* outlining needs of the African American community. The article was signed by Mrs. John Hope, Mrs. Marion Wilkinson, Miss Lucy Laney, Mrs. Charlotte Hawkins Brown, Mrs. Mary Jackson McCrorey, Mrs. Janie Porter Barrett, Mrs. M. L. Crosthwait, and Mrs. Booker T. Washington, in addition to Bethune. The seven main issues put forth were (1) conditions of domestic service; (2) child welfare; (3) conditions of travel; (4) education; (5) lynching; (6) public press; and (7) suffrage. Her colleagues asserted that without resolving discrimination and oppression in these areas, higher education would have limited impact.[14]

Bethune repeatedly talked about the need for rural education facilities for African American tenant farmers, the working poor, and the incarcerated. Between world wars, well over 700,000 black people worked in substandard conditions. Their basic living and working conditions affected their educational access and economic growth. As an educator, Bethune saw a dire need to provide basic skills training and moral guidance to those laboring in tenant farming, turpentine camps, prisons, and other sites of exploitative working conditions. She urged communities to develop schools for all family members and instilled a service-oriented work ethic in her students.[15]

While she was aware of her marginalized position as a black woman in America, she saw service as a duty and struggle as an honor. It was this spirit of collective struggle that spurred her to write to Charlotte Hawkins Brown, "I think of you and Nannie Helen Burroughs and Lucy Laney and myself as being the most sacrificing class." In a cohort with the likes of Terrell, Washington, Wells, and activist Janie Porter Barrett, Bethune inspired a proactive spirit on a collective level despite significant interpersonal differences among these women.[16]

In addition to service as an aspect of community building, Bethune was very heavily involved in national and international politics. She treated her political work as an extension of her teaching, administration, and public service. In her 1926 presidential address to the NCNW, she stated:

> twelve million Negroes are expecting the National Government to remove all hindrances affecting their liberty, opportunities and protection as American citizens. . . . I hold that blood and color does not define an American citizen. . . . This country belongs to Negroes as much as it does to those of any other race. Our forebears and those of us living in this time have suffered, agonized, bled for this—our land. We have helped to make it what it is today. Denied equal share in the fruits

of our sacrificing and suffering, we have protested. We shall protest and protest again.[17]

A patriot who used the language of democracy to argue for equality, she valued her country enough to critique it.

Bethune was involved in government at the highest levels, and her close relationship with President Franklin Roosevelt and Mrs. Eleanor Roosevelt was an example of her willingness to work across boundaries to achieve increased access for black people. Bethune, like Washington, drew criticism from African Americans during her time. She was a dyed-in-the-wool Republican and remained so long after most African Americans had abandoned the party of Lincoln for the party of Roosevelt.

Some of Bethune's contemporaries took issue with her seemingly conciliatory stance toward some powerful but unpopular white public figures. However, her administrative savvy and diplomatic demeanor were effective in moving public policy. Historians note with amazement Bethune's ability to voice disagreement with powerful parties and still maintain the ties necessary to carry out significant political work. Her talent for recruiting, maintaining, and motivating a supportive and loyal staff in her many institutional endeavors testified to her skills as an administrator. Again, like Washington, Bethune has been accused of being a power monger, crushing or removing all who opposed her; even Dorothy Height, Bethune's successor as president of the NCNW, acknowledged challenges in Bethune's personality. Nevertheless, in current historiography, Bethune's brash leadership style has been overshadowed by the gains garnered because of her political and social dominance. Bethune argued that racism was not democratic and that she aimed to further democracy, even by means of autocracy in her own organizations.[18]

Bethune was a patriot but not a U.S. nationalist. Even though she was heavily involved in recruiting black soldiers and nurses for World War II, she rejected the supremacist tendencies that blind American nationalism inspired. She encouraged international collaboration; antiwar and peace activism was part of her educative work. In an address to NCNW, she proclaimed:

> intolerance, commercial enmities, territorial greed, racial and national hatreds [and] lust for power and blood are never swept away by war, nor disposed of by a stroke of the diplomatic pen, even when used by statesmanship of the British Empire, Republic of the United States, French Republic, Germany, Italy, or Japan. So today the peace of the

world is a matter of concern. . . . I speak to you about the world today because of various nations, peoples, contentions, for peaceful adjustments and settlement on the recognition of equal rights established and enforced by a common will.[19]

In her many realms of responsibility, Bethune assumed that education, work, and service were all means toward democratic living, and she consciously employed the language of social contract to advance international peace and human "citizenship."

Education as a right for all was a fundamental component of demands published in Logan's edited volume, *What the Negro Wants.* In her contribution to that volume, a chapter titled "In Pursuit of Unalienable Rights," Bethune brainstormed with leading black politicians and compiled a list demanding equity in nine areas: (1) government leadership in building favorable public opinion; (2) victory of democracy over dictatorship; (3) democracy in the armed forces; (4) protection of civil rights and an end to lynching; (5) the free ballot; (6) equal access to employment opportunities; (7) extension of federal programs in public housing, health, social security, education, and relief under federal control; (8) elimination of racial barriers in labor unions; and (9) realistic interracial cooperation. Without equality in all these areas, college attendance for blacks would be moot.[20]

Bethune made clear that if white Americans did not adhere to principles and practices of universal freedom, they should be prepared for black Americans to fight:

Throughout America today many people are alarmed and bewildered by the manifestation of this world ferment among the Negro masses. We say we are living in a period of "racial tension." They seem surprised that the Negro should be a part of this world movement. Really, all true Americans should not be surprised by this logical climax of American education. For several generations colored Americans have been brought up on the Boston Tea Party and the Declaration of Independence; on the principle of equality of opportunity, the possession of inalienable rights, the integrity and sanctity of the human personality. Along with other good Americans the Negro has been prepared to take his part in the fight against an enemy that threatens all these basic American principles. He is fighting now on land and sea and in the air to beat back the forces of oppression and tyranny and discrimination. Why, then, should we be surprised when at home as well as abroad he fights back against these same forces?[21]

Thus, recurring rebellions and demands for inclusive freedom, true democracy, and equal opportunity in the United States were a logical result of African Americans being educated in a country that espoused these as basic
principles. One of the contributions that black people offered to the United
States was an opportunity to make good on its claims. One main barrier
to national progress was what Bethune termed the "historical hangover" of
American whites. She boldly equated the rebellions by black residents of
Harlem, Detroit, and Los Angeles in 1943 to the Boston Tea Party and similar
acts of self-determination: she foretold unending black revolt for as long as
structural inequalities were maintained.[22]

In her "Last Will and Testament," written in the year of her death, Bethune recorded a legacy that distilled her long life of struggle on the eve of
her passing. She wished to bequeath (1) love; (2) hope; (3) the challenge of
developing confidence in one another; (4) a thirst for education; (5) respect
for uses of power; (6) faith; (7) racial dignity; (8) a desire to live harmoniously
with your fellow men; and (9) responsibility for young people. For each gift,
she offered her vision for beneficiaries. She avowed:

> I leave you a thirst for education. Knowledge is the prime need of the
> hour. More and more, Negroes are taking full advantage of hard-won
> opportunities for learning. . . . We are making greater use of the privi-
> leges inherent in living in a democracy. . . . I leave you a responsibility
> to our young people. . . . Our children must never lose their zeal for
> building a better world. . . . Nor must they forget that the masses of our
> people are still underprivileged, ill-housed, impoverished, and victim-
> ized by discrimination. We have a powerful potential in our youth, and
> we must have the courage to change old ideas and practices so that we
> may direct their power towards good ends.[23]

Bethune's legacy, clearly articulated with a realization that she was not to be
around much longer, demonstrated her dedication to teaching, even as she
knew that she would not see the results of her lessons. Higher education was
tied to community development; her will was for all to realize the connection and work to construct an equitable, and ethical, sustainable world.

Black Pragmatism and National Progressivism: Washington, Du Bois, and Black Women's Service Ideal

The history of African American education is steeped in both experiential
and pragmatist traditions. Shaw makes clear that, although there was disagreement between Du Bois and Washington about the fundamental theo-

ries, goals, and methods of education, the philosophy of community-based learning was a point of intersection between the two thinkers:

> thus, notwithstanding the contemporary and subsequent debates between advocates of classical education and vocational programs, both types of schools shared this public mission. Black communities were to benefit from the existence of these schools, and people everywhere were to profit from the training of the students as they spread out over the country to live and work.[24]

Although it was clear that Washington was interested in training black people to work and serve, it was equally clear (to some) that he did not mean black people's work to be only subservient menial labor. One of Washington's southern white critics wrote in the *Saturday Evening Post* (1905):

> [Washington] is the greatest diplomat his race has produced. Yet he who reads between the lines of his written and spoken words will find the same purpose and the same faith which his more blunt and fearless brethren have honestly and boldly proclaimed. In his book, *The Future of the Negro*, we find this careful sentence: "To state in detail just what place the black man will occupy in the South as a citizen when he has developed in the direction named is beyond the wisdom of any one." Yet on page 69 he says: "The surest way for the Negro to reach the highest positions is to prepare himself to fill well at the present the basic occupations" . . . independent industries, of course—for, mark you *"Tuskegee Institute is not a servant-training school."*[25]

By pointing out that Washington had economic equality in mind, Baptist minister Thomas Dixon Jr.—author of *The Klansman*, the novel on which the 1915 movie *Birth of a Nation* was based—asserted that Washington had total social equality, eventual racial equality, and amalgamation in mind all along. Because Washington was not up front about all of his intentions, there remained much debate about whether he was really a closet radical and just what type of social relations he had in mind. Undoubtedly, though, while he did push social service, Washington did not intend to educate blacks to be a perpetual underclass.

Du Bois's thoughts on education transformed over time, but he too consistently advocated education for collective gain: "The function of the Negro college, then, is clear: it must maintain the standards of popular education, it must seek the social regeneration of the Negro, and it must help in the solution of problems of race contact and co-operation."[26] But beyond education for service, Du Bois concluded:

The function of the university is not simply to teach bread-winning, or to furnish teachers for the public schools, or to be a centre of polite society; it is, above all, to be the organ of that fine adjustment between real life and the growing knowledge of life, an adjustment which forms the secret of progress.[27]

As Bethune recognized, Du Bois asserted that black leadership would, of course, need to be trained at universities in order to produce knowledge and culture for the society.

To Du Bois, Washington's idea of industrial education did not provide sufficient opportunity for black people to fully participate in America as equal citizens. African Americans needed to understand the language and foundation of the American political and social systems if they were to truly participate. Though interpretations differed greatly regarding what "social benefit" should look like in practice, uplift was a universal theme in African American educational thought.

Slogans like "each one, reach one, teach one" and "lifting as we climb" implied the black communal roots of community-based educational philosophy. Further, service-related education was consistent with African educational traditions. In *Non-Western Educational Traditions: Alternative Approaches to Educational Thought and Practice*, Timothy Reagan asserted that community-based and communal learning is one of seven traits offered by African, Islamic, Chinese, Buddhist, and Indigenous American traditions. Obligation to the collective, respect for elders, and a balance between physical, spiritual, emotional, and mental development were overarching themes in Africanist philosophy. Although there is no static comprehensive "African" philosophy but rather a compilation of different regional and ethnic African philosophies, there are striking similarities in insights, processes, and aims in Zulu, Igbo, Asante, Mandinka, and Yoruba that exemplify a general cultural approach that can be seen in various black communities in the African Diaspora.[28]

But Africans had no monopoly on valuing community service. Framers of the American university system constructed leading ideals in contrast to English and German systems:

the English university, [a theorist] concluded, revolved around culture, the production of gentleman aristocrats. The German university found its life not so much in culture as such but in scholarship, in erudition, in the founding of scholars. The American university . . . he saw as a place where the emphasis was placed neither on culture nor scholarship but on service, on the preparation of young Americans for active lives of service. . . . Unquestionably, the service ideal of the American university derived in part from the timing of its flowering . . . when the spirit of what was called Progressivism filled the land.[29]

The ideals of research, teaching, and service not only competed within universities, but they also sometimes determined the focus of entire campuses or national education agendas.

Service of faculty and students of PWIs was not as lingering or immovable as in black women's collegiate experience. Conversations about faculty duties were heated, as Rudolph explained:

> The notion that a college should serve society through the lives of dedicated graduates was not new. . . . What would be new would be the degree to which such purpose would be diluted as the century progressed. . . . As Americans lost their sense of society and substituted for it a reckless individualism, there was less demand on the colleges to produce dedicated leaders. . . . In time colleges would be more concerned about the expectations of their students than about the expectations of society. In time going to college would come very close to being an experience in indulgence rather than an experience in obligation.[30]

Not only did many professors move from community responsibility, but many students no longer attended college out of a sense of duty to others; personal gain became the goal of teaching and learning.

Compared to European institutions, American systems prided themselves on community service. Yet, in deciding a university's role in building community, a significant question was, "Whose community?" Service as an ideal clashed with racist tendencies, sexist hierarchies, and capitalist realities, but—given international interpretations of higher learning—even articulating the ideal of service was significant compared to even more elitist alternatives of remote scholarship.

Bethune's challenge, though directed toward all citizens, begged pressing questions and presented unique challenges regarding black women's community service. Bethune was not the only educator to assert that it was African American college women who held the fate of the black community in their hands. Most assumed, for a myriad of reasons, that black women were destined to be servants of the world. Those who subscribed to the "uplift" ideology asserted that African American women were the only ones capable of effecting social change in the black community, that they were responsible for causes of the degradation in the black community, or that the dominant society was neither capable of nor responsible for changing the structures that hampered African Americans. Those who reified a psychology of self-help and racial uplift often failed to challenge the oppressive systems responsible for the degraded position of black people. Black and white women alike assumed a female moral superiority and internalized a missionary zeal. The uplift ideal was not uncommon at male universities, but there, service was defined much differently: traditionally, because of the gendered perception of power, women engaged in "service" while men engaged in "leadership."[31]

It was this misappropriation of power that Woodson critiqued in his *Mis-education*; he wrote an entire chapter titled "The Need for Service Rather Than Leadership." Because of male chauvinism, women appeared to have merely supporting roles in black American social revolutions.[32]

Yet, black women remained effective in making major changes from the bottom up: they knew their work within the community was as essential as the diplomacy that was taking place in the boardrooms of the aristocracy. Thus, community organizer Ella Baker would later articulate "my theory is strong people don't need strong leaders."[33]

I observe three main themes that emerge from black women's definitions of service: (1) *capability* (we can educate and serve), (2) *responsibility* (we must educate and serve), and (3) *inevitability* (we will educate and serve). For black women, attitudes like that of Burroughs's now-famous "we specialize in the wholly impossible" were prevalent in the relation of service to education. This proved problematic at times because it fed directly into the stereotype of a "strong black woman" who, through the determination of a pack mule, was rumored to offer nothing other than blood, sweat, and tears to the world. But pervasive myths of the "superwoman" and unrecognized intellectual contributions notwithstanding, black women did indeed serve.

African American clubwomen were integral to their communities, but, as Shaw explained, their ideas of "community" often reached beyond racial or national boundaries:

> And when they realized that community development and race uplift would not get them where they wanted to be as long as they were uplifting only the black race, they went to work on uplifting the white race.[34]

Many effective black women educators saw all people of the world as their community.

African American women like Cooper and Bethune were neither the originators nor sole participants in the progressive spirit that swept the United States. They reflected larger ideological movements such as Quaker or Awakening ideas. They were, however, key constituents of a movement to use education for universal freedom, social justice, and equality, and their unique, marginalized social position branded their service as qualitatively different from that of white educators. Their lives and publications provided a blueprint for sustainable balance between scholarly rigor, effective pedagogy, and a service imperative.

* * *

In sum, black collegiate women effectively recorded their challenges, victories, and contributions to colleges and universities. Their narratives of patience, agony, and raw determination are compelling for their creative voice, scholarly rigor, heart-wrenching detail, and theoretical originality.

Black women's research contributed to human thought, their teaching fed those hungry for knowledge, and their tireless advocacy was a beneficent force in the world. Black women educators offered a critical assessment of these three pillars of academe that can assist educators in attaining a goal of truly "higher" education.

Living Legacies–Black Women in Higher Education, Post-1954

In French, one word, *histoire*, translates into both "story" and "history"; this *histoire* tells how black women experienced their striving for advanced scholarly development. Their educational and intellectual legacy is fertile.

A growing body of contemporary scholarship reveals black women's social contract in various arenas. Sharon Harley, Glenda Gilmore, Debra Gray White, Rhonda Willimas, Premilla Nadasen, and Amrita Myers exemplify researchers who explore black women's social relationships in labor, political, civic, housing, welfare, and legal institutions. Recent work, like that of Elizabeth Higginbotham, explores black women's past negotiations in post-1954 universities, and Marshanda Smith has ventured into black women's faculty experiences. Though the *standpoint social contract* that I reveal exists in all public areas, it is the pre-*Brown* academic institutions with which my work has been concerned.[1]

The trials of black women collegians in the first three waves of degree attainment reflected the absence of an equitable system of higher education. Black women have endured atrocities in the dungeons of the Ivory Tower but have nonetheless earned academic pedigree since Lucy Stanton and Mary Jane Patterson first graduated from antebellum Oberlin. Their striving can offer relief and encouragement for those currently struggling to start or complete advanced educational processes.

Historically, African American women highlighted the importance of cultural identity in their research. Their teaching supported a dedication to lifelong learning and demonstrated the necessary awareness of learners' social and historical context. Their service revealed the advantages of collective community building and the imperative to serve for social justice. Themes of uplift, vindication, and reclamation were tools of resistance in their intellectual production; these are vital entry points into understanding the link between cultural standpoint and epistemology. But these themes are just one part of the necessary analysis.

Limitations of Black Women's Thought

Despite their strengths, I have identified four important points of contention in black women's thought that contemporary educators must consider. As controversial scholar Clarence Walker argued in *Deromanticizing Black History*, researchers must look critically at their subjects, especially those held in high regard. Walker argued that historians often paint a "rosy" picture of black experiences to counterbalance the omnipresent portrayal of black life as deviant. Romantic approaches to educational research can ignore the destructive practices of many selfish, egocentric, and triflin' black men—and women—some of whom are in positions of power in academe, which can thus have a limited effect in problem solving. Some problems in education are recurring and must be constantly revisited. Some new problems emerge over time. African American women's experiences and ideas, though in many ways timeless, are significantly challenged by the complexities of twenty-first-century institutions; as problems change over time, so should solutions.[2]

First, race issues are not simple binaries of black and white—discussions must go beyond "us" and "them." Though Cooper's "Women versus the Indian" explicitly made this point, most black women in the past argued from a stagnant, dichotomous racial position. Within "margin to center" arguments by black women, other categories of "Others" (that is, characteristics like ethnicity, nationality, ability, sexuality, and religion) have been obscured. The myth of limited resources that supposes a need for primacy of one marginalized group over another is ineffective for expanding access to education. Race is paramount, but it is not the only factor involved in discrimination.

Additionally, race has historical significance with contemporary ramifications; however, it is a social construct and must be treated as such. The resurgence of arguments for the biological origins of race cannot undo the core relationship of all living things and does not circumvent the mandate to value all life. African American women educators definitely were race women, but humanity takes precedence over race.

Second, extreme selflessness can be as harmful as extreme selfishness. Black women educators' sense of self developed in the "we" of community. Their life's work and philosophies defied the solitary preoccupation of Jung's individuation or Descartes' declaration of thought-being. Black women became real, whole, and conscious through collective action. The ethics of caring and accountability guided their every move. Clearly, many ignored Cooper's warning against exploitative service and through their endless struggle suffered mental and physical exhaustion. Stress was made normative, which robbed many black women of balance, health, peace, and wellness. In uplifting, black women, especially clubwomen, often displayed a martyr complex, becoming self-centered in their claims of selflessness and domineering in the name of freeing "their people." They sought sainthood in their suffering and insisted on dying for the black race instead of living life with measured, balanced enjoyment.

Third, African American women advocated Christian education. They argued that moral, spiritual, ethical, and other metaphysical or religious concepts are essential to formal teaching and learning. Their arguments are convincing because their results were impressive: through faith, they did specialize in "the wholly impossible." Yet, black women's concepts of religion differed drastically. There were fundamental disagreements about the most fitting type of worship for black women and disagreement about to what extent religion should guide education. Contemporary educators must concede that institutionalizing religion in higher education—just as in government—inevitably brings problems. Advocating universal "Christian education" in all colleges and universities would be essentialist, arrogant, and exclusive of other religions or of those who do not identify as monotheists —surely it would rationalize or bolster persecution of non-Christians. Basic interrogation of organized religion often exposes a moral disconnect: historically, not all Christian acts have been moral acts. Obviously, Christian education was not beneficial for most Native Americans or other indigenous peoples of the world.

Nevertheless, Christianity is central to black American life, culture, and thought. Therefore, the discussion of religion in African American education is of great import; how religion is discussed is of great controversy. This is especially relevant given interfaith debates, sectarian divides, and the importance of Islam in the African Diaspora. Unfortunately, many miss the reference to the Qur'an in Jill Scott's song "A Long Walk," which is the epigraph for this history:

> And swell not the cheek (for pride) at men, nor walk in insolence through the earth; for Allah loveth not any arrogant boaster." (Surah 31:18 *Qur'an*)

> Because thou sayest, I am rich, and increased with goods, and have need of nothing; thou knowest not that thou art wretched, and miserable, and poor and blind, and naked. (Revelations 3:17)

In these passages, parallels can be seen in ideas about the virtue of humility. Religious freedom is an important concept and must be upheld in higher education. By moving beyond advocating one religion for all, interfaith collaboration could be rich—especially in the academy. Black women's ardent faith in Christian education, though in line with the origins of most colleges and universities in the United States, reintroduces age-old debates of Awakening versus Enlightenment approaches to education. More important, this history implicates the need for a continued foundation of church and state separation even while religion must remain central to scholarly dialogue. Christian education is a central, but not singular, topic to address in improving the American academy.

Last, challenges to poverty and educational access must be addressed in terms of defying "middle-class" values that marginalize people without property, "skilled" labor, or pedigree. Black women educators engaged in uplift; too often their efforts were directed toward ensuring black participation in an educational hierarchy based on liberal ideals of inclusion rather than radical ideas of institutional revolution. The middle-class notion of educational equity was patronizing and ignored the efficacy of poor people's activism on their own behalf. The historical account of these women as "exceptional" does not honor the efforts of millions of black working-class activists like Fanny Lou Hamer who were not formally educated but were essential in social justice movements. Like appeals to nationalism or the limitations of exclusionary ideas of "citizenship," middle-class values and "talented-tenth" aims in higher education are too narrow a platform from which to address human rights. Future research must connect the narratives of black women in the United States to larger international and transnational histories.[3]

Black women's claimed space, negotiation of social contracts, contribution of ideas, and upholding of social hierarchies all must be explored in future research. Considering marginalized perspectives is essential to evaluation in higher education; alternative narratives offer engaging solutions that address complexities, in new, old, and significant ways.

Due Process and Educational Attainment

In *Breaking Bread*, Cornel West and bell hooks continue the discussion about the "dilemma of the black intellectual." West argues against piecemeal approaches to education such as the "humanist" (liberal/uplift), "revolutionary" (Marxist/structural hierarchies), or "skeptic" (Foucault/power-knowledge/cultural criticism) positions. He advocates for a "catalyst" approach, which creates and reactivates institutional networks for alternative practices. Thus, West advises that clubs, organizations, and entire institutions could be tools for democracy and social justice. I have often said that the academy is a hostile environment with deep-seated organizational failings. However, I agree with West that academe can be a tool for catalytic evolution; yes, schools, colleges, and universities can be catalytic converters![4]

In *Transcending the Talented Tenth*, Joy James makes a case for dismantling elitist notions of degree attainment in higher education. She reveals limitations in historic uplift movements and shows that black scholars need to resist individual heroism by refocusing on communal ethics. In an effort to define what "social justice" means in practical terms, James challenges scholars to assist in the creation of economic, social, and political liberty that meets basic human needs and enhances quality of life for the disenfranchised. James's subsequent research on alarming trends in incarceration, like Angela Davis's scholarship, shows the enduring subjugation of black and poor people. These and other theorists reflect black feminist epistemology as defined by Collins and as practiced by some historic black women academics: to offer potential sites of solidarity with other social movements beyond gender or race.

Further, the focus on African American women's standpoint cannot overshadow or negate the importance of considering other demographics that are shut out of higher education. Native American, Asian, Pacific Islander, Middle Eastern, Jewish, Hispanic/Latino and other demographics all have a distinct, contentious relationship with educational systems in the United States. Above all, black women's standpoint should not contend with these or with black men's voices. Though black women are a "marginalized majority" in the college setting, their voices must be raised primarily to promote coalition and collaboration around causes such as the economic and race-based American prison system and state-sponsored death that is reducing already dismal opportunities for men of color to pursue collegiate study. Black women's legacy can demonstrate how to work for greater political enfranchisement for families that have been victimized for generations by slavery, the convict labor system, police brutality, economic deprivation, and other oppressions that happen both inside and outside of black communities.[5]

In the 1950s, a coalition led by the NAACP asserted that separate-but-equal was an oxymoron. When placed next to the equal protection clause of the Fourteenth Amendment, segregation did not hold up. The Supreme Court ruled, unanimously, that the coalition was right. In the opinion of the Court, Chief Justice Earl Warren wrote:

> In these days, it is doubtful that any child may reasonably be expected to succeed in life if he is denied the opportunity of an education. Such an opportunity, where the state has undertaken to provide it, is a right which must be made available on equal terms.[6]

The significance of the *Brown* ruling, still not adequately implemented, lies in the promised life chances offered by access to quality education. That prisons are funded at the expense of schools will undoubtedly continue to produce social, political, and economic disparities—and therefore social unrest—that compare in magnitude and misfortune to Victor Hugo's rendition of poverty and revolution in *Les Misérables*. The call for reparations, contextualized by Mary Frances Berry's research on Callie House, is based on the reality that the historic robbery of black people has not sufficiently been recognized or rectified. As legal historian Paul Finkelman points out in "Affirmative Action for the Master Class: The Creation of the Proslavery Constitution," even as we use the Constitution to address present inequalities, we must acknowledge the role of the constitutional framers in the propagation of American slavery if we are to effectively dismantle structural systems of inequality embedded in the nation's foundational documents, ideologies, and practices.[7]

Fundamentally, education, social training, and cultural transmission revolve around the volatile ingredients of power, resources, and values. Those who have the greatest access to resources have the power to define themselves—and power to insert that definition into the national curriculum. Cooper convincingly critiqued Eurocentric, paternalistic egotism, and Bethune exposed the farce of democracy in the United States. These perspectives reveal the limitations of "standardized" testing and bring to light the need for reevaluating what the "American mind" should know and what standards should be established in granting access to universities. To gauge the promise of equal educational opportunity in the post-*Brown* era, a state case study is useful. Black women's progress in Florida shows how campus life after desegregation continued to be as difficult as in prior eras.[8]

"I Was One of the First to See Daylight": Florida, a Case Study in Educational Transition

Florida Agricultural and Mechanical School (now FAMU) was founded in 1887 with fifteen students and two instructors. Of the four HBCUs in Florida (Edward Waters founded 1872, Florida Memorial 1879, and Bethune-Cookman College 1904), FAMU has always had the highest enrollment and graduation numbers and remains the only HBCU in the state holding university status to grant doctoral degrees. Accreditation for HBCUs was notoriously slow: FAMU gained college status in 1905 and university status in 1953; it developed its first Ph.D. program, in pharmacology, in 1984. Along with FAMU's success in educating blacks in the Sunshine State, Bethune provided the ultimate example of African Americans' capacity to build institutions. Within its first ten years, Bethune-Cookman had instructed thousands of girls. Bethune provided academic hope for black girls and the network of Florida HBCUs was essential in graduating Florida's black leaders and professional class. However, by Du Bois's second Atlanta study, Florida institutions still had not produced one African American woman graduate from a ranked college. That year, FAMU had an enrollment of 317 students, but it did not grant its first college degrees until 1910.[9]

Along with the devaluation of HBCU degrees by withholding accreditation and equal funding, black students were excluded from well-established state schools like the University of Florida and Florida State. Most of the graduates in the 1910 Atlanta study were born in Georgia (123) or North Carolina (115). Other states followed far behind in the number of graduates: Tennessee (68), Alabama (48), Louisiana (32), Mississippi (28), Kentucky (27), and Maryland (20). Only 7 African Americans born in Florida had graduated from a ranked college by 1910.[10]

In Johnson's 1930s survey, 3,331 revealed their birth state, and the southern numbers were still very uneven. Georgia had 513 black graduates, followed by Texas (443), Virginia (388), Tennessee (253), Alabama (238), and Louisiana (231). By then only 74 African Americans born in Florida reported graduating from college. Further, while other states enjoyed a high number of black graduates as residents, only 94 black college graduates resided in Florida at that time, compared to 505 in Georgia, 413 in Texas, 335 in North Carolina, and 326 in Tennessee. Washington, D.C., alone had 239 black graduates as residents, over two times the number in the whole state of Florida. Of the entire population of almost 20,000 graduates, Florida ranked sixth-lowest in state of residence.[11]

For black students, opportunities to attend universities in Florida were

abysmal. Between 1945 and 1958, there were eighty-five black student applicants to UF; all were denied admission. In 1949, five students applied to
UF: Virgil Hawkins and William Lewis (law), Rose Boyd (pharmacy), Benjamin Finley (agriculture) and Oliver Maxey (chemical engineering). None
were admitted. The first successful black applicants would not be admitted
until the late 1950s, thirty years after UF had graduated its first white female
graduate in 1920 and over a century after its founding in 1853. Daphne Beatrice Alexander Duval (now Duval-Williams), a Florida native, earned three
degrees from FAMU (high school 1924; B.S. in mathematics 1927; and a master's of education 1959). She was the first black woman to enroll at UF and
thus the first black woman in the Florida State University System (FSUS). After graduating from FAMU, she moved to Gainesville and taught at Lincoln
High School, the only high school in town for blacks. Characterizing herself
as "curious" and "ornery," she successfully challenged racial segregation at
UF and enrolled for classes in January 1959. Because she wanted to continue her education, did not want to commute to Tallahassee, and wanted to
lead desegregation efforts in Florida schools like her cousin George Starke
had done, she enrolled for classes in the College of Education. Starke had
graduated from Morehouse College in Atlanta and was admitted to UF's
law school in the fall of 1958. He was the only black student on a campus of
12,000, and though he kept a low profile and did not report any overt resistance to his presence, he left after three months. Daphne's attendance at UF
was similarly uneventful, and though she did not graduate, she cleared the
path for those who came a few years after to earn degrees from UF.[12]

As a child, Duval-Williams had learned to count from her grandmother,
a former slave in Tallahassee; she also valued time spent with her grandfa-
ther, who constructed roads from South Carolina to Florida. Though her
grandparents did not have the advantage of formal education, she credits
them both with offering her more knowledge and technical training than
she often received in school. By the time she enrolled at UF, she was in her
fifties, married to a local businessman, had three children, and had already
earned her M.Ed. Though she already had earned an advanced degree, she
was invested in showing that black students "had just as much gray matter
as the white students." Like black women scholars, teachers, and activists
before her, Duval-Williams was a clubwoman: in 1938, she and four women
founded the Visionaires Club in Gainesville; she was active in the Mt. Car-
mel Baptist Church; and she was involved in many advocacy groups locally
and nationally, including the NAACP and teachers associations. Duval-
Williams passed her academic determination on to her daughters, one of
whom was the first black woman to earn a doctorate from the University of

Miami, and the other of whom (also a math major) worked for NASA. When interviewed a few months shy of her one-hundredth birthday, Daphne Duval-Williams demonstrated a sharp wit and mental determination that was perhaps as intense as when she bucked the Jim Crow system in the 1950s as a community activist who integrated the flagship state school.[13]

After *Brown*, black women were making significant strides in higher education; however, as with other times and places, they were simultaneously being held back in frightening ways. Though there was increased opportunity to attend college, the success was mediated with everyday tragedy. Even while at institutions like FAMU—which were centers of hope and communal growth—black women were subject to social terror. In a stunning example, the same year Duval-Williams successfully enrolled at UF in Gainesville, Betty Jean Owens, a FAMU student, was forced from a car she was in with three other classmates and repeatedly raped by four white Tallahassee men. In contrast to popular rhetoric of American meritocracy, college attendance failed to guarantee professional advancement, economic security, or even offer basic safety for African Americans. Still, black students pursued higher education and sought to improve their chances of success against all odds.[14]

The historical record of Florida's state PWIs shows that most of the eleven state colleges admitted a select few black students in their inaugural classes because all but two were opened in the mid-1960s, when UF and FSU had already begun to desegregate. By 1962, UF had 7 black undergraduates; in 1965, there were 35 of 18,000; and about 100 black students of 25,000 were on campus by 1969. Florida State University admitted its first black student in 1962 (Maxwell Courtney) and growth at FSU was as incremental as growth at UF. The rest of Florida PWIs admitted black students in their opening years: Black students first attended University of South Florida in 1964, Florida Atlantic University in 1964, University of Central Florida in 1968, and were present at the other campuses as they opened.[15]

Though there was attrition in the first cohort of black students at each institution, black graduates nonetheless trickled out of Florida's colleges as surely as they trickled in. At least two black undergraduates earned undergraduate degrees in 1965: Stephen Mickle from UF and Maxwell Courtney from FSU. In the early years of access, there was not much gender disparity between men and women in the enrollment or graduation numbers; enrollment at each location was in the single digits until the 1970s. Faculty appointments in Florida PWIs generally became available in the 1970s as well, and there was not much gender disparity there either because the numbers for both men and women were also in the single digits.[16]

Kitty Oliver, a celebrated journalist, nonfiction writer, and oral historian in Florida, entered the University of Florida in 1965. She was one of only five black freshmen to integrate campus housing. Her story, told in *Multicolored Memories of a Black Southern Girl*, is intriguing for its portrayal of one of the first black students who integrated the PWIs in Florida and builds on past memoirs. Oliver, from Jacksonville, traced her mother's roots to the Gullah people of South Carolina. She was an only child and the first in her family to attend college. The story of her choice to attend UF instead of the more popular FAMU provides an intriguing snapshot of black college life in the South.

In her narrative, Oliver recalled young adulthood in her mid-1960s transition from Jacksonville to Gainesville. Most of her peers attended FAMU or other HBCUs in the state. In Florida as elsewhere, white schools were notorious for presenting problems on campus, in the classroom, and in the local communities that hampered black students' ability to excel academically or socially. Despite this reality, Oliver chose to attend a PWI, and overall she valued the experience. She chronicled her 1960s experiences: her participation in voter-registration drives and pickets against stores that discriminated by race; being "randomly selected" to have a black roommate in the dorm at UF, and the next semester, being immediately rejected by the white roommate assigned; the students' treating her as "exotic" and her foray into flirtations with non-black men; guarded but fruitful relationships with black physical plant workers and residents of Gainesville; intense and shifting intraracial disagreements over "Black Power" or "flower child" campus identities; transition from black church music to Otis Redding, to Peter, Paul, and Mary, to Santana, and ultimately to a sampling of each to create her own musical voice. In her college memoir, Oliver disclosed the hardships of being one of a handful of blacks at a PWI in a southern state. But she also expressed appreciation for those, like Duval-Williams, who had come before her to "kick down the door" so that she could have a choice of institutions and be "one of the first to see daylight and walk on in."[17] Much work must be done to keep the door open: by 2005, there were 25,000 black women students in the FSUS and only 14,000 black men. Meanwhile, there were over 40,000 black men in Florida's state prisons. Conversely, of 5,810 total tenured faculty, the state of Florida has 258 tenured black men faculty, but only 157 tenured black women.

Kitty Oliver's story of student life, her subsequent attainment of a master's of fine arts from Florida International University, and her work for nine years as an associate professor at Florida Atlantic University provide much opportunity for race and gender analysis of higher education in the Sunshine

State. As can be seen, Oliver's cohort of black collegiate women and subsequent numbers in Florida tells much about the complex relationship of race, gender, and higher education. The aggregate numbers in Florida's public colleges and universities and individual narratives of past students provide a unique case study for comparison of the national evolution of higher education for African Americans in the post-*Brown* era.

Nationwide Patterns and the Impact of Black Women Scholar-Activists

Nationally, the increase in college attendance between 1870 and 1970 was drastic: "In 1870 but 1.7 percent of the young people aged 18–21 were enrolled in colleges and universities; by 1970 half of the age group 18–21 would be at college." Although demographic changes were partially responsible for the increase, the larger reason was the proliferation of colleges and the change in college type. The nineteenth-century liberal arts colleges were overtaken by immense university complexes and the rapid growth of the community college systems in the twentieth century: "In 1876 there were 311 colleges and universities; in 1960 there were 2,026."[18]

This expansion in college attendance did not, however, equate to significant increases in opportunities for black women. In 1960, of all black women in the labor force, 53.9 percent were employed in domestic or other service positions, 10.8 percent were in clerical and sales, and 6 percent were in professional positions. In 1980, 30.8 percent were employed in domestic service or other service work, 32.4 percent were in clerical and sales positions, and 14.8 percent were in professional positions. At the turn of the twenty-first century, approximately 12.6 percent (34,658,190) of the U.S. population was classified as black. While 56.3 percent of U.S. black women were employed in the domestic or service fields, only 14.8 percent were employed in professional occupations. Relative to the population, black women's access to economic stability, professional training, and employment opportunity has not drastically changed since the late 1800s. Of course, physical conditions and quality of life have improved beyond measure, but equitable distribution of resources is still not a reality. The sustained disparities become more heinous when factoring in the exponential loss of life, health, and wealth during enslavement and segregation. That this phenomenon is worldwide is scandalous and maddening.[19]

Though school segregation laws were changed in 1954, it became obvious that, as in prior eras, community activism proved the most effective means of enforcing ordinances mandating equal access to education, public accommodation, housing, and employment. Black women were fundamental to the success of the NAACP, the Urban League, and parent-teacher associations, and black collegiate women were fundamental to the black women's clubs that forced implementation of laws. The majority of black women in America worked in "low-skill" agriculture, service, or domestic jobs; they also worked in churches and community organizations. It was the rank-and-file, as activist and organizer Ella Baker called them—most without the aid of "higher" education—whose organization and activism forced growth.[20]

The film *Fundi* documents the importance of organizers like Baker in mobilizing for change, but many of these women were also engaged in the academy. Ella Baker, involved with the NAACP, Southern Christian Leadership Conference (SCLC), and the Student Nonviolent Coordinating Committee (SNCC) was a 1927 graduate of Shaw University.[21]

Septima Clark, a South Carolina activist for equal teacher salaries and adult literacy, attended Columbia and Atlanta University, where she studied briefly with Du Bois. Clark, a member of Alpha Kappa Alpha Sorority, earned a B.A. from Benedict College in 1942 and a master's degree from Hampton Institute in 1945.[22]

Mary Fair Burks and Jo Ann Robinson were central to social change. Burks, the first president of the Women's Political Council, which helped lead the 1955–56 Montgomery Bus Boycott in Alabama, earned a B.A. from Alabama State College, an M.A. from the University of Michigan, and eventually a doctorate in education from Columbia. Burks did postgraduate work at Harvard, Oxford, and the Sorbonne. Jo Ann Robinson, whose mobilizing efforts were central to the success of the Montgomery Bus Boycott, was also a faculty member at Alabama State University. Robinson was the chair of the Women's Political Council but also earned an M.A. from Atlanta University. These women's experiences can help expand notions of college student identities and enhance the idea of "service" in education. Many radical activists of the 1950s and 1960s were college-educated women, but as with advocacy for black studies programs in the 1960s and 1970s, black women scholar-activists were largely recognized only for their hands and hearts, not their heads.[23]

Antebellum and Jim Crow practices left many black youth to be educated by whites who were trained in reading and writing but not functional in antiracist methods. Those students with black teachers were often at the mercy of school boards that mandated curricula that depicted black inferiority. Recent scholarship indicates that not enough has changed: racist scholarship abounds, few resources are allotted to poor schools, and de facto segregation is firmly in place.[24]

Linda Brown, the young girl in the *Brown v. Board* case, is a poignant example of the resiliency demanded of black women and generational problems with education access. Linda Brown's Supreme Court case made history, but the struggle continued long after the ruling: she acted as plaintiff on behalf of her children (1979) and grandchildren (1987) in school desegregation cases in Topeka, Kansas. By the 1990s, Linda Brown Buckner was a Head Start teacher and lecturer who was still fighting for the equity mandated in 1954. Data from the U.S. Census show the direct relation of educational attainment to health status, health care, income, wealth, employment, and home ownership. Generally, if one element is missing, chances for a prosperous life are limited in all areas. African American women, despite gains in college access in relation to black men, still suffer from the cumulative negative effects of racism compounded by the feminization of poverty.[25]

After *Brown* and the civil rights movement, black women continued to create effective advocacy networks: these included the National Welfare Rights Organization (1967), Clara ("Mother") Hale House in Harlem (1969), the Coalition of 100 Black Women (1971), the National Women's Political Caucus (1971), the National Black Feminist Organization (1973), Marian Wright Edelman's Children's Defense Fund (1973), Combahee River Collective (1974), the Black Women's United Front of the Congress of African Peoples (1975), and the National Black Woman's Health Project (1981). In 1979, the Association of Black Women Historians was founded, marking a culmination of the desire for black women to claim, name, and share their own history. A contemporary example of the coupling of research and advocacy, the Women of Color Resource Center of California publishes an annual *National Directory of Women of Color Organizations and Projects*, which lists over seventy national African, African American, and Afro Caribbean organizations that focus on topics including arts, professional development, domestic violence, health, citizenship and voting rights, sexuality rights, religion, as well as economic, housing, and workers' rights. Sweet Honey in the Rock, established in 1973 by Bernice Johnson Reagon, continues to serve as an example of black women's dedication to popular education; in their performances they teach about history, liberation, spirituality, and creativity. Theirs is but one example of the sustained dedication to communal intellectual development that is rigorous in scholarship but not confined to the halls of academe.[26]

Autobiography, novels, plays, and poetry have continued to amplify black women's creative and critical voice. Black woman's nonfiction rapidly grew after the 1960s. *The Black Woman: An Anthology, Tomorrow's Tomorrow,* and *The Afro-American Woman: Struggles and Images* were, respectively, an early anthology of critical essays about black women's experiences, a sociological study of black women, and an anthology of black women's history. During this time, contested definitions of "black art" and the "black aesthetic" abounded, as did the redefinitions of black womanhood. Scholars organized around political education and cultural consciousness.[27]

Scholarly work about black women exploded in the 1980s and 1990s: *All the Women Are White, All the Men Are Black, But Some of Us Are Brave*; *Home Girls: A Black Feminist Anthology*; *When and Where I Enter: The Impact of Black Women on Race and Sex in America*; *Labor of Love, Labor of Sorrow: Black Women, Work, and the Family from Slavery to the Present*; *Afro-American Women of the South and the Advancement of the Race, 1895–1925*; *A Shining Thread of Hope: The History of Black Women in America*; and *Too Heavy a Load: Black Women in Defense of Themselves, 1894–1994* are examples. While not focused solely on education, these works provided resources for better understanding black women's role in American education whether formal or informal, institutional or community-based, cultural or civic. In 1981, Barbara Smith and Audre Lorde began Kitchen Table: Women of Color Press. This signaled an important shift from writing to production, creating a venue for women of color themselves to decide what is fit to print.

There also has been an increase in theorizing black women's experience. Before Collins's *Black Feminist Thought*, black women interpreted their experiences to change representations and social policy. Books such as *Black Macho and the Myth of the Superwoman*; *Ain't I A Woman: Black Women and Feminism*; *Sister Outsider: Essays and Speeches*; *Theorizing Black Feminisms: The Visionary Pragmatism of Black Women*; and *Shadowboxing: Representations of Black Feminist Politics* advanced dialogue, scholarship, and interpretations.[28] Multifaceted discussions of womanism have added depth and breadth to cultural discussions of feminism.

Kantian scholar Robert Wolff defined philosophy as "literally, love of wisdom, philosophy is the systematic, critical examination of the way in which we judge, evaluate, and act, with the aim of making ourselves wiser, more self-reflective, and therefore better men and women." Black women's philosophies—their wise examinations—are sorely needed to maximize the potential in higher education.[29]

Cultural Identity and Academic Production: Dr. Player's Challenge

After Bethune and Cooper, Willa Player, Niara Sudarkasa, Gloria Randall Scott, Mary Frances Berry, Johnnetta Cole, and Ruth Simmons all became college or university presidents, breaking new ground in leadership. Angela

Davis and Lani Guinier have served communities and institutions, proving that their heads, hearts, and hands are still connected. Literary giants (Toni Morrison, Maya Angelou, Sonia Sanchez, and Ntozake Shange), historians (Nell Irvin Painter, Evelyn Higginbotham and Darlene Clark Hine), and scientists (Jewell Plummer Cobb and Mae Jameson) have led by developing extensive bodies of research and providing scholarly venues in which to redefine African American women's experiences. Each has confirmed principles of measuring learning by applied outcome, coalition building, and working with ethics of accountability and care. Through these women, and thousands of others, Bethune's and Cooper's legacy of "building a better world" continues.[30]

Of the above-named scholars, most are known internationally. One intellectual often overlooked but significant in her scholarly contributions is Willa Player (1909–2003). Player (highlighted earlier for her research on Bennett College) earned her B.A. from Ohio Wesleyan (1929), M.A. from Oberlin (1930), and Ph.D. in education from Columbia (1948); she also studied in France. In February 1959, she delivered an address titled "Over the Tumult—The Challenge" at Ohio Wesleyan as a powerful post–World War II entreaty for the redirection of institutional research.

Her admonition to maintain a strong link between scientific inquiry and ethical action exposed the failings of technological advancement and limitations of nationalism. Her comments—referencing the wake of the August 1945 bombing of Hiroshima and Nagasaki—ring eerily true as the United States orchestrates a "War on Terror" in the twenty-first century and explores space to Pluto:

> Today we are dangling in an uneasy balance between world deliverance and world destruction. These circumstances have come about so rapidly that we have not had time to close the ever-widening gap between scientific discovery and moral commitment. Although our colleges are desperately re-examining their goals and re-appraising their values, we have not yet found the solution to the problem of how to establish the appropriate organic relationship between the search for truth and the moral responsibility inherent therein.[31]

Like Cooper's call for social justice, Player's solution for institutional improvement was deceptively simple: love was her answer to the crisis academics faced. But the love she advocated was not a "Pollyanna" panacea; it required physical, moral, and intellectual rigor:

We desperately need a leadership of inclusiveness. May I say that this is possible in proportion as we are able to put our love of humanity above the love of self. Responsible leadership must be characterized by love. . . . We need desperately a leadership of intellectual integrity. We have to say this over and over again—for we are prone to want the world at too cheap a price, and nothing really worthy is ever achieved except by hard, intellectual effort, and the development of the power of straight thinking.[32]

Player challenged academics to admit and ensure the right of all living beings to grow instead of taking the more often traveled road of dominance, arrogance, exclusion, and hatred.

Black women academics have a history of organizing to share resources, ideas, and agendas that are in line with Player's focus on the need for academe to become more positive and inclusive. In 1976, the newly formed National Association of Black Professional Women in Higher Education held a conference at Wingspread in Racine, Wisconsin. The association was founded to discuss "national policy concerns . . . to benefit higher education by identifying, clarifying and resolving issues affecting institutions and individuals, especially black females." In 1994, Johnetta Cole, Angela Davis, and Lani Guinier gave keynote addresses, "In Defense of Our Names," at a conference that drew two thousand black women academics to the Massachusetts Institute of Technology (MIT). Each speaker addressed the need for black women to learn the history of intellectual struggle provided in this volume. In their call to strengthen resolve to fully incorporate black women in the academy, they also called for a close inspection of the foremothers in order not to duplicate past shortcomings. The call they sounded at the MIT conference has not yet been fully answered. Ten years after that conference, in 2004, leading women scholars addressed a "Gender, Race, and Rights in American Women's History" conference at the Radcliffe Institute for Advanced Study. Among the comments on institutional cultures, panelist Nell Irvin Painter poignantly acknowledged the severity of the physiological stresses that negatively affect black women academics as we strive to create space for ourselves in the cultural vacuity known as the Ivory Tower.[33]

Smart and Sassy: Sisters of the Academy and an Unwounded Spirit

Black women at all levels are caught in the politics of respectability, much as they were in the last two centuries. In order to demonstrate her worthiness of a place at the seminar table, a black woman professor must prove herself to be better than all colleagues. One mistake and, much as Fanny Coppin observed, the scholarly credibility of the whole race—and gender—lies in question. Consequently, excellence is at once repressive and compelling: while buying into ideas of excellence reifies the trappings of ego and merit, it is nonetheless necessary to demonstrate that achievement is commonplace in black women's collegiate history so that when scholars do excel, it is seen as normative rather than exceptional.[34]

Research reveals particular ways that black women strive to gain access to increasingly higher levels of the academy despite constant mental, psychological, and physical pressure. This striving, however, is often done in a historical vacuum.[35]

Universities often publicize their desire to be "engaged" campuses that value community service. There is much lip service given to diversity and valuing community partnership; however, if these were true institutional values, the campus and community service activities that minorities are disproportionately called to take part in would be part of the tenure and promotion review. In addition, contemporary movements in experiential education, especially community service-learning, seek to define the relationship of education to public service. However, much like the settlement house movement of the nineteenth century, advocates of the service-learning movement are often racist in their publications and practices. Not enough advocates of community service-learning critically reflect on their own relationship to community or counteract elitist notions of service. Black women have contributed valuable educational and experiential philosophies, yet these ideas are rarely cited in leading research publications in the field.[36]

Perhaps this history can remove the professional and ideological barriers that continue to hamper intellectual production and deny a rightful place to the "Other" in the academy. The documentary *Shattering the Silences: Minority Professors Break into the Ivory Tower* outlines issues that academic minorities face when attempting to work in an institutional bureaucracy that was not constructed for them, that assumes their inferiority, that undermines their ability to succeed, and that denies their ability to contribute to the "thought of great thinkers."

Professional academicians should be held accountable for continually contributing civic ideas and actions based on ideals of community empowerment . . . and real justice for all. Otherwise, why should academics be respected? In a deeply stirring and insightful speech, Evelyn Brooks Higginbotham of Harvard gave the keynote address at the 2005 meeting of the Association of Black Women Historians annual luncheon in Buffalo, New

York. Her comments, titled "An Open Letter to Condoleezza Rice," assured Rice, the political powerhouse, that black women historians continue to carry on the tradition of critical assessment and would certainly record how Rice used, or withheld, her power for the social advancement of the least privileged. Similarly, my standard of excellence, like Cooper's and Bethune's, is based not on the prestige of a diploma but on the contribution someone makes to the sustainability of the least advantaged in her/his community.

The academy, though central in society, is not central to the majority of African American women's lives. Black women academics are held accountable to many constituencies, not the least of which is that of black women who successfully negotiate their lives without any need of academic institutions. So, though I acknowledge the importance of higher education, I do not assert that it is the most important sphere in black women's communal experience; the central institutions of import are black families, churches, and social organizations.[37]

I am invested in reclaiming the black organizations and institutions in higher education and challenging the assertion that anything black is inferior. As black Greek-letter organizations (BGLOs) reach their centennial celebrations, they provide an excellent opportunity to reflect on the horrendous practices of hazing, hateful exclusionary habits, and conspicuous consumption. They also offer a chance to recall the vision of BGLO organization founders and use the precious pearls of wisdom and effective activist strategies embedded therein by the black educated class.

HBCUs are as valuable, problematic, and promising as historically women's or private religious colleges, but they are rarely granted due legitimacy. Although HBCUs have experienced an alarmingly high incidence of mismanagement of funds and loss of accreditation, it is certainly less shocking than comparable failings of other academic institutions, not to mention criminal greed, inefficacy, and neglect of white leaders in private corporations and governmental agencies that the "most prestigious" institutions train. Despite problems, HBCUs work. Statistically, the majority of black elite have graduated from black schools, including Ed Bradley, Thurgood Marshall, Martin Luther King Jr., John Hope Franklin, W.E.B. Du Bois, Althea Gibson, Kwame Kilpatrick, Ruth Simmons, Medgar Evers, Alex Haley, Toni Morrison, Mary Frances Berry, Alice Walker, Betty Shabazz, Ralph Ellison, Tom Joyner, Ronald McNair, Jesse Jackson, and Oprah Winfrey. That HBCUs continue to educate students regardless of race, creed, or status warrants a continued—and increased—investment in those institutions. HBCUs, like religious and single-sex institutions, offer a unique critical and valuable academic perspective. When Du Bois assessed the issue in 1941 ("The Future of the Negro State University") and in 1946 ("The Future and Function of the Private Negro College"), he warned of the dangers of education belonging only to the rich and white. Supporting HBCUs enriches education by resisting streamlined racist privatization of college and university access.[38]

In addition, this history supports an increased interest in community colleges and their renewed status in the educational social order. The assessment of institutional worth in higher education needs a drastic overhaul, as demonstrated by Jamie Johnson's documentary *Born Rich*, which revealed that children of wealthy donors to prestigious schools were sometimes awarded college diplomas without attending class, taking exams, or demonstrating basic academic competency. Clearly, higher education has not yet reached its potential heights. Not all black women will succeed in fundamentally changing structures by "speaking truth to power," as Anita Hill's congressional testimony and status as a tenured faculty member accomplished. But attempts are being made.

Problems such as low birth rates, poor nutrition, dilapidated buildings, overpoliced but still unsafe schools, racist curricula and teachers, limited books and materials, overrepresentation in special education classes, tracking to vocational education, tracking away from liberal arts education, limited access to technology, and lack of academically challenging classes all work against equitable learning opportunities for black or poor children. Significantly, racist pseudoscientific "research" adds to the already devastating effects that poverty has on the poor. For example, the "mid-1990s Kennedy Krieger study that encouraged landlords to rent lead-contaminated homes to . . . 107 poor, [predominantly black] Baltimore families with young children" was housed at Johns Hopkins University. When public outcry exposed the study, the researchers admitted no wrongdoing.[39]

The World War I–era "psychometric" propositions spawned a generation of more overtly racist research during the 1960s and 1970s: Arthur Jensen, in the *Harvard Educational Review* (1969), argued that since he found social success depended on IQ, public resources needed to be directed to the elites of society; Nobel Prize physicist William Shockley suggested coerced sterilizations for people with low IQs and propagation of "genius" sperm banks; and Richard Herrnstein, in an article on the "habitability of IQ" in the *Atlantic Monthly* (1971), compiled evidence that combined metaphysics, biology, and psychology to state why and how white people—and some Asians—were cognitively superior to all other races. Though the questions, methodologies, methods, and arguments differed greatly between these researchers, and though reasons to which the deficit was ascribed varied, all arguments pointed to African inferiority (albeit with slight variation by nationality). That they differed so greatly in means yet all arrived at the same end reveals the pervasiveness of race supremacy in academic knowledge production.

In research findings such as those produced by *The Bell Curve: Intelligence and Class Structure in American Life* (1994), authors dehumanize ethnic minorities, thereby providing a seemingly rational basis that makes research like the Krieger study possible. Since *The Bell Curve*'s authors asserted that the "*g*" factor, or general intelligence, does not measure human excellence, perhaps we should strive to construct a measure of higher education that more accurately reflects virtues that are routinely espoused in a nation that touts itself as being democratic. When Rose Browne objected to including standardized intelligence measurements popular in the 1930s as part of her doctoral study, Truman Kelly, a Harvard statistics professor supported her with this assurance: "Mrs. Browne, just omit any reference to the I.Q. tests. . . . After all, the I.Q. is merely a relative measure. It shows us what knowledge we have been able to give the child, but does not tell us how much more knowledge the child might have gained by other environmental conditions. Personally, I think you are quite justified in omitting the I.Q. tests." Beyond the need for mere statistical representation in faculty and graduate student ranks, black women's analyses must be incorporated into disciplinary epistemology and academic praxis in order to alleviate the heinous pseudoscience and harmful pedagogical practices being carried out under the guise of objective scholarship.[40]

Certainly, the women in this study demonstrated "classic" characteristics of intelligence, but this history shows that educational success came in different forms, thus supporting Dr. Howard Gardner (also a Harvard professor) in an argument for using multiple intelligence theory as a standard measure of competency and worth rather than the essentialist IQ testing. The authors of *The Bell Curve* readily admit that the "intelligence quotient" (IQ) simply measures one characteristic in a range of intelligence indicators. Moreover, they confess, "the thing we know as IQ is important but not a synonym for human excellence." IQ measures cognitive functioning in response to a specific type of test. Why then, is IQ, or the "g factor," used in standardized test construction? Why, if standardized tests admittedly do not measure academic or human potential, are they among the most important criteria for determining access to college and graduate school? Scholars in black women's history provide a vital perspective from which to address and weigh these questions. Certainly, it is essential to have relatively uniform understanding of academic subjects, and it is imperative to develop reasonable criteria with which to determine academic competency. What is not essential is the historic cultural bias with which the tests have been constructed, the big business that they generate in order to keep the rich on an inside track to economic domination, or the equation of narrowly defined academic excellence to a "meritocracy" that, thinly veiled, rationalizes withholding resources from those in need.[41]

.   Now, as ever, race is a slippery and elusive variable (as proven by the 2000 Census multiracial categorization), and debates about race, gender, economic class, and cognitive difference are as alive and well as religion versus science debates. What also remains dynamic is the messiness of constructing the American college curriculum. Choosing what to keep and what to change in pursuit of academic excellence is not a simple matter of rejecting all things in the "dead white men" canon. Lawrence Levine's *The Opening of the American Mind: Canons, Culture, and History* provided a convincing rejoinder to Allan Bloom's *The Closing of the American Mind: How Higher Education Has Failed Democracy and Impoverished the Souls of Today's Students.* As Levine argued, the challenge to a conservative, traditional curriculum is not a uniform rejection of the "classics" but rather a rigorous, and fearless, intellectual debate about a wide range of texts and approaches. Just like race is not as simple as black and white, a truly excellent college curriculum is neither a traditional canon (conservative), a deconstruction of the existing canon (liberal), nor a new canon of "marginalized" texts (radical). I argue that academic excellence comes with a combination of these approaches.[42]

Based on archaic and faulty notions of excellence, the "eminence" of a university still is measured in direct reverse proportion to the number of minority graduate students and tenured, full-time black women faculty. Early in this twenty-first century, leadership of Harvard University openly disparaged black and women's scholarship. The challenge to African American studies as a field coupled with the biological determinist assertion of women's intellectual inferiority—particularly in mathematics and science—provides rough academic ground. True, it is a fact that black women, Willie Hobbs Moore (Michigan, 1972) and Shirley A. Jackson (MIT, 1976), did not earn a Ph.D. in physics until one hundred years after Edward Bouchet earned his doctorate from Yale and eighty years after the first white woman, Margaret Eliza Malby, earned her Ph.D. in that field (1895). Reasons for this phenomenon are deeply contested; I argue that this history effectively disputes the simplistic positions of Harvard's Larry Summers and others.[43]

I, like my predecessors, "talk back" to the gatekeepers. As in my dissertation, "Living Legacies: Black Women, Educational Philosophies, and

Community Service, 1865–1965," I stand steadfast that my research remain radically subjective, even when, as a junior scholar, I am rightly challenged to improve the quality of my scholarship. I readily admit to "partisan pleading" on behalf of the underrepresented and disenfranchised populations of which I am a member. This history tells my story. While attending college and graduate school over the past decade, I have identified with the feelings of helplessness, academic insecurity, victimization, and determined strategizing revealed in historic memoirs. Many gatekeepers have told me (essentially), "you can't win, you can't break even, and you can't get out of the game"—and I have felt just like the scarecrow in the 1970s black musical *The Wiz*. Too often, students, administrators, colleagues, and journal reviewers who assumed I had no knowledge of the academic history referenced herein or scholarly skills required to make it in academe have subjected me to *extraordinary scrutiny*. Though sometimes it pays to be underestimated, quite honestly, many folks have simply gotten on my very last nerve, and I have felt like turning into the stereotypical angry black woman and just throwing a fit. All this for the pleasure of having debilitating school loans because, economically, my ancestors were not only "left behind" but kept behind.[44]

I have faced barriers that are specific to my identity as a black woman. Researching this history bolstered my resolve to succeed despite internal anxieties or external blockades. As Joyce West Stevens theorizes in *Smart and Sassy*, my contentious relationship with academies of higher education has strengthened my will to be "smart" (making sense of the world in a way that makes sense to me) and "sassy" (challenging others' interpretations if, after due investigation, they do not jibe with my experience, ethical research, global perspectives, or lessons of my elders). I think for myself, knowing full well that historic definitions of higher education insist that I cannot or should not do so.[45]

This research is my life's work. This is my word, my law, my experiment. My journey. My prophecy. But this history is not my story alone. It can no longer be said that Plato's dialogues are "universal" while black women's writings are merely simple or particular. Though originating from a unique standpoint, black women have spoken to themes of universal human interest at least as much as Greek men. Additionally, without reading black women's and other marginalized scholarship, one may very well miss a full appreciation of the enduring relevance of the *Pyramid Texts*, the implications of the *Phaedrus* or the *Republic*, or the philosophical significance of "The Beginning of Time." Black women complicate ideas of innocence and judgment found in ancient Egypt; they embody the relationship between love and written word and challenge ideas of citizenship or freedom in Plato's dialogues; and they engage Stephen Hawking's assessment of impending forward motion of time in ways that give deeper meaning to these and other stories.

Black women in the Ivory Tower exemplify the best of scholarship-activism. Their views of education offer a foil to Machiavellian models that don't provide a sustainable future for the country or world. I offer my *standpoint social contract* and black feminist approaches to higher education, but not to assert all black women are genius-saints (trust me, we're not). Rather, I argue that by researching black women's academic history, we may find hints on how to alleviate inequalities through humane research, culturally sensitive teaching, active learning, and informed service. Colleges and universities in the United States have increasingly become central to defining cultural, political, and economic reality on a global scale. For those interested in ensuring that the academy does not continue to reify impenetrable social hierarchies, history is instructive. I pray that this story helps create more equitable and ethical institutions as time, technology, and circumstance reconfigure the international human landscape.

Education is both a human and civil right—all human beings deserve "this right to grow." I submit that all who wish to lend their head, hearts, and hands in earnest rigor, for the betterment of all, should have keys to the Ivory Tower. Gatekeepers and hoarders of power have played a shell game with resources long enough. Many in the academy have been ignobly prideful, arrogant, and wretched. Institutional change will no doubt be a long journey, but please, as Jill Scott has suggested, let's take that long walk.

Notes

Introduction. "This Right to Grow": Higher Education as Both a Human and Civil Right

1. Cooper, "Souvenir," in *Voice*, 339–40. The term *Ivory Tower* originates in the Bible (Songs of Solomon), but is commonly used to mean "pure" intellectual striving in the abstract sanctuary of an academic campus.

2. Bethune, *Building a Better World*, 108–11.

3. Mills, *Racial Contract*, 88; Rousseau, "The Social Pact," in *Social Contract*, 18–19; Pateman, *Sexual Contract*, 17–25, 41. For race and gender intersections in history, see Louise Newman, *White Women's Rights: The Racial Origins of Feminism in the United States*, 20, and Leslie Alexander, "Challenge of Race," 50–51. This work also builds on Patricia Hill Collins's articulation of black women's standpoint throughout *Black Feminist Thought*.

4. Hine, Brown, and Terborg-Penn, *Historical Encyclopedia*, vol. 2, 1320–25, 1347–48. Charlotte Grimké (1855–62), Anna Cooper (1892–1945), Sarah Early (1894), Fannie Coppin (1913), Emma Hackley (1916), Charlotte Brown (1919; 1941), Hallie Brown (1926), Harriet Marshall (1930), Mary McLeod Bethune (1902–55), Augusta Baker (1957), and Septima Clark (1962) all produced major works, as designated by their inclusion in the Library of Congress catalogue. Though two of the women (Bethune and Grimké) did not produce manuscripts themselves, their work has been published in book form.

5. Martin, *Reclaiming a Conversation*, 3–7.

6. Ibid., 3.

7. Shaw, *What a Woman Ought to Be and to Do*, 74. See also Cooper, "Higher Education of Women," in *Voice*, 72–88; Cuthbert, *Education and Marginality*; Noble, *Negro Woman's College Education*; Ihle, *Black Women in Higher Education*; Slowe, "Higher Education of Negro Women"; Noble, "Higher Education of Black Women in the Twentieth Century," Linda Perkins, "Education of Black Women in the Nineteenth Century," 64–86.

8. Lawson, *Three Sarahs*, 203–8; Anderson Papers, Middlebury College Archives.

9. Collins, *Black Feminist Thought*, 251–71.

10. Ibid., 14, 21–43, 210–16, 228.

11. John Hope Franklin, "On the Evolution of Scholarship," 13–18. I demarcate four periods in black education: (1) pre-1865, a period of suppression; (2) 1865–1910, emergence from enslavement, growth of opportunity, and academic elitism; (3) 1910–54, a period when the number of collegiate black women exceeded black men, but black women remained marginalized; and (4) post-1954, in which black women increased their demands for citizenship both in American society and academe. I focus on the first three eras as "waves" of educational attainment.

12. Significantly, feminist research also supports the use of this framework. Sandra Harding identified three types of feminist scholarship: work that recovers women's theories, research that examines contributions, and history that exposes women's victimization by male dominance. These themes in feminist methodology are accompanied by resistance narratives, mirroring approaches in black studies. See also Sitkoff, "Segregation, Desegregation, Resegregation"; Kirsch, *Ethical Dilemmas in Feminist Research*, 21; V. P. Franklin, "New Perspectives on African American Educational History."

13. Collier-Thomas, "Impact of Black Women," 173.

14. Rorty, *Philosophers on Education*, 1–2, 37, 54, 82, 136, 154, 184, 374–75. I don't argue that classical philosophers should not be studied but rather that other perspectives need to be considered.

15. Feagin, Vera, and Imani, *Agony of Education*; Cleveland, *Long Way to Go*; U.S. Dept. of Education, *Digest of Education Statistics 2001 Edition*, table 8; U.S. Dept. of Education, *Digest of Education Statistics 2002*, table 228; Nettles and Perna, *African-American Education Data Book*, 27, 434; Trower and Chait, "Faculty Diversity: Too Little for Too Long," 35; *Florida State University System Fact Book*.

16. All biographical information on Cooper found in Hutchinson, *Anna J. Cooper: A Voice from the South*; Lemert and Bhan, "The Colored Woman's Office," in Cooper, *Voice*, 1–43. There is no conclusive documentation of the year of her birth.

17. Biographical information on Bethune found in Bethune, *Building a Better World*, 3–17; Giddings, *In Search of Sisterhood*, 16; Hine, *Hine Sight*, 16–17; and Hanson, *Bethune and Black Women's Political Activism*, 1–10. See also Bethune, "The Adaptation of the History of the Negro to the Capacity of the Child"; and Elaine Smith, *A Guide to the Microfilm Edition of Mary McLeod Bethune Papers*, pt. 1, 1918–1955. McCluskey and Smith utilized the following periodicals to assess Bethune's work: *Aframerican Women's Journal* (renamed *Women United*, 1940–49); *Chicago Defender* (1848–1955); *National Notes* (1924–28); *Pittsburgh Courier* (1937–38).

18. Flemming, *Answered Prayer to a Dream*, 23.

19. Bethune, *Building a Better World*, 11.

20. Ibid., 4, 15.

Chapter 1. "A Plea for the Oppressed": Educational Strivings, Pre-1865

1. Lawson and Merrill, "Antebellum 'Talented Thousandth,'" 143–48; Paul Nelson, "Experiment in Interracial Education at Berea College," 91; Pulliam and Van Patten, *History of Education in America*, 134; Rudolph, *American College and University*, 47; Woodson, *Education of the Negro Prior to 1861*, 265; Baumann, "History of Recording Black Students at Oberlin College." Pulliam and Van Patten incorrectly list John Russwurm as the first African American college graduate.

2. Hine, *A Shining Thread*, 122–23.

3. "In Motion," Schomburg map collection; see maps titled, "African Americans Going West," "Free African Population in the 19th Century," and "Principal States

of Origin of the Migrants 1870–1890"; Lawson and Merrill, "Antebellum 'Talented Thousandth,'" 143–48.

4. Ihle, *Black Women in Higher Education*, 5; Lawson and Merrill, "Antebellum 'Talented Thousandth'"; Lawson and Merrill, "Antebellum Black Codes at Oberlin College"; Slowe, *Higher Education of Negro Women*, 352.

5. Brown, *Homespun Heroines*, 244–45; Ihle, *Black Women in Higher Education*. Solomon's oversight of Lucy Stanton resulted in the incorrect identification of 1858 as the date that the first woman spoke at an Oberlin commencement. Solomon, *In the Company of Educated Women*, 29. The Cleveland Hall of Fame incorrectly records Stanton's death date as 1912.

6. Mary Jane Patterson was born in Raleigh, North Carolina; some sources list her birth date as 1840, but Ohio state census records suggest that 1843 is probably correct.

7. Mary Patterson Papers, O.H.I.O. Resource Center.

8. Lawson and Merrill, *Three Sarahs*, 3–46.

9. Hartigan, "Edmonia Lewis," in Hine, Brown, and Terborg-Penn, *Historical Encyclopedia* vol. 1, 716–19.

10. Linda Perkins, *Fanny Jackson Coppin and the Institute for Colored Youth*; Linda Perkins, "Heed Life's Demands"; Linda Perkins, "Quaker Beneficence and Black Control." Morgan, in *Historical Perspectives on the Education of Black Children*, incorrectly identifies Coppin as the first black woman college graduate, 25.

11. Lawson and Merrill, *Three Sarahs*, 16; Lawson and Merrill, "Antebellum 'Talented Thousandth.'"

12. Woodson, *Education of the Negro Prior to 1861*, 2–12.

13. Cross, "Earliest Black Graduates," 104; Lawson and Merrill, "Antebellum 'Talented Thousandth.'"

14. Woodson, *Education of the Negro Prior to 1861*, 28, 72, 112–13.

15. Woodson, *Education of the Negro Prior to 1861*; McPherson, *Abolitionist Legacy*; Du Bois, *College-Bred Negro*, Du Bois and Dill, *College-Bred Negro American*; Linda Perkins, "Education" in Hine, Brown, and Terborg-Penn, *Historical Encyclopedia*; James Anderson, *Education of Blacks in the South*; Heather Williams, *Self-Taught*.

16. James Anderson, *Education of Blacks in the South*; Bond, *Education of the Negro in the American Social Order*; V. P. Franklin, *Education of Black Philadelphia*; Morgan, *Historical Perspectives on the Education of Black Children*; Heather Williams, *Self-Taught*; Terrell, "History of the High School for Negroes in Washington"; Richardson, *Maria W. Stewart*.

17. Linda Perkins, "Education"; Bond, *Education of the Negro in the American Social Order*; Woodson, *Education of the Negro Prior to 1861*; James Anderson, *Education of Blacks in the South*; Jacqueline Jones, *Labor of Love*.

18. James Anderson, *Education of Blacks in the South*; Bond, *Education of the Negro in the American Social Order*.

19. James Anderson, *Education of Blacks in the South*, 7–9; Linda Perkins, "Education" in Hine, Brown, and Terborg-Penn, *Historical Encyclopedia*, 380–87; Haywood, *Prophesying Daughters*; Peterson, *Doers of the Word*; Woodson, *Education of the Negro Prior to 1861*; Wright, *Education of Negroes in New Jersey*.

20. Heather Williams, *Self-Taught*, 57–58; Rudolph, *American College and University*, 8–13.

21. For example, Rust College was one of the several schools supported by the Methodist Episcopal Church and the Stewart Missionary Foundation. There were eleven of these schools in the South and one in the West. Rudolph, *American College and University*, 11, 19, 55, 70. Congregationalists founded Yale, Dartmouth, Williams, Amherst, Oberlin, and Western Reserve. Ihle, *Black Women in Higher Education*, 140.

22. Rudolph, *American College and University*, 4–47. The first American colleges were Harvard College (Massachusetts, 1636), the College of William and Mary (Virginia, 1692), the Collegiate School/Yale (Connecticut, 1701), and New Jersey College/Princeton (New Jersey, 1746).

23. Ibid., 185.

24. Ibid., 211.

25. Pulliam and Van Patten, *History of Education in America*, 82–83; Rudolph, *American College and University*, 24–26, 120.

26. Pulliam and Van Patten, *History of Education in America*, 34; Rudolph, *American College and University*, 27, 76, 104, 139.

27. Pulliam and Van Patten, *History of Education in America*, 102; Rudolph, *American College and University*, 134, 151, 239.

28. Pulliam and Van Patten, *History of Education in America*, 103–4; Rudolph, *American College and University*, 249–52.

29. Rudolph, *American College and University*, 255.

30. Ibid., 308.

31. Ibid., 307–28.

32. Ihle, *Black Women in Higher Education*, 223; Rudolph, *American College and University*, 311–12.

33. Rudolph, *American College and University*, 314.

34. Kluger, *Simple Justice*, 75–77.

35. Jacqueline Jones, *Labor of Love*, 35–75; "Chronology" in Hine, Brown, and Terborg-Penn, *Historical Encyclopedia*, vol. 2, 1309–13; Morris, *Southern Slavery and the Law*; Sinha, *Counterrevolution of Slavery*.

36. Ihle, *Black Women in Higher Education 5*, 223; Jacqueline Jones, *Labor of Love*.

37. McHenry, *Forgotten Readers*; Royster, *Traces of a Stream*.

38. Gaspar and Hine, *Beyond Bondage*; Woodson, *Education of the Negro Prior to 1861*, 256–82; Rudolph, *American College and University*, 7, 52, 55, 68–85; Neverdon-Morton, *Afro-American Women of the South*; Karen Johnson, *Uplifting the Women and the Race*; White, *Too Heavy a Load*.

39. Carby, *Reconstructing Womanhood*, 95–120.

40. White, *Too Heavy a Load*. For discussion of social politics involved in black women's middle-class values, see Lemert's, "Colored Woman's Office," in Cooper, *Voice*.

Chapter 2. "The Crown of Culture": Educational Attainment, 1865–1910

1. Paul Nelson, "Experiment in Interracial Education at Berea College, 1858–1908," 91.

2. The original *Voice* was published in Xenia, Ohio; even though Cooper was living in D.C., Ohio still was a mainstay for black resources. Black men also wrote on black women's social position. Views ranged, but most notable are Alexander Crummell, "The Black Woman of the South: Her Neglects and Her Needs" (1883), in *Africa and America*, and Du Bois, "The Damnation of Women" (1920), in *Darkwater*.

3. Cooper, "Higher Education of Women," in *Voice*, 84; Carby, *Reconstructing Womanhood*, 95–120.

4. Cooper, "Higher Education of Women," in *Voice*, 85; Linda Perkins, "Education," 384.

5. Du Bois, *College-Bred Negro*, 56. These numbers closely mirrored the conservative-liberal split of the Hayes-Tilden Compromise in the 1876 presidential election: Republican (northern) states had 37 graduates and Democrat (southern) states only 16. Hine, *Odyssey*, 302.

6. Du Bois, *College-Bred Negro*, 55–56. There are a few recent surveys of blacks in higher education that help give insight into the lives that these numbers represent. For example, the first black graduate of Cornell was a woman, Sara Brown, a Virginia native, and her sister also graduated from Cornell in 1899. Slater, "Blacks Who First Entered the World of White Higher Education," 52.

7. Paul Nelson, "Experiment in Interracial Education at Berea College, 1858–1908," 9.

8. Du Bois and Dill, *College-Bred Negro American*, 46–47; Rudolph, *American College and University*, 250–55, 263, 281, 287, 424–27; Ihle, *Black Women in Higher Education*, xvii.

9. Du Bois and Dill, *College-Bred Negro American*, 46–47.

10. Ibid., 46–47; Burnside, "Black Symbols," in Berea College, *U.S. Traditions*, 116–23; Taylor and Moore, *African American Women Confront the West*, 293–311; Ihle, *Black Women in Higher Education*, 140.

11. Du Bois, *College-Bred Negro*, 37; Du Bois and Dill, *College-Bred Negro American*, 45.

12. Du Bois, *College-Bred Negro*, 12–13; Du Bois and Dill, *College-Bred Negro American*, 12–13.

13. Pulliam and Van Patten, *History of Education in America*, 130–31; Rudolph, *American College and University*, 263, 281.

14. James Anderson, *Education of Blacks in the South*, 114, 251, 256; Ward, *Black*

Physicians in the Jim Crow South, 24; Willie and Edmonds, *Black Colleges in America*, 111.

15. Ihle, *Black Women in Higher Education*, 185; Cooper, "Higher Education of Women," in *Voice*, 84; Linda Perkins, "Education," 386–87.

16. Du Bois and Dill, *College-Bred Negro American*.

17. Ward, *Black Physicians in the Jim Crow South*, 20–24; Willie and Edmonds, *Black Colleges in America*, 80–83.

18. Du Bois and Dill, *College-Bred Negro American*.

19. Gilmore, *Gender and Jim Crow*.

20. Du Bois and Dill, *College-Bred Negro American*; Ihle, *Black Women in Higher Education*, 141.

21. Charles Johnson, *Negro College Graduate*, 47–48.

22. Watkins, *White Architects of Black Education*.

23. Watkins, *White Architects of Black Education*; Anderson and Moss, *Dangerous Donations*.

24. Willie and Edmonds, *Black Colleges in America*, 80–83.

25. Spelman was rated as a college in 1901. In 1938, *Opportunity* featured an article that outlined Bennett's development. Ihle, *Black Women in Higher Education*, 210. See the following entries in *Historical Encyclopedia*, vol. 1: Brown, "Hartshorn Memorial College," 543–47; Guy-Sheftall, "Bennett College" and "Spelman College," 109, 1091–95; Linda Perkins, "Education," 384.

26. Guy-Sheftall, "Black Women and Higher Education," 278–87; Collins, "Socialization at Two Black Women's Colleges," 2.

27. Ihle, *Black Women in Higher Education*, 77.

28. Lane, *Documentary of Mrs. Booker T. Washington*; Ihle, *Black Women in Higher Education*, xiii–xxx, 122; Easter, *Nannie Helen Burroughs*; James Anderson, *Education of Blacks in the South*, 34–35; Anderson and Moss, *Dangerous Donations*; Brazzell, "Bricks without Straw," 26–49; Watkins, *White Architects of Black Education*.

29. Rudolph, *American College and University*, 232, 442.

30. Ibid., 244.

31. Linda Perkins, "Racial Integration of the Seven Sister Colleges," 104–8.

32. Rudolph, *American College and University*, 317; Du Bois and Dill, *College-Bred Negro American*, 46; Linda Perkins, "Racial Integration of the Seven Sister Colleges."

33. Rudolph, *American College and University*, 319–22.

34. Ibid., 322.

35. Ibid., 326–27.

36. Ibid., 325.

37. African American communities also established exclusive intellectual clubs. See Lemert's, "The Colored Woman's Office," about discrimination in the American Negro Academy (founded by Alexander Crummell in 1897), in Cooper, *Voice*.

38. Rudolph, *American College and University*, 322; Cross, "Earliest Black Graduates," 105; Titcomb, "Earliest Members of Phi Beta Kappa," 92.

39. Linda Perkins, "Racial Integration of the Seven Sister Colleges," 106; Giddings, *In Search of Sisterhood*, 84; Fauset authored *There Is Confusion* (1924), *Plum Bun* (1929), *The Chinaberry Tree* (1931), and *Comedy, American Style* (1933).

40. By the turn of the twenty-first century, there were 262 chapters with 722,914 members. Controversy surrounds the organization because top-ranked HBCUs were not awarded chapters for decades after students met requirements. Spelman was not granted a chapter until 1997. In his account, "Earliest Black Members of Phi Beta Kappa" (2001), Titcomb documented George Washington Henderson as the first inductee (1877, University of Vermont). Before Titcomb's research, scholars believed that Edward Bouchet was also the first ΦBK. Bouchet was not elected to ΦBK until 1884, though he graduated in 1874. Because of the obscurity of black women, research also overlooked Anderson.

41. Shaw, *What a Woman Ought to Be and to Do*, 42.

42. Pateman, *Sexual Contract*; Mills, *Racial Contract*; Cooper, "My Racial Philosophy," in *Voice*, 236–37.

43. Butler, "Black Fraternal and Benevolent Societies in Nineteenth-Century America," in Brown, Parks, and Phillips, *African American Fraternities and Sororities*, 67–93; Ihle, *Black Women in Higher Education*, 40, 45; White, *Too Heavy a Load*, 27. Skee-wee!

44. Alexander, "History of the Colored Race in America" (1887), in Ihle, *Black Women in Higher Education*, 45.

45. Rudolph, *American College and University*, 189.

46. Ibid., 263, 281–93.

47. Pulliam and Van Patten, *History of Education in America*, 162–63; Rudolph, *American College and University*, 281, 293.

48. Rudolph, *American College and University*, 289.

49. Litwack, *Trouble in Mind*; Painter, *Standing at Armageddon*.

50. Litwack, *Trouble in Mind*, 11.

51. Ibid., 12.

Chapter 3. "Beating Onward, Ever Onward": A Critical Mass, 1910–1954

1. Charles Johnson, *Negro College Graduate*, 39.

2. Du Bois, *College-Bred Negro American*, 47, 52; Charles Johnson, *Negro College Graduate*, 8.

3. Rudolph, *American College and University*, 146, 546–47.

4. Height, *Open Wide the Freedom Gates*, 30–31, 297; Cross, "Earliest Black Graduates," 104; Du Bois, *College-Bred Negro*, 55; Du Bois and Dill, *College-Bred Negro American*, 46; Charles Johnson, *Negro College Graduate*, 7–8. Very few black women sought graduate or professional degrees outside of the nursing field. Black nurses were second in number to normal school teachers but were the largest number of

students trained in the professions. *The College-Bred Negro American* published the survey of 800 African American college graduates, from 107 PWIs and 34 HBCUs. Johnson's study, though more current, mistakenly listed John Russwurm as the first African American college graduate (Bowdoin, Maine, 1826).

5. Charles Johnson, *Negro College Graduate*, 20, 292–98.

6. Cuthbert, *Education and Marginality*, 18; Noble, "Negro Woman's College Education," 34, table 3.

7. Gibson and Lennon, "Historical Census Statistics on the Foreign-born Population of the United States: 1850–1990." Cuthbert calculated that a total of 2,458 had earned degrees, so Johnson's survey included a significant portion of the black women college graduates. Cuthbert, *Education and Marginality*, 18.

8. Cuthbert, *Education and Marginality*, 138; Solomon, *In the Company of Educated Women*, 145, 242n2.

9. Charles Johnson, *Negro College Graduate*, 10, 22. Of these, 14,078 had done so in the South; 2,465 in New England; 2,117 in the Midwest; and 258 in the West.

10. Du Bois, *Philadelphia Negro*, 93, 95; Solomon, *In the Company of Educated Women*, 76, 131.

11. Charles Johnson, *Negro College Graduate*, 38–40; Slater, "First Black Graduates," 72; Slater, "Blacks Who First Entered the World of White Higher Education"; Woodson to Dykes, April 7, 1921, in Eva Dykes Papers, MSRC Collections; Harley, "Black Women in a Southern City."

12. Cuthbert, *Education and Marginality*, 141–45; Du Bois and Dill, *College-Bred Negro American*.

13. Bethune, *Building a Better World*, 72.

14. Charles Johnson, *Negro College Graduate*, 20; Ihle, *Black Women in Higher Education*, 107, 140, 186, 213–14; Linda Perkins, "Education," 384–85.

15. Harley and the Black Women's Work Collective, *Sister Circle*.

16. Marlowe, *Right and Worthy Grand Mission*, 204–5; Brown, Parks, and Phillips, *African American Fraternities and Sororities*, 79, 163.

17. Evans, "Black Greek-Lettered Organizations and Civic Responsibility"; Giddings, *In Search of Sisterhood*, 16, 84. See Turk, *Bound by a Mighty Vow*; and Kimbrough, *Black Greek 101*. The five black fraternities are Alpha Phi Alpha (1906), Kappa Alpha Psi (1911), Omega Psi Phi (1911), Phi Beta Sigma (1914), and Iota Phi Theta (1963). For analysis of the first sororities, see Giddings's *In Search of Sisterhood* and Parker's *Past Is Prologue*.

18. Ihle, *Black Women in Higher Education*, 86; Giddings, *When and Where I Enter*; Turk, *Bound by a Mighty Vow*.

19. Linda Perkins, "Black Feminism and 'Race Uplift,' 1890–1900"; Linda Perkins, "Black Women and the Philosophy of 'Racial Uplift' prior to Emancipation"; Wilson, "All of the Glory. . . Faded . . . Quickly"; Johnson, "Georgiana Simpson," in *Historical Encyclopedia*, vol. 2, 1038–39.

20. Ihle, *Black Women's Higher Education*, xxiii, xxv, 101.

21. White, *Too Heavy a Load*, 67–68, 81, 148, 159. For variances in black women's

ideologies, compare Lane, *Documentary of Mrs. Booker T. Washington*; Terrell, *Colored Woman in a White World*; Cooper, *Voice*; Hanson, *Bethune and Black Women's Political Activism*; and Height, *Open Wide the Freedom Gates*.

22. White, *Too Heavy a Load*, 87–109, 157; Ihle, *Black Women in Higher Education*, 202; Evelyn Higginbotham, *Righteous Discontent*, 14–15; Ula Taylor, speech at the Association of Black Women Historians annual luncheon, 2003 ASALH conference, Orlando, Florida.

23. Ihle, *Black Women in Higher Education*, xxix, 199–201; Flemming, *Answered Prayer to a Dream*, 15; Bethune, *Building a Better World*, 5, 50–53, 285.

24. James, *Transcending the Talented Tenth*. Ihle asserts that women like Patterson, Coppin, and Terrell were "exceptional"; this interpretation must be further investigated. True, they overcame extraordinary barriers, but they did not possess a capacity lacking in other black women. Ihle, *Black Women in Higher Education*, xv.

25. James Anderson, *Education of Blacks in the South*, 269, 273.

26. Ihle, *Black Women in Higher Education*, xxxvii n2; James Anderson, *Education of Blacks in the South*, 266–73; Rudolph, *American College and University*, 427, 443.

27. V. P. Franklin, *Living Our Stories*, 11–20; Franklin and Collier-Thomas, "Biography, Race Vindication, and African-American Intellectuals," 1–16; Malveaux, "When the Personal Is Political," 36; Harrison and Harrison, *African American Pioneers in Anthropology*, 1–22; Sundiata, *Brothers and Strangers*, 2–8, 41–45, 339–40.

28. Ihle, *Black Women in Higher Education*, 169.

29. Ihle, *Black Women in Higher Education*, 161; Linda Perkins, "Black Women and the Philosophy of 'Uplift'"; Linda Perkins, "Black Feminism and 'Race Uplift'"; Howard University student manual, Lucy Diggs Slowe Papers, MSRC Collections.

30. Ihle, *Black Women in Higher Education*, xxviii; Slowe, "Higher Education of Negro Women"; Slowe, "Colored Girl Enters College"; *Journal of the College Alumnae Club of Washington*, memorial edition, January 1939, Lucy Diggs Slowe Papers, MSRC Collections.

31. Ihle, *Black Women in Higher Education*, 165.

32. White, *Too Heavy a Load*, 40–41; Ihle, *Black Women in Higher Education*, 189; Slowe, "Higher Education of the Negro Woman," 354, 356.

33. Ihle, *Black Women in Higher Education*, 190; Terrell, *Colored Woman in a White World*, 52–53.

34. Ihle, *Black Women in Higher Education*, 190.

35. Cuthbert, *Education and Marginality*, 117–18; Charles Johnson, *Negro College Graduate*, 60.

36. Cuthbert, *Education and Marginality*, 134–51.

37. Player, *Improving College Education*, 35–40.

38. Ibid., 36, 204–8.

39. Cuthbert, *Education and Marginality*, 92; Ihle, *Black Women in Higher Education*, 86; Kimbrough, *Black Greek 101*; Giddings, *In Search of Sisterhood*; Parker, *Past Is Prologue*.

40. As evidenced by her bibliographic essay, Noble consciously built her study on research by Woodson, Slowe, Johnson, Cuthbert, and Player. Noble, "Negro Woman's College Education," 32, appendix A.

41. Ibid., 4–8, 76–93; Ula Taylor, *Veiled Garvey*, chap. 1.

42. Noble, "Negro Woman's College Education," 137–39.

43. Ibid., 34–35.

44. U.S. Dept. of Education, *Digest of Education Statistics 2001*, table 8; Noble, "Negro Woman's College Education," 29; Elizabeth Higginbotham, *Too Much to Ask*.

45. Sundiata, *Brothers and Strangers*, 7. *Birth of a Nation* was based on Thomas Dixon's 1905 novel *The Klansman*; *Gone with the Wind* was based on Margaret Mitchell's 1936 novel.

46. Scott, *Contempt and Pity*, 12, 32, 81.

47. Zieger and Gall, *American Workers*, 33–65; Maxine Jones, "No Longer Denied," 241.

48. Hine, *Historical Encyclopedia*, 1309–32.

49. Harley, "Black Women in a Southern City"; Logan, *What the Negro Wants*.

50. Jacqueline Jones, *Labor of Love*, 215; Ihle, *Black Women in Higher Education*, xxxvii n3. Legislation relating to the *Brown* case: *Roberts v. Boston* (1848); *Murray v. University of Maryland Law School* (1936); *Gaines v. Missouri* (1938); *Sweat v. Painter* (1950); *Sipuel v. University of Oklahoma Law School* (1948); *McClauren v. Oklahoma* (1950); *Brown v. Topeka, Kansas Board of Education* (1954); *Lucy v. Adams* (1955); *Bakke v. UC Davis* (1978); *Gratz v. Bollinger* (2003); and *Grutter v. Bollinger* (2003). Tushnet's *NAACP's Strategy against Segregated Education* (1987) and Kluger's *Simple Justice* (1975) describe these cases in great detail. James Patterson's *"Brown v. Board of Education"* (2001) provides helpful context for the cases.

51. Takaki, *A Different Mirror*, 228–36; 327–29.

52. Dewey, *Democracy and Education*, 19–20, 122–23; Dewey, *Experience and Education*, 40. Not only did black women's identity influence their own education, but education impacted families through generations: Mary Jane Patterson's cousin was Langston Hughes's grandmother; Sadie Tanner Mossell Alexander was the niece of artist Henry O. Tanner; Charlotte Hawkins Brown's niece is Natalie Cole.

53. Cooper, "Souvenir," in *Voice*, 339–40.

Chapter 4. "Reminiscences of School Life": Six College Memoirs

1. V. P. Franklin, *Living Our Stories*, 11–20; Braxton, *Black Women Writing Autobiography*; Margo Perkins, *Autobiography as Activism*. For a comprehensive list of black women's autobiographies, see Evelyn Higginbotham, *Harvard Guide to African-American History*, 777–839. These six were chosen for their focus on the college experience. In "Being and Living in Research," Theodorea Berry uses contemporary autobiography to consider how cultural identity can inform teaching diverse populations.

2. Ihle, *Black Women in Higher Education*, xxvi.

3. Linda Perkins, *Fanny Jackson Coppin and the Institute for Colored Youth*.

4. Coppin wrote under the pseudonym "Catherine Casey" and began the column in 1878. She delivered the World's Fair address as one of a triad of speeches given by herself, Anna Cooper, and activist Fannie Barrier Williams.

5. In 1919, Levi Coppin published his own autobiography, *Unwritten History*. Here, the reader was treated to a more personal view, albeit from the perspective of her husband.

6. Coppin, *Reminiscences*, 15. Coppin's papers are located at Oberlin College; Friends Historical Library, at Swarthmore College; and the Quaker Records, at Haverford College. In 1922, the Quakers transferred the school to the State of Pennsylvania. It is now Cheyney State Teachers College.

7. Ihle, *Black Women in Higher Education*, 24; Coppin, *Reminiscences*, 12.

8. Coppin, *Reminiscences*, 15–17.

9. Ibid., 13.

10. Ibid., 12.

11. Ibid., 14.

12. Ibid., 17–18.

13. Terrell, *Colored Woman in a White World*, 40; Ihle, *Black Women in Higher Education*, 25, 32–34.

14. Terrell, *Colored Woman in a White World*.

15. White, *Too Heavy a Load*, 87–109, Terrell's papers are held at the Library of Congress in Washington, D.C.

16. Terrell, *Colored Woman in a White World*, 21.

17. Ihle, *Black Women in Higher Education*, 28–29.

18. Terrell, *Colored Woman in a White World*, 42–43.

19. Ibid., 32, 42, 48; Cooper, "Higher Education of Women," and "Early Years in Washington," in *Voice*, 85–86, 312; Ihle, *Black Women in Higher Education*, 23, 28–29, 81; Coppin, *Reminiscences*, 12.

20. Terrell, *Colored Woman in a White World*, 40.

21. Ibid., 43.

22. Ibid., 46–47.

23. Ibid., 48.

24. Patterson, "Hurston," in *Historical Encyclopedia*, vol. 1, 598–603.

25. Mary Helen Washington, introduction to Walker, *I Love Myself When I Am Laughing*; Hurston quoted in *Historical Encyclopedia*, vol. 1, 602.

26. Now Morgan State University.

27. Hurston, *Dust Tracks*, 129.

28. Ibid.

29. Ibid.

30. Ibid., 130.

31. Ibid., 131–32.

32. Ibid., 139–40.

33. Ibid., 140.

34. Ibid.

35. Ibid., 143; Mikell, "Feminism and Black Culture," 51–61.

36. Hurston, *Dust Tracks*, 144–45.

37. No available source confirms Morton's death date. The *Harvard Guide* does not list a date, and my attempts to locate information from Delta Sigma Theta's national office and Texas College were unsuccessful. Her last publication appeared in 1972.

38. Morton, *My First Sixty Years*, 16–30.

39. Ibid., 128–43.

40. Ibid., 32.

41. Ibid., 40–43.

42. Ibid., 39.

43. Ibid.

44. Ibid., 40–42.

45. Ibid., 52–53.

46. Browne, *Love My Children*, 25–30.

47. Browne, *Love My Children*, 25–87.

48. Browne, *Love My Children*, 55.

49. Ibid., 99–111.

50. Ibid., 18–19.

51. Ibid., 20.

52. Murray, *Autobiography*, 1–27.

53. Ibid., "To Maida" (dedication); Bell-Scott, "To Write Like Never Before"; Drury, "Experimentation on the Male Side"; Rupp and Taylor, "Pauli Murray: The Unasked Question."

54. Murray, *Autobiography*, 60–64.

55. Ibid., 64–68.

56. Ibid., 68.

57. Ibid., 83–91.

58. Ibid., 85–86.

59. Pauli Murray Papers, MSRC Collection; Murray, *Autobiography*, 182–83.

60. Murray, *Autobiography*, 183–84.

61. Ibid.

62. Ibid., 261.

63. Ibid., 260–64.

Chapter 5. "I Make Myself Heard": Comparative Collegiate Experiences

1. Delany and Delany, *Having Our Say*, 162.

2. Ihle, *Black Women in Higher Education*, 137.

3. Alpha Kappa Alpha Sorority Ivy Leaf Papers, MSRC Collections; Parker, *Past Is Prologue*, 29, 83–86; Ihle, *Black Women in Higher Education*, 142–43.

4. Parker, *Past Is Prologue*, 157; Ihle, *Black Women in Higher Education*, 148; Shaw, *What a Woman Ought to Be*, 50–51.

5. Ihle, *Black Women in Higher Education*, xxii, 96.

6. Ibid., 151.

7. Ibid., xxx.

8. Ibid., 217–18.

9. Sollors, "Owls and Rats in the American Funnyhouse."

10. Willie and Edmonds, *Black Colleges in America*, 68–87, 100–114; Ihle, *Black Women in Higher Education*, 53, 77.

11. Ihle, *Black Women in Higher Education*, 53.

12. Flemming, *Answered Prayer to a Dream*, 47–64; Ihle, *Black Women in Higher Education*, 213–14.

13. Ihle, *Black Women in Higher Education*, 196.

14. Usher, quoted in Ihle, *Black Women in Higher Education*, 71.

15. Dunnigan's autobiography was titled *A Black Woman's Experience—From Schoolhouse to White House* (1974), quoted in Ihle, *Black Women in Higher Education*, 121.

16. Ihle, *Black Women in Higher Education*, 121.

17. Ibid., 114–17.

18. Ibid., 115.

19. Ibid., 114–16, 122.

20. Ibid., 120.

21. Ibid., 63.

22. Ibid., 85–86, 117–18.

23. Ibid., 39–47, 53–54.

24. Ibid., 87.

25. Ibid., 118.

26. Ibid.

27. Pulliam and Van Patten, *History of Education in America*, 209; Ihle, *Black Women in Higher Education*, 73.

28. Ihle, *Black Women in Higher Education*, xxv, xxviii, 87.

29. Slowe, "Higher Education of Negro Women," 356.

30. Coppin, *Reminiscences*, 13, 15.

31. Terrell, *Colored Woman in a White World*, 47–48.

32. Ihle, *Black Women in Higher Education*, 121.

33. Ibid., 81; Newman, *White Women's Rights*, 86–87.

34. Delany and Delany, *Having Our Say*, 147–63.

35. Ihle, *Black Women in Higher Education*, 148.

36. Ibid., 138.

37. Ibid., 31.

38. Ibid., 138.

39. Browne, *Love My Children*, 24.

40. Ihle, *Black Women in Higher Education*, 64.

41. Neverdon-Morton, *Afro-American Women of the South*, 10–67; Bumstead, "What the Normal Graduates of Atlanta University Are Doing" (1895), in Ihle, *Black Women in Higher Education*, 165, 210, 202.

42. Shaw, *What a Woman Ought to Be and to Do*, 68–104.

43. Ihle, *Black Women in Higher Education*, 54.

Chapter 6. "The Third Step": Doctoral Degrees, 1921–1954

1. Charles Johnson, *Negro College Graduate*, 11; Greene, *Holders of Doctorates*, 23, 219; Rudolph, *American College and University*, 335. The regional breakdown for the 19,883 who earned degrees is 14,078 (South); 2,465 (New England); 2,117 (Midwest); and 258 (West).

2. Greene, *Holders of Doctorates*, 23, 219. Greene's study surveyed 368 of the 381 recipients of doctoral degrees. Of the 13 nonrespondents, some may have been women, and some who earned degrees were not represented, so 48 is an estimate. Perkins counted 45 total, but that was the number of degree earners in the field of education. Linda Perkins, "Education," 386.

3. Charles Johnson, *Negro College Graduate*, 8; Greene, *Holders of Doctorates*, 33. Cross, "Earliest Black Graduates," 104; Du Bois, *College-Bred Negro*, 55; Du Bois and Dill, *College-Bred Negro American*, 46; Solomon, *In the Company of Educated Women*, 134–37.

4. Greene, *Holders of Doctorates*, 29–31.

5. Linda Perkins, "Education," 386.

6. Ibid., 385.

7. Ihle, *Black Women in Higher Education*, 144.

8. Woolf, *A Room of One's Own*, 106; Mazon, *Gender and the Modern Research University*, 6.

9. William Clark, "On the Ironic Specimen of the Doctor of Philosophy"; Mickens, *Edward Bouchet*, vii; Greene, *Holders of Doctorates*, 22–23; Rudolph, *American College and University*, 232, 237, 289, 335, 397, 442; Solomon, *In the Company of Educated Women*, 134–37; Mazon, *Gender and the Modern Research University*; Greene, *Holders of Doctorates*; Tobin, *Black Female Ph.D.*; Willie, Grady, and Hope, *African-Americans and the Doctoral Experience*.

10. Rudolph, *American College and University*, 269, 335, 397.

11. Ibid., 397.

12. Pulliam and Van Patten, *History of Education in America*, 143–35; Rudolph, *American College and University*, 273.

13. Matson, "Phillis Wheatley—Soul Sister?" 222–30; Sterling, *We Are Your Sisters*; Stewart, *Maria W. Stewart*.

14. Dykes, "Pope and His Influence in America from 1715–1850"; Simpson, "Herder's Conception of 'Das Volk'"; Mossell, "The Standard of Living among One Hundred Negro Migrant Families in Philadelphia."

15. A notable exception is Pero Dagbovie, "Black Women Historians from the Late Nineteenth Century to the Dawning of the Civil Rights Movement," 241–61; Charles Johnson, *Negro College Graduate*, 39.

16. Greene, *Holders of Doctorates*, 78–84.

17. Francille Wilson delivered the 2002 address to ABWH; she clarified that the order of degrees earned was Dykes, Mossell, Simpson, but the order of graduation

was Simpson, Mossell, Dykes. This was confirmed in Dykes's 1977 interview for the Black Women Oral History Project (p. 11) in Dykes Papers MSRC.

18. Linda Perkins, "Radical Integration of the Seven Sister Colleges," 104–5; Rudolph, *American College and University*, 296, 469; James Anderson, *Education of Blacks in the South*, 251; letter from Woodson, April 7, 1921, Eva Dykes Papers, MSRC.

19. Dykes, "Pope and His Influence," 12–14, 31, 102–5, 581.

20. Ibid., 13–17, 84, 445, 564.

21. Ibid., 34–35, 96–99; 597–614.

22. Ibid., 110, 117.

23. Dykes, *Negro in English Romantic Thought*, 127–52.

24. Johnson, "Georgiana Simpson," in *Historical Encyclopedia*, vol. 2, 1038–39; "Frelinghuysen University" catalogue, n.d., Anna Julia Cooper Papers, MSRC Collections.

25. Simpson, "Herder's Conception of 'das Volk,'" 7, 9, 14–35, 49, 53–57.

26. Mossell, "Standard of Living," 5–7, 9–13.

27. Ibid., 10, 31; Giddings, *In Search of Sisterhood*, 71–73; Malveaux, "Missed Opportunity," 307–10.

28. Mossell, "Standard of Living," 5.

29. Malveaux, "Missed Opportunity," 307–10; Mossell, "Standard of Living," 21, 23, 49–50; Du Bois, *Philadelphia Negro*, 45, 192–221.

30. Quite a few African Americans studied in Paris, including Bishop Daniel Payne (1868), Mary Church Terrell (1888), and Carter G. Woodson (1907). Greene, *Holders of Doctorates*.

31. Cooper, "Introduction to *Pelerinage*," in *Voice*, 230; Keller, "An Educational Controversy."

32. The Xi Omega chapter of Alpha Kappa Alpha Sorority sponsored a ceremony for Cooper on December 29, 1925, at Howard University's Rankin Chapel, where her degree was presented by William Tindal, D.C. commissioner, on behalf of Emile Daeschner, the French ambassador to the United States (1924–25). Her speech was published in an event program, which was reprinted as part of the sorority's Boulé review in the 1926 *Ivy Leaf*, 16–17. A memento of Daeschner's letter of congratulations, with Cooper's photo, was reprinted in "A Course in Progressions with Dates of Accomplishments," in the *Aframerican Women's Journal*, vol. 1 (summer 1940): 32.

33. Cooper, "L'Attitude de la France," 1; Anna Julia Cooper Papers, MSRC Collections.

34. Cooper, "Third Step," in *Voice*, 327–28.

35. Ibid., 324–29.

36. Ibid., 328–29.

37. Mikell, "Zora Neale Hurston," 61–65; James Patterson, *"Brown v. Board of Education,"* 105; 241n37; McFadden, "Septima Clark and the Struggle for Human Rights," in Crawford, Rouse, and Woods, *Women in the Civil Rights Movement*.

38. Hine et al., *Black Women in United States History*, vol. 6, 459.

39. Dagbovie, "Black Women Historians from the Late Nineteenth Century to the Dawning of the Civil Rights Movement"; "Chronology" in Hine, Brown, and Terborg-Penn, *Historical Encyclopedia*, 1320–25; Ihle, *Black Women in Higher Education*, xvi; Cross, "Tributes and Tokens," 70–71. Bethune's eleven honorary degrees included four LL.D.s (Lincoln [Penn.] 1935, Howard 1942, Atlanta 1943, and Wiley 1943).

40. Meier and Rudwick, *Black History and the Historical Profession*, 104.

Chapter 7. Research: "The Yard Stick of Great Thinkers"

1. Hine, *A Shining Thread*, 3–4.

2. Cooper, "Equality of Races" in *Voice*, 291–93; Baker-Fletcher, *A Singing Something*, 21.

3. Cooper, "Ethics of the Negro Question," 212; "The Social Settlement," 218; "Black Slavery and the French Nation," 283; all in *Voice*.

4. Cooper, "Higher Education of Women" in *Voice*, 82.

5. Du Bois, *Souls of Black Folk*, 102.

6. Cooper, "Early Years in Washington," in *Voice*, 312–13.

7. Ibid., 313; Jefferson, "Query 14" in *Notes on the State of Virginia*; Frees, *Founding Fathers*, 36.

8. Cooper, "Status of Women in America," in *Voice*, 112–16.

9. Cooper, "Higher Education of Women," 85; and "Our Raison d'Être," 51; both in *Voice*.

10. Cooper, "Higher Education of Women," in *Voice*, 84; Lemert, "Colored Woman's Office" in Cooper, *Voice*, 266; Carby, *Reconstructing Womanhood*, 95–120.

11. Cooper, "Higher Education of Women," in *Voice*, 84.

12. Cooper, "Higher Education of Women," in *Voice*, 75, 76, 78.

13. Cooper, "Higher Education of Women," in *Voice*, 72, 79–80, 82, 86–87.

14. Cooper, "Humor of Teaching," in *Voice*, 233–34.

15. Ibid., 233–35, 258.

16. Ibid., 235.

17. Cooper, "Higher Education of Women," in *Voice*, 73–74.

18. Cooper, "Has America a Race Problem?" in *Voice*, 132.

19. In "Angry Saxons and Negro Education," in *Voice*, she chided Washington for his 1895 Atlanta Compromise Speech.

20. Cooper, "Woman versus the Indian," in *Voice*, 88–108.

21. Cooper, "Negro in American Literature," 149; "Writer Flays 'Native Son,'" 342–43; and "Dr. Cooper Doesn't Like the Hughes Poem," all in *Voice*, 341–42.

22. Cooper, "Negro's Dialect," in *Voice*, 240–41.

23. Ibid.

24. Cooper, *Voice*, 116, 186, 259.

25. Cooper, "Intellectual Progress of Colored Women," in *Voice*, 202–3.

26. Cooper, "The Third Step," 329; and "My Racial Philosophy," 237; both in *Voice*.

27. Bethune, *Building a Better World*, 4, 35–36, 39–40.

28. Ibid., 213–14. The organization is now the Association for the Study of African American Life and History (ASALH).

29. Ibid., 215. Bethune gave an account of the progress: "Illiteracy has decreased from about 95 percent in 1865 to only 16.3 percent in 1930. In the very states that during the dark days of Reconstruction prohibited the education of Negroes by law, there are today over 2 million pupils . . . and 25,000 students in the more than 100 Negro colleges and universities. Some 116 Negroes have been elected to Phi Beta Kappa in white Northern colleges; over 60 have received the degree of Doctor of Philosophy."

30. Ibid.

31. Ibid., 52, 191.

32. Ibid., 6–7, 223.

33. Ibid., 69, 71.

34. Ibid., 53, 78–79.

35. Ibid., 54, 56, 77.

36. Rudolph, *American College and University*, 415–16.

37. Ibid., 352.

38. Ibid., 273, 279.

39. Ibid., 211.

40. Ibid., 406.

41. Rudolph, *American College and University*, 399–400; Newman, *White Women's Rights*, 39.

42. Cooper, "Third Step," in *Voice*, 325.

43. Cooper, "Women versus the Indian," in *Voice*, 104.

44. Cooper, "They Also," in Cooper Papers, MSRC Collections.

Chapter 8. Teaching: "That Which Relieves Their Hunger"

1. Watkins, *White Architects of Black Education*, 14; James Anderson, *Education of Blacks in the South*, 9; Bond, *Education of the Negro*, 28–32; Heather Williams, *Self-Taught*, 3.

2. Linda Perkins, "Education"; Harley, "Beyond the Classroom"; Collier-Thomas, "The Impact of Black Women," 254–65; Rudolph, *American College and University*, 339.

3. Litwack, *Trouble in Mind*; Allen, *Without Sanctuary*.

4. Painter, *Standing at Armageddon* and *Exodusters*; Litwack, *Been in the Storm So Long* and *Trouble in Mind*; Cooper, "Sketches from a Teacher's Notebook" in *Voice*, 229.

5. Cooper, *Voice*, 175–76, 251, 255–57.

6. Cooper, "What Are We Worth?" in *Voice*, 257.

7. Cooper, "Higher Education of Women, 79; "Humor of Teaching," 234; both in *Voice*.

8. Cooper's papers at MSRC contain photos of her Dunbar years, including her play production. She also acted in the play, in the role of Sentinel.

9. Cooper, "Humor of Teaching," in *Voice*, 235.

10. Bethune, *Building a Better World*, 84, 76, 276.

11. Ibid., 35.

12. Ibid., 35–40, 82, 114.

13. Ibid., 94, 98; Ihle, *Black Women in Higher Education*, 91.

14. Bethune, *Building a Better World*, 213–14.

15. Ibid., 79, 82–85, 191.

16. Ibid., 81–82.

17. Ibid., 96–97.

18. Ibid., 91–92.

19. White, *Too Heavy a Load*, 72; Bethune, *Building a Better World*, 67, 76–77, 118.

20. Bethune, *Building a Better World*, 84–86.

21. Ibid.

22. Ibid., 67, 71–79, 82, 85, 118, 215.

23. Ibid., 85.

24. Flemming, *Answered Prayer to a Dream*, 28; Stewart-Dowdell and McCarthy, *African Americans at the University of Florida*, 55.

25. Higginbotham's analysis made three contributions to the historiography: she highlighted the centrality of religion in education; she interrogated the "politics of respectability" by exploring social and economic class differences between the "common" masses and the club leader elites; and she demonstrated the permeability between supposedly dichotomous ideologies of vocational versus liberal education. Evelyn Higginbotham, *Righteous Discontent*, 40–42, 212. Ihle, *Black Women in Higher Education*, 107, 186; Perkins, "Education," 384–85.

26. James Anderson, *Education of Blacks in the South*, 34–35; Hunter, *Correct Thing*.

27. Terrell, "History of the High School for Negroes in Washington"; Sowell, "Education of Minority Children."

28. See "About Voorhees College: History," www.voorhees.edu/vchistory/index.htm (accessed May 7, 2006).

29. Patton, "Lucy Craft Laney," in *Historical Encyclopedia*, vol. 1, 693–94.

30. Wadelington and Knapp, *Charlotte Hawkins Brown*, 179.

31. Evelyn Higginbotham, *Righteous Discontent*.

32. Ihle, *Black Women in Higher Education*, 26–27.

33. Coppin, *Reminiscences*, 40, 59, 64.

34. Ibid., 44.

35. Ibid., 9–44.

36. Dewey, *Democracy and Education*, 110; Dewey, *Experience and Education*, 45, 67.

37. Browne, *Love My Children*, 107.

38. Ibid., 24.

39. *Journal of Blacks in Higher Education*, 118; Lawson, "Sarah Woodson Early," 15–26; Robinson, *Contributions of Black American Academic Women*, 134; Height, *Open Wide the Freedom Gates*, 40–41, 46; Hoyt, "Dorothy Height," in *Historical Encyclopedia*, vol. 1, 553.

40. Ihle, *Black Women in Higher Education*, 156–57.

41. Ibid., 181.

42. Ibid., xxvii, 175–78.

43. Rudolph, *American College and University*, 230.

44. Ibid., 160, 226.

45. Ibid., 163–64, 200–226.

46. Ibid., 415.

47. Ibid., 59–60, 65.

48. Collins, *Black Feminist Thought*, 39.

49. Ibid., 43.

50. hooks, *Teaching to Transgress*; Murrell, *African-Centered Pedagogy*; Pollard and Ajirotutu, *African-Centered Schooling*; Reagan, "Wise Child Is Talked to in Proverbs," in Reagan, *Non-Western Educational Traditions*.

51. Cooper, "No Flowers Please, 1940," in *Voice*, 344.

Chapter 9. Service: "A Beneficent Force"

1. Guzman, "Social Contributions," 86–94.

2. Cooper, "Woman versus the Indian," in *Voice*, 105.

3. Cooper, *Voice*, 103, 106–7, 204, 259, 297.

4. Cooper, "What Are We Worth?" in *Voice*, 178, 237, 261.

5. Cooper, "My Racial Philosophy," in *Voice*, 237.

6. Ibid., 236–37.

7. Cooper, "Higher Education of Women," 75–77, 83; Cooper, "Woman versus the Indian," in *Voice*, 96–100.

8. Pulliam and Van Patten, *History of Education in America*, 178–79; Rudolph, *American College and University*, 368.

9. Rudolph, *American College and University*, 368.

10. Cooper, "The Social Settlement," in *Voice*, 219.

11. Ibid., 222–23.

12. Bethune, *Building a Better World*, 40, 124, 158.

13. Hanson, *Mary McLeod Bethune*, 98; Bethune, *Building a Better World*, 125.

14. Ibid., 78, 140, 145–49.

15. Ibid., 231.

16. Ibid., 24, 52–56, 68, 83–85, 94.

17. Ibid., 159–61, 191, 193.

18. Height, *Open Wide the Freedom Gates*, 156. Bethune cited her mother's philosophy of life—she could not be discouraged—as a source of power in times of need. Bethune, *Building a Better World*, 36, 274.

19. Bethune, *Building a Better World*, 84, 112, 159–60, 245–58, 273.

20. Logan, *What the Negro Wants*, 248–59; Height, *Open Wide the Freedom Gates*, 89.

21. Bethune, "Certain Unalienable Rights," in *Building a Better World*, 248–58.

22. Bethune, *Building a Better World*, 20–27.

23. Ibid., 60–61.

24. Shaw, *What a Woman Ought to Be and to Do*, 98.

25. Dixon, "Booker T. Washington and the Negro," *Saturday Evening Post*, August 19, 1905, 1.

26. Du Bois, *Souls of Black Folk*, 101.

27. Ibid., 87.

28. Reagan, "A Wise Child Is Talked to in Proverbs," in Reagan, *Non-Western Educational Traditions*. See also Hord and Lee, *I Am Because We Are*; Asante, *Afrocentricity*; Karenga, *Black Studies*; Conyers, *Africana Studies*; White, *Too Heavy a Load*, 17.

29. Rudolph, *American College and University*, 356–57.

30. Ibid., 440–61,

31. See Mueller, "Ella Baker and the Origins of 'Participatory Democracy,'" in Crawford, Rouse, and Woods, *Women in the Civil Rights Movement*, 1–12, 51; Height, "'We Wanted the Voice of a Woman to Be Heard': Black Women and the 1963 March on Washington," in Collier-Thomas and Franklin, *Sisters in the Struggle*, 86; Giddings, *When and Where I Enter*, 302; Hine, *A Shining Thread*, 281; Shaw, *What a Woman Ought to Be and to Do*, 69.

32. Newman, *White Women's Rights*, 8, 42, 54.

33. Mueller, "Ella Baker and the Origins of 'Participatory Democracy,'" in Crawford, Rouse, and Woods, *Women in the Civil Rights Movement*.

34. Shaw, *What a Woman Ought to Be and to Do*, 2.

Chapter 10. Living Legacies—Black Women in Higher Education, Post-1954

1. See bibliography for the full citations to these authors' works.

2. Clarence Walker, *Deromanticizing Black History*, xv.

3. Wallace, *Black Macho and the Myth of the Superwoman*; Boris, "On Grassroots Organizing," 140; Zieger and Gall, *American Workers*, 54.

4. hooks and West, *Breaking Bread*, 131–46.

5. Reagon, "Coalition Politics"; Takaki, *A Different Mirror*.

6. *Brown v. Board of Education*, 347 U.S. 483 (1954).

7. Finkelman, "Affirmative Action for the Master Class."

8. Watkins, *White Architects of Black Education*; Butchart *Northern Schools, Southern Blacks, and Reconstruction*; Anderson and Moss, *Dangerous Donations*.

9. Du Bois and Dill, *College-Bred Negro Americans*, 46–47; Flemming, *Answered Prayer to a Dream*, 28; Stewart-Dowdell and McCarthy, *African Americans at the University of Florida*, 55; "History," Florida Agricultural and Mechanical University Web site, http://www.famu.edu/a&m.php?page=history.

10. Du Bois and Dill, *College-Bred Negro American*, 46–47, 54–55.

11. Charles Johnson, *Negro College Graduate*, 10, 22–23, 42, 50.

12. Duval-Williams, interview by author, February 1, 2006, Orlando, Fla.; Daphne Duval-Williams Papers; Stewart-Dowdell and McCarthy, *African Americans at the University of Florida*, 55; Maxine Jones, "Black Women in Florida, 1920–1950," in Colburn and Landers, *African American Heritage of Florida*, 264.

13. From interviews by author with Daphne Duval-Williams and her two daughters, Dr. Daphne Duval-Harrison and Sally Duval-Evans, January 22–February 1, 2006. See also "Jones High Alumni Reminisce," *Orlando Times*, December 21, 1995, and "Desegregation of UF: Black Pioneers Marched Bravely into History," *Gainesville Sun*, September 18, 1998.

14. McGuire, "It Was Like All of Us Had Been Raped."

15. Florida State University System *Fact Book 2003–2004* (race and gender student criteria selected), accessed October 1, 2005.

16. The first black faculty appointment in the Florida State University System, outside of FAMU, was in 1966, when Eva Pride was appointed assistant professor at the University of South Florida. In 1969, her husband, Richard Pride, also joined the faculty at USF. "A Dynasty of Pride—40 Years of Memories," University of South Florida, University Relations, http://usfweb2.usf.edu/history/pride.html. Florida's gender patterns in higher education mirror national trends: there are many more black women enrolled in college, but they are drastically behind black men in faculty appointments and pay. Florida State University System *Fact Book 2003–2004* (faculty by gender and race criteria selected); *Florida Department of Corrections 2003–2004 Annual Report*, p. 36, and Inmate Population Table; http://www.fldcu.org/factbook/default.asp, accessed October 1, 2005

17. Oliver, *Multicolored Memories*, 58–96.

18. Rudolph, *American College and University*, 486–87.

19. Newsome and Dodoo, "Reversal of Fortune: Explaining the Decline in Black Women's Earnings," 442–65; Hine, *Historical Encyclopedia*, vol. 2, 1309–32; Orlando Taylor, "New Directions for American Education."

20. Baker represents an interesting case because she operated somewhat outside of the circles of elite black clubwomen. As in earlier decades, college education did mean an increased social status, but family history, geographic location, economics, sorority membership, political affiliation, and church group often determined who worked with whom and who would be considered rogue elements in the world of black activists. Height, *Open Wide the Freedom Gates*; Grant, *Fundi*.

21. Crawford, Rouse, and Woods, *Trailblazers and Torchbearers*; Height, *Open Wide the Freedom Gates*, 152.

22. Septima Clark, *Echo in My Soul*.

23. Burns, "Mary Fair Burks," in *Historical Encyclopedia*, vol. 1, 196; Height, *Open Wide the Freedom Gates*, 41.

24. Tucker and Herman, "Using Culturally Sensitive Theories"; West Stevens, *Smart and Sassy*; Bond, *Education of the Negro in the American Social Order*, 264;

U.S. Dept. of Education, *Digest of Education Statistics 2002 Edition*, tables 68, 96. More than one-half (53.4 percent) of African American public school teachers in 1993–94 received their undergraduate degrees from HBCUs. Nettles and Perna, *Data Book II Executive Summary*, 18, 21. *Data Book II*, 217–18.

25. Davis and James, *Angela Y. Davis Reader*; Finkelman, "Affirmative Action for the Master Class"; "Linda Carol Brown" in Hine, Brown, and Terborg-Penn, *Historical Encyclopedia*, vol. 1, 181.

26. "Chronology," in Hine, Brown, and Terborg-Penn, *Historical Encyclopedia*, vol. 2, 1327–30.

27. Other autobiographies of interest include *The Long Shadow of Little Rock* (Daisy Bates, 1962), *Coming of Age in Mississippi* (Ann Moody, 1968), and *No Disrespect* (Sistah Souljah, 1996). Bracey, "Afro-American Women," 106–10.

28. See also Phillips, *Womanist Reader*; Winbush, *Warrior Method*.

29. Wolff, "Narrative Time," 4; Collier-Thomas, "The Impact of Black Women"; Jennings, "Black Intellectuals: The Perennial Question."

30. As of 2004, there were sixteen black women presidents of HBCUs; these schools included Bennett, Fisk, Texas Southern, and Spelman. See "Black College Presidents: Pioneering on the Frontiers of Education," *Ebony* (September 2001); "New Black College Presidents," *Ebony* (October 1999); "The Status of the Academic Professions: 2003–2004," *NEA Higher Education Advocate* (Summer 2004); Nettles and Perna, *Data Book I*.

31. Player, "Over the Tumult," 4.

32. Ibid., 8.

33. Davis, "Black Women and the Academy"; Eva Dykes Papers, MSRC Collections.

34. Mary Frances Berry, "Twentieth-Century Black Women in Education," 288–300; Davis, "Black Women and the Academy," 422–31; Moses, *Black Women in Academe*; Phillip, "Breaking the Silence: Black Women Academics Meet," 14; Patricia Williams, *Alchemy of Race and Rights*; Aptheker, *Woman's Legacy*; Lee Jones, *Making It on Broken Promises*; Schiller, "A Short History of Black Feminist Scholars," 19.

35. Burke, Cropper, and Harrison, "Real or Imagined—Black Women's Experiences in the Academy"; Crosson, "Public Service in Higher Education: Practices and Priorities"; Baez, "Faculty of Color and Traditional Notions of Service."

36. Reardon, "Institutionalizing Community Service-Learning"; Cruz and Giles, "Where's the Community in Service-Learning Research?; Stanton, Giles, and Cruz, *Service-Learning*; Eyler and Giles, *Where's the Learning in Service-Learning?*; Zlotkowski, *Successful Service-Learning Programs*.

37. Collins, *Black Feminist Thought*, 39.

38. Du Bois, *Education of Black People*, 169–80; 181–93, 185.

39. Roig-Franzia, "My Kids Were Used as Guinea Pigs," *Washington Post*, August 25, 2001; Bond, *Education of the Negro in the American Social Order*; Kozol, *Savage Inequalities*; Nettles and Perna, *Data Book II*.

40. Herrnstein and Murray, *Bell Curve*, 8–19; Browne, *Love My Children*, 149.

41. Herrnstein and Murray, *Bell Curve*, 21, 442.

42. Levine, *Opening of the American Mind*, 13, 25–27; Bloom, *Closing of the American Mind*, 344, 356–57, 381.

43. Nettles and Perna, *Data Book III*, xx, 27, 434; Trower and Chait, "Faculty Diversity: Too Little for Too Long," 35; "Science," in Hine, Brown, and Terborg-Penn, *Historical Encyclopedia*, vol. 2, 1015; Mickins, *Edward Bouchet*, 97.

44. Lumet, Sidney. *The Wiz*. Universal City Studios film, 1978; Jill Nelson, *Straight, No Chaser*, 201.

45. West Stevens, *Smart and Sassy*, 22–48; Springer, "Third Wave Black Feminism?" and Springer, *Still Lifting, Still Climbing*.

Bibliography

Primary Sources

ARCHIVES

Middlebury College Archives
  Mary Annette Anderson Papers.
Moreland-Spingarn Research Center (MSRC) Collections
  Alexander, Sadie T. M., Papers.
  Alpha Kappa Alpha Sorority Ivy Leaf Papers.
  Cooper, Anna Julia, Papers.
  Dykes, Eva, Papers.
  Murray, Pauli, Papers.
  Simpson, Georgiana, Papers.
  Slowe, Lucy Diggs, Papers.
  Terrell, Mary Church, Papers.
Oberlin College Archives Collections
  African American Alumni Records.
  Cooper, Anna Julia, Papers.
  Coppin, Fanny, Papers.
  Patterson, Mary, Papers.
  Terrell, Mary Church, Papers.
O.H.I.O. (Oberlin Historical and Improvement Organization) Resource Center
  Patterson, Mary, Papers.
University of Pennsylvania
  Alexander, Sadie Mossell, Papers.

PERSONAL PAPERS

Duval-Williams, Daphne, Papers. Courtesy of Sally Duval-Evans.

PUBLISHED RESOURCES

Baumann, Roland. "A History of Recording Black Students at Oberlin College and the Story of the Missing Record." Oberlin: Minority Student Records, 2002.
Lewin, Tamar. "U.S. Investigating Johns Hopkins Study of Lead Paint Hazard," *New York Times*, sec. A, p. 11, August 24, 2001.
National Educational Association. "The Status of the Academic Professions: 2003–2004." Special issue, *NEA Higher Education Advocate* 20 (summer 2004).
Nettles, Michael, and Laura Perna. *The African-American Education Data Book: Preschool through High School Education.* Fairfax, Va.: Frederick D. Patterson Research Institute of the College Fund/UNCF, 1997.

Player, Willa. "Over the Tumult—The Challenge." *Bennett College Social Justice Lecture Series Volume I.* 1959. Reprint. Greensboro: Bennett College Press, 1998.

Roig-Franzia, Manuel. "My Kids Were Used as Guinea Pigs: Lead Paint Study Adds to Debate on Research." *Washington Post,* August 25, 2001.

Shilton, Katherine. "'This Scholarly and Colored Alumna': Anna Julia Cooper's Troubled Relationship with Oberlin College." Oberlin College Archives.

Smith, Elaine. *A Guide to the Microfilm Edition of Mary McLeod Bethune Papers, pt. 1, 1918–1955.* Editorial advisor, Randolph H. Boehm. Bethesda, Md.: University Publications of America, 1997.

U.S. Department of Education. *Digest of Education Statistics 2000 Edition.* Washington, D.C.: National Center for Education Statistics, 2000.

———. *Digest of Education Statistics 2001 Edition.* Washington, D.C.: National Center for Education Statistics, 2001.

———. *Digest of Education Statistics 2002 Edition.* Washington, D.C.: National Center for Education Statistics, 2002.

WORLD WIDE WEB RESOURCES

Florida State University System Factbook.
http://www.flbog.org/factbook

Gibson, Campbell, and Emily Lennon. "Historical Census Statistics on the Foreign-born Population of the United States: 1850–1990." http://www.census.gov/population/www/documentation/twps0029/twps0029.html (accessed May 7, 2006).

Hawking, Stephen. "The Beginning of Time." http://www.hawking.org.uk/lectures/index.html (accessed May 7, 2006).

"In Motion: The African-American Migration Experience." Schomburg Center for Research in Black Culture. Maps available at http://www.inmotionaame.org/ (accessed May 7, 2006).

Jefferson, Thomas. *Notes on the State of Virginia.* University of Virginia Library. http://etext.lib.virginia.edu/toc/modeng/public/JefVirg.html (accessed May 7, 2006).

DISSERTATIONS

Collins, Alicia. "Socialization at Two Black Women's Colleges: Bennett College and Spelman College." Ed.D. diss., University of Pittsburgh, 2001.

Cooper, Anna Julia. "L'attitude de la France a l'egard de l'esclavage: Pedant la Revolution." Ph.D. diss., University of Paris, 1925.

Drury, Doreen. "Experimentation on the Male Side": Race, Class, Gender, and Sexuality in Pauli Murray's Quest for Love and Identity, 1910–1960." Ph.D. diss., Boston College, 2000.

Dykes, Eva. "Pope and His Influence in America from 1715–1850." Ph.D. diss., Radcliffe College, 1920.

Evans, Stephanie Y. "Living Legacies: Black Women, Educational Philosophies, and

Community Service, 1865–1965." Ph.D. diss., University of Massachusetts, Amherst, 2003.

Mossell, Sadie. "The Standard of Living among One Hundred Negro Migrant Families in Philadelphia." Ph.D. diss., University of Pennsylvania, 1921.

Myers, Amrita. "Negotiating Women: Black Women and the Politics of Freedom in Charleston, South Carolina, 1790–1860." Ph.D. diss., Rutgers University, 2004.

Noble, Jeanne. "The Negro Woman's College Education." Ph.D. diss., Columbia University, 1956.

Perkins, Linda. "Fanny Jackson Coppin and the Institute for Colored Youth: A Model of Nineteenth Century Black Female Educational and Community Leadership, 1837–1902." Ph.D. diss., University of Illinois at Urbana-Champaign, 1978.

Robinson, Omelia. "Contributions of Black American Academic Women to American Higher Education." Ph.D. diss., Wayne State University, 1978.

Simpson, Georgiana. "Herder's Conception of 'Das Volk.'" Ph.D. diss., University of Chicago, 1921.

Smith, Marshanda. "Black Women in the Academy: The Experience of Tenured Black Women Faculty on the Campus of Michigan State University, 1968–98." Master's thesis, Michigan State University, 2002.

Zola, Makosana. "Social Factors in the Positioning of Black Women in South African Universities." Ed.D. diss., Columbia University, 1997.

Secondary Sources

Alexander, Leslie. "The Challenge of Race: Rethinking the Position of Black Women in the Field of Women's History." *Journal of Women's History* 16 (summer 2004): 50–60.

Allen, James, ed. *Without Sanctuary: Lynching Photography in America.* Santa Fe, New Mex.: Twin Palms Publishers, 2000.

Anderson, Eric, and Alfred Moss. *Dangerous Donations: Northern Philanthropy and Southern Black Education, 1902–1930.* Columbia: University of Missouri Press, 1999.

Anderson, James. *The Education of Blacks in the South, 1860–1935.* Chapel Hill: University of North Carolina Press, 1988.

Aptheker, Bettina. *Woman's Legacy: Essays on Race, Sex, and Class in American History.* Amherst: University of Massachusetts Press, 1982.

Asante, Molefi. *Afrocentricity: The Theory of Social Change.* Buffalo: Amulefi Publishing, 1980.

Baez, Benjamin. "Faculty of Color and Traditional Notions of Service." *Thought and Action: The NEA Higher Education Journal* 15 (fall 1999): 131–38.

Baker-Fletcher, Karen. *A Singing Something: Womanist Reflections on Anna Julia Cooper.* New York: Crossroad, 1994.

Bates, Daisy. *The Long Shadow of Little Rock: A Memoir.* Fayetteville: University of Arkansas Press, 1962.

Bell-Scott, Patricia. "'To Write Like Never Before': Pauli Murray's Enduring Yearning." *Journal of Women's History* 14 (summer 2002): 58–61.

Benjamin, Lois, ed. *Black Women in the Academy: Promises and Perils.* Gainesville: University Press of Florida, 1997.

Berea College. *U.S. Traditions: A Reader.* Littleton, Mass.: Tapestry Press, 2003.

Berry, Mary Frances. "Twentieth-Century Black Women in Education." *Journal of Negro Education* 51 (summer 1982): 288–300.

Berry, Theodorea. "Being and Living in Research: A Discussion on Cultural Experience and Cultural Identity as Referents in Knowledge Production." *Journal of Thought* 40 (spring 2005): 27–38.

Bethune, Mary McLeod. "The Adaptation of the History of the Negro to the Capacity of the Child." *Journal of Negro History* 24 (June 1939): 9–13.

———. *Mary McLeod Bethune: Building a Better World.* Edited by Audrey McCluskey and Elaine Smith. Bloomington: Indiana University Press, 2002.

Bloom, Allan. *The Closing of the American Mind: How Higher Education Has Failed Democracy and Impoverished the Souls of Today's Students.* New York: Simon and Schuster, 1987.

Bond, Horace Mann. *The Education of the Negro in the American Social Order.* New York: Octagon, 1966.

Boris, Eileen. "On Grassroots Organizing, Poor Women's Movements, and the Intellectual as Activist." *Journal of Women's History* 14 (summer 2002): 140–43.

Bracey, John. "Afro-American Women: A Brief Guide to Writings from Historical and Feminist Perspectives." *Contributions in Black Studies* 8 (1986–87): 106–10.

Braxton, Joanne. *Black Women Writing Autobiography: A Tradition within a Tradition.* Philadelphia: Temple University Press, 1989.

Brazzell, Johnetta Cross. "Bricks without Straw: Missionary-Sponsored Black Higher Education in the Post-Emancipation Era." *Journal of Higher Education* 63 (1992): 26–49.

Breaux, Richard. "Maintaining a Home for Girls: The Iowa Federation of Colored Women's Clubs at the University of Iowa, 1919–1950." *Journal of African American History* 87 (spring 2002): 236–55.

Brown, Hallie Q. *Homespun Heroines and Other Women of Distinction.* 1926. Reprint. New York: Oxford University Press, 1992.

Brown, Linda. *The Long Walk: The Story of the Presidency of Willa B. Player at Bennett College.* Greensboro: Bennett College Press, 1998.

Brown, Tamara, Gregory Parks, and Clarenda Phillips. *African American Fraternities and Sororities: The Legacy and the Vision.* Lexington: University of Kentucky Press, 2005.

Browne, Rose Butler. *Love My Children: An Autobiography, The Education of a Teacher.* 2nd ed. New York: Meredith Press, 1969.

Brown v. Board of Education 347 U.S. 483 (1954).

Burke, Beverly, Andrea Cropper, and Philomena Harrison. "Real or Imagined—Black

Women's Experience in the Academy." In *Community, Work, and Family* 3 (December 2000): 297–310.

Butchart, Ronald. *Northern Schools, Southern Blacks, and Reconstruction: Freedmen's Education, 1862–1875*. Westport, Conn.: Greenwood, 1980.

Callender, Christine. *Education for Empowerment: The Practice and Philosophies of Black Teachers*. Stoke on Trent, UK: Trentham, 1997.

Carby, Hazel. *Reconstructing Womanhood: The Emergence of the Afro-American Woman Novelist*. New York: Oxford University Press, 1987.

Carroll, Rebecca. *Sugar in the Raw: Voices of Young Black Girls in America*. New York: Crown, 1997.

Clark, Septima Poinsette. *Echo in My Soul*. New York: Dutton, 1962.

Clark, William. "On the Ironic Specimen of the Doctor of Philosophy." *Science in Context* 5 (March 1992): 97–137.

Cleveland, Darrell. *A Long Way to Go: Conversations about Race by African American Faculty and Graduate Students*. New York: Peter Lang, 2004.

Colburn, David, and Jane Landers, eds. *The African American Heritage of Florida*. Gainesville: University Press of Florida, 1995.

Coleman, Trevor. "Whose Battle?: The Latest Fight Surrounding Affirmative Action Underscores What's at Stake—Not Just for Minorities, but for the Next Generation of Women, Black and White." *Crisis* 109 (May/June 2002): 35–38.

Collier-Thomas, Bettye. "The Impact of Black Women in Education: An Historical Overview." *Journal of Negro Education* 51 (summer 1982): 254–65.

Collier-Thomas, Bettye, and V. P. Franklin. *Sisters in the Struggle: African American Women in the Civil Rights–Black Power Movement*. New York: New York University Press, 2001.

Collins, Patricia Hill. *Black Feminist Thought: Knowledge, Consciousness, and the Politics of Empowerment*. 1991. Reprint. New York: Routledge, 2000.

Conyers, J. L. *Africana Studies: A Disciplinary Quest for Both Theory and Method*. Jefferson, N.C.: McFarland, 1997.

Cooper, Anna Julia. *Slavery and the French Revolutionists, 1788–1805*. Translated by Frances Richardson Keller. New York: Edwin Mellen, 1988.

———. *The Voice of Anna Julia Cooper: Including a Voice from the South and Other Important Essays, Papers, and Letters*. Edited by Charles Lemert and Esme Bhan. Lanham, Md.: Rowman and Littlefield, 1998.

Coppin, Fanny Jackson. *Reminiscences of School Life and Hints on Teaching*. 1913. Reprint. New York: G. K. Hall, 1995.

"A Course in Progressions with Dates of Accomplishments." *Aframerican Women's Journal* 1 (summer 1940): 32.

Crawford, Vicki, Jacqueline Rouse, and Barbara Woods, eds. *Women in the Civil Rights Movement: Trailblazers and Torchbearers, 1941–1965*. Bloomington: Indiana University Press, 1993.

Cross, Theodore. "The Earliest Black Graduates of the Nation's Highest Ranked Liberal Arts Colleges." *Journal of Blacks in Higher Education* 38 (winter 2002–3): 104.

———. "Tributes and Tokens: The Record of Honorary Degrees for Blacks." *Journal of Blacks in Higher Education* 6 (winter 1994–95): 70–71.

Crosson, Patricia. *Public Service in Higher Education: Practices and Priorities.* Washington, D.C.: Association for the Study of Higher Education, 1985.

Crummell, Alexander. *Africa and America: Addresses and Discourses.* Miami: Mnemosyne, 1969.

Cruse, Harold. *Crisis of the Negro Intellectual.* 1967. Reprint. New York: Quill, 1984.

Cruz, Nadinne, and Dwight Giles. "Where's the Community in Service-Learning Research?" *Michigan Journal of Community Service-Learning* 7 (fall 2000): 28–34.

Cuthbert, Marion. *Education and Marginality: A Study of the Negro Woman College Graduate.* New York: Garland, 1987.

Dagbovie, Pero. "Black Women Historians from the Late Nineteenth Century to the Dawning of the Civil Rights Movement." *Journal of African American History* 89 (summer 2004): 241–61.

Daniels, Sadie. *Women Builders.* Washington, D.C.: Associated Publishers, 1970.

Davis, Angela. "Black Women and the Academy." *Callaloo* (spring 1994): 422–31.

Davis, Angela, and Joy James. *The Angela Y. Davis Reader.* Malden, Mass.: Blackwell, 1998.

Delany, Bessie, and Sadie Delany. *Having Our Say: The Delany Sisters' First Hundred Years.* New York: Dell, 1993.

Dewey, John. *Democracy and Education.* 1916. Reprint. New York: Free Press, 1997.

———. *Experience and Education.* 1938. Reprint. New York: Free Press, 1997.

Du Bois, W.E.B. *The College-Bred Negro.* Atlanta: Atlanta University Press, 1900.

———. *Darkwater: Voices from within the Veil.* 1920. Reprint. New York: Dover, 1999.

———. *The Education of Black People: Ten Critiques, 1906–1960.* Edited by Herbert Aptheker. 1973. Reprint. New York: Monthly Review Press, 2001.

———. *The Philadelphia Negro: A Social Study.* 1899. Reprint. Philadelphia: University of Pennsylvania Press, 1998.

———. *The Souls of Black Folk.* 1903. Edited by David Blight. Boston: Bedford Books, 1997.

Du Bois, W.E.B., and Augustus G. Dill. *The College-Bred Negro American.* Atlanta: Atlanta University Press, 1910.

Dykes, Eva. *The Negro in English Romantic Thought.* Washington, D.C.: The Associated Publishers, 1942.

Easter, Opal. *Nannie Helen Burroughs.* New York: Garland, 1995.

Evans, Stephanie Y. "Black Greek-Lettered Organizations and Civic Responsibility." *Black Issues in Higher Education* 21 (October 7, 2004): 98.

———. "Recent Research Rewrites Society's History with Identity of First Black Woman Member." *Key Reporter* 70 (February 2005): 3–14.

Eyler, Janet, and Dwight Giles. *Where's the Learning in Service-Learning?* San Francisco: Jossey-Bass, 1999.

Fargher, John Mack, and Florence Howe, eds. *Women and Higher Education in American History: Essays from the Mount Holyoke College Sesquicentennial Symposia.* New York: Norton, 1988.

Feagin, Joe, Hernán Vera, and Nikitah Imani. *The Agony of Education: Black Students at White Colleges and Universities.* New York: Routledge, 1996.

Finkelman, Paul. "Affirmative Action for the Master Class: The Creation of the Proslavery Constitution." *Akron Law Review* 32 (1999): 423–70.

Fleming, John. "Blacks in Education to 1954: A Historical Overview." In *The Case for Affirmative Action for Blacks in Higher Education,* edited by John Fleming, Gerald Gill, and David Swinton. Washington, D.C.: Howard University Press, 1978.

Flemming, Sheila. *The Answered Prayer to a Dream: Bethune-Cookman College, 1904–1994.* Virginia Beach: Donning, 1995.

Franklin, John Hope. "On the Evolution of Scholarship in Afro-American History." In *The State of Afro-American History: Past, Present, and Future,* edited by Darlene Clark Hine. Baton Rouge: Louisiana State University Press, 1986.

———. *Mirror to America: The Autobiography of John Hope Franklin.* New York: Farrar, Straus and Giroux, 2005.

Franklin, V. P. *The Education of Black Philadelphia: The Social and Educational History of a Minority Community, 1900–1950.* Philadelphia: University of Pennsylvania Press, 1979.

———. "Hidden in Plain View: African American Women, Radical Feminism, and the Origins of Women's Studies Programs, 1967–1974." *Journal of African American History* 87 (fall 2002): 433–46.

———. *Living Our Stories, Telling Our Truths: Autobiography and the Making of the African-American Intellectual Tradition.* New York: Oxford University Press, 1996.

Franklin, V. P., and James Anderson. *New Perspectives on Black Educational History.* Boston: G. K. Hall, 1978.

Franklin, V. P., and Bettye Collier-Thomas. "Biography, Race Vindication, and African-American Intellectuals: Introductory Essay." *Journal of African American History* 87 (winter 2002): 160–74.

Freeman, Kassie, ed. *African American Culture and Heritage in Higher Education Research and Practice.* Westport, Conn.: Praeger, 1998.

Frees, Andrew. *The Founding Fathers and the Politics of Character.* Princeton, N.J.: Princeton University Press, 2004.

Freire, Paulo. *Pedagogy of the Oppressed.* 1970. Reprint. New York: Continuum, 1993.

Gaspar, David Barry, and Darlene Clark Hine, eds. *Beyond Bondage: Free Women of Color in the Americas.* Urbana: University of Illinois Press, 2004.

Generett, Gretchen, and Rhonda Jeffries. *Black Women in the Field: Experiences Un-*

derstanding Ourselves and Others through Qualitative Research. Cresskill, N.J.: Hampton Press, 2003.

Giddings, Paula. *In Search of Sisterhood: Delta Sigma Theta and the Challenge of the Black Sorority*. New York: William Morrow, 1988.

———. *When and Where I Enter: The Impact of Black Women on Race and Sex in America*. New York: Quill, 1984.

Gilmore, Glenda. "Admitting Pauli Murray." *Journal of Women's History* 14 (summer 2002): 62–68.

———. *Gender and Jim Crow: Women and the Politics of White Supremacy in North Carolina, 1896–1920*. Chapel Hill: University of North Carolina Press, 1996.

Grant, Joanne. *Fundi: The Story of Ella Baker*. Icarus Films, 1981.

Greene, Harry. *Holders of Doctorates among American Negroes: An Educational and Social Study of Negroes Who Have Earned Doctoral Degrees in Course, 1876–1943*. Boston: Meador, 1946.

Guy-Sheftall, Beverly. "Black Women and Higher Education: Spelman and Bennett College Revisited." *Journal of Negro Education* 51 (summer 1982): 278–87.

Guzman, Jessie. "The Social Contributions of the Negro Woman since 1940." *Negro History Bulletin* 33 (January 1948): 86–94.

Hanson, Joyce. *Mary McLeod Bethune and Black Women's Political Activism*. Columbia: University of Missouri Press, 2003.

Harley, Sharon. "Beyond the Classroom: The Organizational Lives of Black Female Educators in the District of Columbia, 1890–1930." *Journal of Negro Education* 51 (summer 1982): 254–64.

———. "Black Women in a Southern City: Washington, D.C., 1890–1920." In *Sex, Race, and the Role of Women in the South*, edited by Joanne V. Hawks and Sheila Skemp. Jackson: University Press of Mississippi, 1983.

Harley, Sharon, and the Black Women's Work Collective. *Sister Circle: Black Women and Work*. New Brunswick, N.J.: Rutgers University Press, 2002.

Harrison, Ira, and Faye Harrison. *African American Pioneers in Anthropology*. Champaign: University of Illinois Press, 1999.

Haywood, Chanta. *Prophesying Daughters: Black Women Preachers and the Word, 1823–1913*. Columbia: University of Missouri Press, 2003.

Height, Dorothy. *Open Wide the Freedom Gates: A Memoir*. New York: Public Affairs, 2003.

Herrnstein, Richard, and Charles Murray. *The Bell Curve: Intelligence and Class Structure in American Life*. New York: Free Press, 1994.

Higginbotham, Elizabeth. *Too Much to Ask: Black Women in the Era of Integration*. Chapel Hill: University of North Carolina Press, 2001.

Higginbotham, Evelyn, ed. *The Harvard Guide to African-American History*. Cambridge: Harvard University Press, 2001.

———. *Righteous Discontent: The Women's Movement in the Black Baptist Church, 1880–1920*. Cambridge: Harvard University Press, 1993.

Hine, Darlene Clark. *Black Women in United States History: From Colonial Times to the Present.* Brooklyn, N.Y.: Carlson, 1990.

———. *Hine Sight: Black Women and the Re-construction of American History.* Bloomington: Indiana University Press, 1994.

———. *A Shining Thread of Hope: The History of Black Women in America.* New York: Broadway, 1998.

Hine, Darlene Clark, and American Historical Association, eds. *The State of Afro-American History: Past, Present, and Future.* Baton Rouge: Louisiana State University Press, 1986.

Hine, Darlene Clark, Elsa Barkley Brown, and Rosalyn Terborg-Penn, eds. *Black Women in America: An Historical Encyclopedia.* Bloomington: Indiana University Press, 1994.

Hine, Darlene Clark, William Hine, and Stanley Harrold. *The African-American Odyssey.* Upper Saddle River, N.J.: Prentice Hall, 2005.

hooks, bell. *Teaching to Transgress: Education as the Practice of Freedom.* New York: Routledge, 1994.

hooks, bell, and Cornel West. *Breaking Bread: Insurgent Black Intellectual Life.* Boston: South End Press.

Hord, Fred, and Jonathan Lee. *I Am Because We Are: Readings in Black Philosophy.* Amherst: University of Massachusetts Press, 1995.

Hull, Gloria, Patricia Bell Scott, and Barbara Smith, eds. *All the Women Are White, All the Blacks Are Men, But Some of Us Are Brave: Black Women's Studies.* New York: Feminist Press, 1982.

Hunter, Tera. "The Correct Thing: Charlotte Hawkins Brown and the Palmer Institute." *Southern Exposure* 11 (Sept/Oct 1983): 37–43.

Hurston, Zora Neale. *Dust Tracks on the Road.* 1942. New York: Harper Perennial, 1996.

———. *Their Eyes Were Watching God.* 1937. New York: Harper Collins, 1990.

Hutchinson, Louise Daniel. *Anna J. Cooper: A Voice from the South.* Washington, D.C.: Smithsonian Institution Press, 1981.

Ihle, Elizabeth. *Black Women in Higher Education: An Anthology of Essays, Studies, and Documents.* New York: Garland, 1992.

James, Joy. *Transcending the Talented Tenth.* New York: Routledge, 1996.

James, Joy, and T. Denean Sharpley-Whiting, eds. *The Black Feminist Reader.* Oxford, UK: Blackwell, 2000.

James, Stanlie, and Abena Busia. *Theorizing Black Feminisms: The Visionary Pragmatism of Black Women.* London: Routledge, 1993.

Jennings, James. "Black Intellectuals: The Perennial Question." *Souls* 4 (spring 2002): 65–76.

Johnson, Charles. *The Negro College Graduate.* 1938. Reprint. New York: Negro Universities Press, 1969.

Johnson, Jamie. *Born Rich.* Home Box Office film, 2003.

Johnson, Karen. *Uplifting the Women and the Race: The Lives, Educational Philoso-phies, and Social Activism of Anna Julia Cooper and Nannie Helen Burroughs.* New York: Garland, 2000.

Jones, Jacqueline. *Labor of Love, Labor of Sorrow: Black Women, Work, and the Fam-ily from Slavery to the Present.* New York: Basic, 1985.

Jones, Lee, ed. *Making It on Broken Promises: African American Male Scholars Con-front the Culture of Higher Education.* Sterling, Va.: Stylus Publishing, 2002.

Jones, Maxine. "No Longer Denied: Black Women in Florida, 1920–1950." In *Afri-can American Heritage of Florida,* edited by David Colburn and Jane Landers. Gainesville: University Press of Florida, 1995.

Karenga, Maulana. *Introduction to Black Studies.* Los Angeles: University of Sankore Press, 1993.

Keller, Frances. "An Educational Controversy: Anna Julia Cooper's Vision of Resolu-tion." *NWSA Journal* 11 (fall 1999): 49–67.

Karenga, Maulana. *Selections from the Husia: Sacred Wisdom of Ancient Egypt.* Los Angeles: University of Sankore Press, 1984.

Kimbrough, Walter. *Black Greek 101: The Culture, Customs, and Challenges of Black Fraternities and Sororities.* Madison, N.J.: Fairleigh-Dickinson University Press, 2003.

Kirsch, Gesa. *Ethical Dilemmas in Feminist Research: The Politics of Location, Inter-pretation, and Publication.* Albany: State University of New York Press, 1999.

Kluger, Richard. *Simple Justice: The History of "Brown v. Board of Education" and Black America's Struggle for Equality.* New York: Vintage, 1975.

Kozol, Jonathan. *Savage Inequalities: Children in America's Schools.* New York: Crown, 1991.

Krenshaw, Kimberle. "Mapping the Margins, Intersectionality, Identity Politics, and Violence against Women of Color." *Stanford Law Review* 43 (1991): 1241–79.

Ladner, Joyce. *Tomorrow's Tomorrow: The Black Woman.* Lincoln: University of Ne-braska Press, 1971.

Lane, Linda. *A Documentary of Mrs. Booker T. Washington.* New York: Edwin Mellen Press, 2001.

Lasch, Christopher, ed. *The Social Thought of Jane Addams.* Indianapolis: Bobbs-Merrill, 1965.

Lawson, Ellen. "Antebellum Black Codes at Oberlin College." *Oberlin Alumni Maga-zine,* January/February 1980, 18–21.

———. "Sarah Woodson Early: 19th Century Black Nationalist 'Sister.'" *Umoja* 2 (sum-mer 1981): 15–26.

Lawson, Ellen, and Marlene Merrill. "The Antebellum 'Talented Thousandth': Black College Students at Oberlin before the Civil War." *Journal of Negro Education* 52 (spring 1983): 142–55.

———, comps. *The Three Sarahs: Documents of Antebellum Black College Women.* New York: Edwin Mellen Press, 1985.

Levine, Lawrence. *The Opening of the American Mind: Canons, Culture, and History.* Boston: Beacon Press, 1996.

Litoff, Judy, and David Smith, eds. *What Kind of World Do We Want?: American Women Plan for Peace.* Wilmington: Scholarly Resource Books, 2000.

Litwack, Leon. *Trouble in Mind: Black Southerners in the Age of Jim Crow.* New York: Knopf, 1998.

Logan, Rayford, ed. *What the Negro Wants.* Chapel Hill: University of North Carolina Press, 1944.

Mabokela, Obakeng, and Anna Green, eds. *Sisters of the Academy: Emergent Black Women Scholars in Higher Education.* Sterling, Va.: Stylus, 2001.

Malveaux, Julianne. "Missed Opportunity: Sadie Tanner Alexander Mossell and the Economics Profession." *American Economic Review* 81 (1991): 307–10.

———. "When the Personal Is Political: Telling and Selling Our Stories." *Black Issues in Higher Education* 19 (November 21, 2002): 36.

Marlowe, Gertude Woodruff. *A Right Worthy Grand Mission: Maggie Lena Walker and the Quest for Black Economic Empowerment.* Washington, D.C.: Howard University Press, 2003.

Martin, Jane. *Reclaiming a Conversation: The Ideal of the Educated Woman.* New Haven: Yale University Press, 1985.

Matson, Lynn. "Phillis Wheatley—Soul Sister?" *Phylon* 33 (fall 1972): 222–30.

Mazon, Patricia. *Gender and the Modern Research University: The Admission of Women to German Higher Education, 1865–1914.* Palo Alto: Stanford University Press, 2003.

McGuire, Danielle L. "'It Was Like All of Us Had Been Raped': Sexual Violence, Community Mobilization, and the African American Freedom Struggle." *Journal of American History* 91 (December 2004): 906–31.

McHenry, Elizabeth. *Forgotten Readers: Recovering the Lost History of African American Literary Societies.* Durham, N.C.: Duke University Press, 2002.

McPherson, James. *The Abolitionist Legacy: From Reconstruction to the NAACP.* Princeton, N.J.: Princeton University Press, 1975.

Meier, August, and Elliott Rudwick. *Black History and the Historical Profession, 1915–1980.* Urbana: University of Illinois Press, 1986.

Mickens, Ronald. *Edward Bouchet: The First African American Doctorate.* River Edge, N.J.: World Scientific, 2002.

Mikell, Gwendolyn. "Feminism and Black Culture in the Ethnography of Zora Neale Hurston." In *African American Pioneers in Anthropology,* edited by Ira Harrison and Faye Harrison. Champaign: University of Illinois Press, 1999.

Mills, Charles. *The Racial Contract.* Ithaca: Cornell University Press, 1997.

Morgan, Harry. *Historical Perspectives on the Education of Black Children.* Westport, Conn.: Praeger, 1995.

Morris, Thomas. *Southern Slavery and the Law.* Chapel Hill: University of North Carolina Press, 1999.

Morton, Lena Beatrice. *My First Sixty Years: Passion for Wisdom.* New York: Philosophical Library, 1965.

Moses, Yolanda. *Black Women in Academe: Issues and Strategies.* Washington, D.C: Association of American Colleges and Universities, 1989.

Murray, Pauli. *Pauli Murray: The Autobiography of a Black Activist, Feminist, Lawyer, Priest, and Poet.* Knoxville: University of Tennessee Press, 1987.

Murrell, Peter. *African-Centered Pedagogy: Developing Schools of Achievement for African American Children.* Albany: State University of New York, 2002.

Myers, Lena. *A Broken Silence: Voices of African American Women in the Academy.* Westport, Conn.: Bergin and Garvey, 2002.

Nelson, Jill. *Straight, No Chaser: How I Became a Grown-Up Black Woman.* New York: J. P. Putnam's Sons, 1997.

Nelson, Paul. "Experiment in Interracial Education at Berea College, 1858–1908." In *U.S. Traditions: A Reader,* edited by Berea College General Education Board. Littleton, Mass.: Tapestry Press, 2003.

Nelson, Stanley, and Gail Pellett. *Shattering the Silences: Minority Professors Break into the Ivory Tower.* California Newsreel, 1997.

"Negro Higher Education as Seen through the Antebellum Black Press." *Journal of Blacks in Higher Education* 30 (summer 1998): 36–38.

Neverdon-Morton, Cynthia. *Afro-American Women of the South and the Advancement of the Race, 1895–1925.* Knoxville: University of Tennessee Press, 1991.

Newman, Louise. *White Women's Rights: The Racial Origins of Feminism in the United States.* New York: Oxford University Press, 1999.

Newsome, Yvonne, and Nii-Amoo Dodoo. "Reversal of Fortune: Explaining the Decline in Black Women's Earnings." *Gender and Society* 16 (August 2002): 442–65.

Noble, Jeanne. "The Higher Education of Black Women in the Twentieth Century." In *Women and Higher Education in American History: Essays from the Mount Holyoke College Sesquicentennial Symposia,* edited by John Mack Fargher and Florence Howe. New York: Norton, 1988.

Oliver, Kitty. *Multicolored Memories of a Black Southern Girl.* Lexington: University of Kentucky Press, 2001.

Ozmon, Howard, and Samuel Craver, eds. *Philosophical Foundations of Education.* Columbus: Merrill, 1990.

Painter, Nell. *Exodusters: Black Migration to Kansas after Reconstruction.* New York: Norton, 1986.

———. *Standing at Armageddon: The United States, 1877–1919.* 1976. Reprint. New York: Norton, 1987.

Parker, Marjorie. *Past Is Prologue: The History of Alpha Kappa Alpha, 1908–1999.* Washington, D.C.: Alpha Kappa Alpha Sorority, Incorporated, 1999.

Pateman, Carol. *The Sexual Contract.* Palo Alto: Stanford University Press, 1988.

Patterson, James. *"Brown v. Board of Education": A Civil Rights Milestone and Its Troubled Legacy.* New York: Oxford University Press, 2001.

Perkins, Linda. "Black Feminism and 'Race Uplift,' 1890–1900." Working paper, Radcliffe Institute. Cambridge, Mass.: Mary Ingraham Bunting Institute, 1981.

———. "Black Women and the Philosophy of 'Racial Uplift' prior to Emancipation." Working paper, Radcliffe Institute. Cambridge, Mass.: Mary Ingraham Bunting Institute, 1980.

———. "Education." In *Black Women in America: An Historical Encyclopedia*, vol. 1, 380–87, edited by Darlene Clark Hine, Elsa Barkley Brown, and Rosalyn Terborg-Penn. Brooklyn, N.Y.: Carlson, 1993.

———. "Education of Black Women in the Nineteenth Century." In *Women and Higher Education in American History: Essays from the Mount Holyoke College Sesquicentennial Symposia*, edited by John Mack Fargher and Florence Howe. New York: Norton, 1988.

———. *Fanny Jackson Coppin and the Institute for Colored Youth, 1865–1902*. New York: Garland, 1987.

———. "Heed Life's Demands: The Educational Philosophy of Fanny Jackson Coppin." *Journal of Negro Education* 51 (summer 1982): 181–90.

———. "Introduction: New Perspectives on African American Educational History." *Journal of African American History* 87 (fall 2002): 369–71.

———. "Quaker Beneficence and Black Control: The Institute for Colored Youth, 1852–1903." In *New Perspectives of African American Educational History*, edited by V. P. Franklin, 19–43. Boston: G. K. Hall, 1978.

———. "The Radical Integration of the Seven Sister Colleges." *Journal of Blacks in Higher Education* 19 (spring 1998): 104–8.

Perkins, Margo. *Autobiography as Activism: Three Black Women of the Sixties*. Jackson: University of Mississippi Press, 2000.

Peterson, Carla. *Doers of the Word: African-American Women Speakers in the North 1830–1880*. Piscataway, N.J.: Rutgers University Press, 1995.

Phillip, Mary-Christine. "Breaking the Silence: Black Women Academics Meet, Send Message to Clinton." *Black Issues in Higher Education* 11 (1994): 14.

Phillips, Layli, ed. *THE Womanist Reader: The First Quarter Century of Womanist Thought*. New York: Routledge, 2006.

Player, Willa. *Improving College Education for Women at Bennett College: A Report of a Type A Project*. New York: Garland, 1987.

Plato. "Phaedrus." In *Plato: The Collected Dialogues*, edited by Edith Hamilton and Huntington Cairns. Princeton, N.J.: Princeton University Press, 1961.

Pollard, Diane, and Cheryl Ajirotutu. *African-Centered Schooling in Theory and Practice*. Westport, Conn.: Bergin and Garvey, 2000.

Pulliam, John, and James Van Patten. *History of Education in America*. Upper Saddle River, N.J.: Prentice Hall, 1999.

Reagan, Timothy. *Non-Western Educational Traditions: Alternative Approaches to Educational Thought and Practice*. Mahwah, N.J.: Lawrence Erlbaum, 1996.

Reagon, Bernice Johnson. "Coalition Politics: Turning the Century." In *Home Girls:*

A Black Feminist Anthology, edited by Barbara Smith. 1983. Reprint. New Brunswick, N.J.: Rutgers University Press, 2000.

Reardon, Kenneth. "Institutionalizing Community Service-Learning at a Research Campus." *Michigan Journal of Community Service-Learning* 4 (May 1997): 130–36.

Rorty, Amélie, ed. *Philosophers on Education: New Historical Perspectives*. London: Routledge, 1998.

Rousseau, Jean-Jacques. *The Social Contract and Discourse on the Origin and Foundation of Inequality among Mankind*. 1762. Reprint. New York: Washington Square Press, 1967.

Royster, Jacqueline. *Traces of a Stream: Literacy and Social Change among African American Women*. Pittsburgh: University of Pittsburgh Press, 2000.

Rudolph, Frederick. *The American College and University: A History*. 1962. Reprint. Athens: University of Georgia Press, 1990.

Rupp, Leila, and Verta Taylor. "Pauli Murray: The Unasked Question." *Journal of Women's History* 14 (summer 2002): 83–88.

Schiller, Naomi. "A Short History of Black Feminist Scholars." *Journal of Blacks in Higher Education* 32 (autumn 2000): 119–25.

Scott, Daryl. *Contempt and Pity: Social Policy and the Image of the Damaged Black Psyche, 1880–1996*. Chapel Hill: University of North Carolina, 1997.

Scott, Jill. "A Long Walk." *Who Is Jill Scott? Words and Sound*, vol. 1. Compact disc B00004UARR. Hidden Beach Records, 2000.

Shaw, Stephanie. *What A Woman Ought to Be and to Do: Black Professional Women Workers during the Jim Crow Era*. Chicago: University of Chicago Press, 1996.

Sinha, Manisha. *The Counterrevolution of Slavery: Politics and Ideology in Antebellum South Carolina*. Chapel Hill: University of North Carolina, 2000.

Sitkoff, Harvard. "Segregation, Desegregation, Resegregation: African American Education, A Guide to the Literature." *OAH Magazine of History* 15 (winter 2001): 6–13.

Slater, Robert. "The Blacks Who First Entered the World of White Higher Education." *Journal of Blacks in Higher Education* 4 (summer 1994): 47–56.

———. "The First Black Graduates of the Nation's 50 Flagship State Universities." *Journal of Blacks in Higher Education* 12 (September 1996): 72–82.

Slowe, Lucy. "The Colored Girl Enters College—What Shall She Expect?" *Opportunity: Journal of Negro Life* 15 (September 1937): 276–79.

———. "Higher Education of Negro Women." *Journal of Negro Education* 2 (July 1933): 352–58.

Smith, Valerie. *Not Just Race, Not Just Gender: Black Feminist Readings*. New York: Routledge, 1998.

Sollors, Werner. "Owls and Rats in the American Funnyhouse: Adrienne Kennedy's Drama." *American Literature* 63 (September 1991), 507–32.

Solomon, Barbara. *In the Company of Educated Women: A History of Women and Higher Education in America*. New Haven: Yale University Press, 1986.

Sowell, Thomas. "The Education of Minority Children." In *Education in the Twenty-first Century*, edited by Edward Lazear. Stanford, Calif.: Hoover Institution Press, 2002, 79–93.

Springer, Kimberly. *Still Lifting, Still Climbing: Contemporary African American Women's Activism*. New York: New York University Press, 1999.

———. "Third Wave Black Feminism?" *Signs: Journal of Women in Culture and Society* 27 (2002): 1059–82.

Stanton, Timothy, Dwight Giles, and Nadinne Cruz. *Service-Learning: A Movement's Pioneers Reflect on its Origins, Practice, and Future*. San Francisco: Jossey-Bass, 1999.

Sterling, Dorothy. *We Are Your Sisters: Black Women in the Nineteenth Century*. New York: Norton, 1997.

Stewart, Maria. *Maria W. Stewart: America's First Black Woman Political Writer*, edited by Marilyn Rishardson. Bloomington: Indiana University Press, 1987.

Stewart-Dowdell, Betty, and Kevin McCarthy. *African Americans at the University of Florida*. Gainesville: Privately printed, 2003.

Sundiata, Ibrahim. *Brothers and Strangers: Black Zion, Black Slavery, 1914–1940*. Durham: Duke University Press, 2003.

Takaki, Ronald. *A Different Mirror: A History of Multicultural America*. Boston: Little, Brown, 1993.

Taylor, Orlando. "New Directions for American Education: A Black Perspective." *Journal of Black Studies* 2 (September 1970): 101–11.

Taylor, Quintard, and Shirley Ann Wilson Moore, eds. *African American Women Confront the West: 1600–2000*. Norman: University of Oklahoma Press, 2003.

Taylor, Ula. *The Veiled Garvey: The Life and Times of Amy Jacques Garvey*. Chapel Hill: University of North Carolina Press, 2002.

Terrell, Mary Church. *A Colored Woman in a White World*. 1940. Reprint. New York: Arno Press, 1980.

———. "History of the High School for Negroes in Washington." *Journal of Negro History* 2 (July 1917): 252–66.

Titcomb, Caldwell. "The Earliest Members of Phi Beta Kappa." *Journal of Blacks in Higher Education* 33 (October 2001): 92–101.

———. "New Discovery of an Earlier Black Female Member of Phi Beta Kappa." *Journal of Blacks in Higher Education* 49 (autumn 2004): 95–98.

Tobin, McLean. *The Black Female Ph.D.: Education and Career Development*. Washington, D.C.: University Press of America, 1980.

Trower, Cathy, and Richard Chait. "Faculty Diversity: Too Little for Too Long." *Harvard Magazine* 104 (March–April 2002): 33–37, 98.

Tucker, Carolyn, and Keith Herman. "Using Culturally Sensitive Theories and Research to Meet the Academic Needs of Low-Income African American Children." *American Psychologist* 57 (October 2002): 762–73.

Turk, Diana. *Bound by a Mighty Vow: Sisterhood and Women's Fraternities, 1870–1920*. New York: New York University Press, 2004.

Tushnet, Mark. *The NAACP's Legal Strategy against Segregated Education, 1925–1950*. Greensboro: University of North Carolina Press, 2006.

Wadelington, Charles, and Richard Knapp. *Charlotte Hawkins Brown and Palmer Memorial Institute: What One Young African American Woman Could Do*. Chapel Hill: University of North Carolina Press, 1999.

Walker, Alice, ed. *I Love Myself When I Am Laughing . . . And Then Again When I Am Looking Mean and Impressive: A Zora Neale Hurston Reader*. New York: Feminist Press, 1979.

Walker, Clarence. *Deromanticizing Black History: Critical Essays and Reprisals*. Knoxville: University of Tennessee Press, 1991.

Wallace, Michelle. *Black Macho and the Myth of the Superwoman*. 1978. Reprint. New York: Verso, 1999.

Ward, Thomas. *Black Physicians in the Jim Crow South, 1880–1960*. Fayetteville: University of Arkansas Press, 2003.

Washington, Booker T. *My Larger Education: Chapters from My Experience*. 1911. Reprint. Miami: Mnemosyne, 1969.

———. *Up from Slavery*. 1901. Reprint. New York: Penguin, 1986.

Watkins, William. *The White Architects of Black Education: Ideology and Power in America, 1865–1954*. New York: Teachers College Press, 2001.

West Stevens, Joyce. *Smart and Sassy: The Strength of Inner-City Black Girls*. New York: Oxford, 2002.

White, Deborah Gray. *Too Heavy a Load: Black Women in Defense of Themselves, 1894–1994*. New York: Norton, 1999.

Williams, Heather. *Self-Taught: African American Education in Slavery and Freedom*. Chapel Hill: University of North Carolina Press, 2005.

Williams, Patricia. *The Alchemy of Race and Rights: Diary of a Law Professor*. Cambridge: Harvard University Press, 1991.

Willie, Charles, and Ronald Edmonds, eds. *Black Colleges in America: Challenge, Development, Survival*. New York: Teachers College Press, 1978.

Willie, Charles, Michael Grady, and Richard Hope, eds. *African-Americans and the Doctoral Experience: Implications for Policy*. New York: Teachers College Press, 1991.

Wilson, Francille. "'All of the Glory . . . Faded . . . Quickly': Sadie T. M. Alexander and Black Professional Women, 1920–50." In *Sister Circle: Black Women and Work*, edited by Sharon Harley, 164–83. New Brunswick, N.J.: Rutgers University Press, 2002.

Winbush, Raymond. *The Warrior Method: A Program for Rearing Healthy Black Boys*. New York: Amistad, 2001.

Wolff, Robert Paul. "Narrative Time: The Inherently Perspectival Structure of the Human World." *Midwest Studies in Philosophy* 15 (1989): 210–23.

Wolters, Raymond. *The New Negro on Campus: Black College Rebellions of the 1920s*. Princeton, N.J.: Princeton University Press, 1975.

Woodson, Carter G. *The Education of the Negro Prior to 1861*. 1919. Reprint. Manchester, N.H.: Ayer, 1991.

———. *The Mis-Education of the Negro*. 1933. Reprint. Trenton, N.J.: Africa World Press, 1999.

Woolf, Virginia. *A Room of One's Own*. 1929. Reprint. San Diego: Harvest, 1989.

Wright, Marion Thompson. *The Education of Negroes in New Jersey*. New York: AMS Press, 1972.

Zieger, Robert, and Gilbert Gall. *American Workers, American Unions: The Twentieth Century*. 3rd ed. Baltimore: Johns Hopkins University Press, 2002.

Zlotkowski, Edward. *Successful Service-Learning Programs: New Models of Excellence in Higher Education*. Bolton, Mass.: Anker Publishing, 1998.

Index

Definition of academic, 2
Delany sisters, 104, 115
Delta Sigma Theta Sorority (1913), 63, 71;
Alexander, 132; Bethune, 16, 68; Dykes,
130; Fauset, 50; Height, 175; Morton, 89;
Terrell, 81; Washington, 68
Demerit system, 110–12
Democracy, 1, 2, 7, 9, 13, 56, 75, 117; Bethune,
2, 141, 153, 165–68, 186–88; Cooper, 146;
Dewey, 138, 173; Hurston, 84; "intellectual
democracy" (Evans), 11; Levine, 214; West,
189–99. *See also* Aristocratic and democratic educational ideals
Dewey, John, 12, 138, 151, 157–58, 165; Ameri-
can Association of University Professors
(AAUP), 155; Coppin and, 173
Discrimination, 7, 11, 104, 138, 185–88, 195;
gender and, 46, 222n37; race and, 87, 88,
105, 108, 137; work, 50, 75. *See also* Race;
Sexism
Dissertations: Alexander, 132–34; Cooper,
134–37, 143; defense, 91, 94–95, 135–37;
doctoral, v, xiv, 6, 58, 71–72, 87, 122, 127,
138; Dykes, 128–30; Evans, 214; order of
black women's first, 230n17; Simpson,
130–32. *See also* Doctoral degree
District of Columbia. *See* Washington, D.C.
Diversity in higher education, 11–12, 178,
203, 210, 218n15, 239n43
Dixon, Thomas, 189, 226n45, 236n25
Doctoral degree: black women, 4, 6, 63,
88, 91–95, 97, 101, 119–38, 150, 158, 170,
175–78, 201, 205, 213, 214; earned by
African Americans, 57–58, 120–22, 200;
honorary, 17, 125, 132, 138, 232n39; origin
of, 125. *See also* Dissertations
Domesticity, 52, 70, 167
Domestic work, 3, 34, 65, 69, 74, 106, 118,
164, 172, 185, 204–5
"Double bind" of race and sex (Baltimore), 7,
77, 102, 207
Douglass, Frederick, 34, 81
Douglass, Sarah Mapps, 27
Du Bois, W.E.B., 12, 36–43, 57–60, 64, 133,
158, 200, 205; *Black Reconstruction*, 151,
165; "double consciousness," 17; education-

al philosophies, 188–90; on HBCUs, 211;
The Souls of Black Folk, 54, 144; "Talented
Tenth," 65, 168, 197, 198. *See also* Atlanta
Studies
Dunbar High School, 38, 47, 63; Alexander,
132; Burroughs, 171; Cooper, 13–14, 135,
158, 163, 233n8; Dykes, 128; Fauset, 50;
Patterson, 170; Simpson, 131; Terrell, 81,
170, 234n27
Dunnigan, Alice, 109–10, 112, 114, 229n15
Dust Tracks on a Road (Hurston), 84
Duval-Williams, Daphne, 201–3, 237n13
Dykes, Eva Beatrice, 4, 63, 121, 123, 127, 131,
137, 175; dissertation, 128–30, 149, 230n17

Early, Sarah Woodson, 175
Eastern Star (Prince Hall Free Masons), 62
Economics: as academic discipline, 31, 69, 87,
99, 127–32, 168; social class, 36. *See also*
Elitism; Home economics
Education: as a human right and civil right,
2, 4, 180, 216
Educational experiences (black women's), 5,
76, 197; articulated philosophies, 2–10, 28,
171, 190, 195, 207, 210, 214; claimed space,
2, 5, 7–8, 34, 48, 50, 124, 197, 209; negotiated social contract, 5, 46, 69, 71, 168,
194, 198, 215, 217n3; reflected aristocratic/
democratic dilemma, 5, 7, 8, 12, 31, 47, 49,
53, 58, 66, 131, 190
Educational philosophies (black women's),
2, 3, 6, 8, 194–97; applied learning, 8,
113, 159, 208; in contrast to mainstream,
158, 176–77; critical epistemology, 1, 8–9,
12, 28, 36, 69, 71, 96, 126, 146, 148, 150,
158–59, 162, 178, 190, 194–95, 206, 210, 211;
limitations, 64, 67, 117, 149, 160, 195; moral
existentialism, 8–9, 28–35, 51–53, 73, 129,
133, 141, 149–51, 153, 162, 164, 167, 172,
196; Player, 208; standpoint and cultural
identity, 2, 5, 9, 10, 69, 130, 149, 178, 215;
women as moral compass, 182, 192. *See
also* Bethune, Mary McLeod; Cooper,
Anna Julia
Education of the Negro Prior to 1861 (Woodson), 26, 27. *See also* Woodson, Carter G.

Johns Hopkins University (Maryland), 126, 212

Johnson, Charles, 36, 57–61, 70–71, 120, 130, 133, 158, 164, 200, 224nn4,7, 230n15; interview of Bethune, 164; interview of Cooper, 182; *Opportunity*, 87

Johnson C. Smith University (Biddle University, North Carolina), 41

Kansas, 21, 44; Topeka, 206, 226n50; University of Kansas, 38, 40, 44

Kemp, Maida Springer (Murray), 97

Kennedy, Adrienne, 107–8, 254

Kentucky, 21, 36, 39, 88, 200; Kentucky State College, 109, 111, 114. *See also* Berea College

Keyser, Frances Reynolds, 165

King, Martin Luther, Jr., 211

Kinson, Sarah Magru, 3, 24, 217n8, 219nn8,11

Ku Klux Klan (KKK), 55

Labor. *See* Work

Labor of Love, Labor of Sorrow (Jones), 219n17, 220nn35,36, 226n50

Land-grant schools, 32, 40, 123

Lane College (Tennessee), 89

Laney, Lucy Craft: as activist, 185, 234n29; Atlanta University, 15; Bethune's mentor, 167; Haines Institute (Georgia), 169–70

Language: as academic discipline, 30, 45, 86, 144, 156, 163; Bethune "language of the workers" and democracy, 141, 167, 186–87; black women's doctorates, 127; Cooper, 14, 131, 134, 144, 149–50, 167; Coppin, 79; Simpson, 131; Terrell, 83

Latino Americans, 13, 54, 75, 198

"L'Attitude de la France à l'égard de l'esclavage pedant la Revolution" (Cooper), 133, 231n33

Laws and legislation: as academic discipline, 30, 58, 61, 201; antiliteracy, 27, 33, 55, 233n29; black women academics, 116, 132, 137; discrimination, segregation, and desegregation, 33, 39, 61, 173, 201, 204, 220n35, 226n50; Murray, 95–102, 137

Law school. *See* Professions

Leadership, 29, 187, 190; black women and, 10, 47, 63–64, 69, 71, 178, 186; institutional, 27, 123, 169–71, 184, 207, 238n30; Player defines, 209; resistance to black women's, 145, 182, 192, 214. *See also* Service

Leland University (Louisiana), 38

Lemert, Charles, 149, 218n16, 221n40, 222n37, 232n10

Le Pèlerinage de Charlemagne (Cooper), 14, 134, 231n31

Lesbian. *See* Sexuality

Lewis, Edmonia, 24–25, 219n9

Liberal arts education, xiii, 8, 27, 38, 41–45, 49, 61, 72, 123, 162, 164, 204, 212. *See also* Classics

Library of Congress, 12, 217n4

Linguistics, 131; race and dialect, 150, 232n22. *See also* Language

Literacy, 26, 28, 34, 38, 162, 233; antiliteracy laws, 27, 33, 55, 233n29; Browne, 94–95; Coppin, 80

Literary clubs, 23, 31, 44, 52, 83, 86

Litwack, Leon, 55

Livingstone College (North Carolina), 38, 41

Locke, Alaine, 73, 87

Logan, Rayford, 187, 226n49, 236n20

Longfellow, Henry Wadsworth, 82, 148

Lorde, Audre, 207. *See also* Sexuality

Louisiana, 33, 200; Morton, 88

Love: Allah, 196; Bethune, 188; Browne, 174; of college and study, 85, 102, 115, 143–44, 148, 150, 215; Cooper, 143, 149, 181; Coppin, 172; Dykes, 130; Player, 208–9; of teaching, 80; of wisdom, 207; of work, 102. *See also* Values and virtues

Love My Children, An Autobiography: The Education of a Teacher (Browne), 92

Lucy, Autherine, 138

Lyle, Ethel Hedgeman, 52

Lynching, 55, 74, 161; Bethune, 185, 187; Cooper, 161; Jackson, 117; Wells (Lynch Law), 126

Mann, Rowena Morse, 125

Marriage, 10, 23, 49, 50, 68, 70, 143, 146. *See also* Family

Marshall, Thurgood, 211

Marxism, 197

Social work, 54, 66, 68, 72
Socrates, 143
Sorbonne University (Paris), xiii, 1, 14, 50,
134–35, 205
Sororities: Addams, 64; Alexander, 132;
Anderson, 49; Bethune, 16, 68; black
women's, 7, 52, 62–63, 69, 71–72; Browne,
92; Clark, 205; Cooper, 14; and doctor-
ate earners, 63; Dykes, 130; Fauset, 51;
Height, 175; Hurston, 85; Jackson, 105;
Lyle, 52; Morton, 89; Noble, 71; Roosevelt,
64; Simpson, 131; Slowe, 67; Terrell, 81;
Washington, 68; white women's, 49, 106.
See also Alpha Kappa Alpha (1908); Delta
Sigma Theta (1913); Sigma Gamma Rho
(1922); Zeta Phi Beta (1920)
The Souls of Black Folk (Du Bois), 54, 144
South Carolina, 27, 33, 40, 43, 60, 201;
Bethune, 15, 138, 164; Clark, 205; Gullah,
203; Murray, 97; Slowe, 67; Wright, 123,
169–70. *See also* Benedict; Bethune,
Mary McLeod; Claflin College; Voorhees
College
Southern Christian Leadership Conference
(SCLC), 205
Southern region: educational attainment,
xiv, 3, 16, 21, 32, 38–43, 60, 98, 106, 174,
176, 200; repression in, 25, 33, 60, 126,
170, 189, 221n5; womanhood, 182–84,
203
Spelman College (Georgia), 41, 42, 45–46,
65, 81, 113, 118, 222n25, 223n40, 238n40
Standardized tests: Browne, 213; Cooper, 148,
163, 199; and IQ, 213
Standpoint and cultural identity (black wom-
en's). *See* Educational philosophies
Standpoint social contract (Evans), 5, 69, 76,
126, 131, 194, 197. *See also Racial Contract*;
Sexual Contract; *Social Contract*
Stanton, Lucy. *See* Sessions, Lucy Stanton
St. Augustine's College (North Carolina), 42;
Cooper, 13; Delany sisters, 115; Murray's
family, 95
Stereotypes, 34, 46, 52, 66, 69, 73, 95, 97, 113,
192, 215. *See also* Gender; Race
Stewart, Maria, 10, 28, 126, 145

Straight College (Louisiana), 38, 42, 50
Student Nonviolent Coordinating Commit-
tee (SNCC), 205
Suffrage, 1, 42, 69, 181, 184, 185. *See also*
Voting
Swarthmore College (Pennsylvania), 58,
227n6
Sweet Honey in the Rock, 206
Swimming pools, 90, 105. *See also* Recre-
ation

"Talented Tenth" (Du Bois), 65, 168, 197,
225n24; Joy James, 198
Talladega College (Alabama), 41, 97
Teaching. *See* Professions
Temperance movement, 7, 34, 35, 118, 184
Tennessee, 38, 43, 109, 118, 200; Ku Klux
Klan, 55; Morton, 89; Tennessee State
College, 66; Terrell, 81. *See also* Fisk
University
Tenure, 13, 155, 203. *See also* Faculty
Terrell, Mary Church, xi, 4, 37, 77, 102, 132,
134, 178, 225n24; Bethune on, 168; *A
Colored Woman in a White World*, 81–84,
85; frustration with racism and sexism,
115–16; graduate study and degrees, 123,
138, 231n30; joy of learning, 114; NCNW
and club work, 52, 63–64, 74, 170, 171, 185;
on Patterson, 170
Texas, 21, 33, 40, 44, 61, 75, 200; Texas Col-
lege, xiii, 89, 228n37; Tillotson College,
175–76
Theater, drama, and plays, 82, 84, 105, 106,
107, 110, 118, 126, 137, 148, 158, 163, 206,
233n8
Their Eyes Were Watching God (Hurston), 85,
88. *See also* Recreation
Theology. *See* Professions
The Third Step (Cooper), ix, 4, 14, 127, 134,
136
Tillotson College (Houston-Tillotson, Texas),
175–76. *See also* Branch, Mary
Too Heavy a Load (White), 207
Tougaloo College (Mississippi), 42–43
Troy Seminary (New York), 32
Truman, Harry, 17, 132

Stephanie Y. Evans is assistant professor in the African American Studies Program and Center for Women's Studies and Gender Research at the University of Florida.